Kittens For

Questions to Ask Your Vet When Your Kitten's Sick

Take this handy list with you to the vet the next time your kitten feels under the weather.

- ✔ What are my treatment options?
- ✔ How much will this treatment cost?
- ✔ How long before I can expect improvement?
- ✔ How do I give him the medicine (and what are the doses)?
- ✔ Are there any side effects I should watch for?
- ✔ Will he get worse before he gets better?
- ✔ Besides giving him medication is there anything I can do to make him more comfortable?
- ✔ What other symptoms might he come down with that are related?
- ✔ Does he need a follow-up appointment?
- ✔ Is he contagious to the other cats, dogs, kids, and so on?
- ✔ Does he need to be confined or quarantined?
- ✔ Will this illness affect his long-term health?
- ✔ How can I keep this from happening again?

Weeding out Kitten Candidates

When picking out a kitten, look for one that is

- ✔ Curious
- ✔ Outgoing
- ✔ Playful
- ✔ Purring
- ✔ Comfortable with being picked up
- ✔ Complete with healthy, pink gums

Pass on a kitten with the following warning signs, which tell you he's not healthy or well socialized:

- ✔ Listlessness
- ✔ Gooey eyes, running nose, or sneezing
- ✔ Visible third eyelid (like a film or goo on the inside corner of his eye)
- ✔ Crusty stuff around butt or runny poop
- ✔ Scabs or missing fur
- ✔ Black stuff in the ears
- ✔ Fleas or flea dirt
- ✔ Thin with potbelly
- ✔ An incorrigible nipper or hard biter
- ✔ Frightened or shy

For Dummies: Bestselling Book Series for Beginners

Detecting Kitten Emergencies

Take your kitten to the vet immediately if you notice

- Bleeding you can't stop
- Difficulty breathing
- Unconsciousness or lethargy
- Staggering or seizures
- Bloody pee or poop
- Pooping more than twice in an hour or straining in the litter box with no results
- Repeated bouts of vomiting in a short time or diarrhea with vomiting
- Signs that he's swallowed something poisonous such as mouth irritation, drooling, vomiting, seizures, or fever
- Signs of pain, such as swelling or inability to use his legs

If you suspect that your kitten has swallowed something toxic, call ASPCA Animal Poison Control Center at 800-548-2423 or 888-426-4435. The call costs $45, but it could save your kitten's life.

Providing the Basics

The following items will make your kitten feel right at home (for more details, see Part II):

- Sturdy carrier
- High quality kitten food
- Litter box, unscented cat litter, and scoop
- Shallow food bowl and deep water bowl (neither should be made of plastic)
- Sturdy scratching post or cardboard scratcher
- Safe toys (without sewn-on bells or eyes that could be chewed off)
- Brush/comb
- Nail clipper

For Dummies: Bestselling Book Series for Beginners

Kittens
FOR
DUMMIES®

by Dusty Rainbolt

WILEY

Wiley Publishing, Inc.
11700 Telegraph Road
Santa Fe Springs, CA 90670

Kittens For Dummies®

Published by
Wiley Publishing, Inc.
111 River Street
Hoboken, NJ 07030-5774
www.wiley.com

For general information on our other products and services or to obtain technical support, please contact our Customer Care Department within the U.S. at 800-762-2974, outside the U.S. at 317-572-3993, or fax 317-572-4002.

Wiley also publishes its books in a variety of electronic formats. Some content that appears in print may not be available in electronic books.

Library of Congress Control Number: 2003114615

ISBN: 0-7645-4150-1

Manufactured in the United States of America

10 9 8 7

1B/TR/QX/QX/IN

WILEY   is a trademark of Wiley Publishing, Inc.

About the Author

Dusty Rainbolt became involved in kitten rescue in 1986 when she cared for an abandoned pregnant cat. She found homes for Mom and the kittens but kept her two favorites: Chani and Wretched. She had no idea that one act of kindness would later bless her with a career writing about cats. She and her husband, Weems, have been raising orphans ever since. In a small way they also helped elevate the Turkish Van breed to championship status in the Cat Fanciers' Association.

Today, Dusty is a member of the Cat Writers' Association. In addition to her own cats, including Chani and Wretched (now both 17 years old), she cares for a house full of foster kittens. She's the cat product reviewer for *Catnip*, the magazine published in cooperation with Tufts University School of Veterinary Medicine. Her award-winning monthly column — "Dear Hobbes" — written with a feline muse named Hobbes (who was one of Dusty's bottle babies), appears in *City + Country Pets*. She's written for *Cat Fancy, CatsUSA, Whole Cat Journal, Cats Magazine, I Love Cats,* and *PetLife* among others. Her articles have won the CWA/ACFA Cat Safety Award, The Purina Nutrition Award, and The Tidy Cat Behavior Award. Dusty's humorous science fiction novel, *All The Marbles*, which prominently features a Turkish Van cat, was released in July 2003.

Dusty's husband, Weems Smith Hutto, provided the photographs for this book. His cat photos have appeared in *Complete Kitten Care* and *The Purina Encyclopedia of Cat Care* by Amy D. Shojai; as well as *The Guide to Handraising Kittens* by Susan Easterly. His pictures appear monthly in *Catnip*. His photos have also been published in *Whole Cat Journal, Cat Fancy Magazine, Cats Magazine,* and *I Love Cats*.

Dedication

To my sister, Margaret Rainbolt, who gave me my very reluctant first lesson in Felinese; to Houston, my first cat — I still miss you; and to Chani and Wretched, my first kittens and my first intoxicating taste of kitten rescue. To Mary Hamilton, who stuck her neck out to save Chani and Wretched's mother. And finally, to Streamer, the Doberman pinscher who loved his baby foster kittens.

Author's Acknowledgments

There are so many people who contributed to this book. I first want to thank Beth Adelman for recommending me, Natasha Graf for believing in me, Jill Burke for walking me through the process, Alissa Schwipps for adopting me and my book like I was always hers, Weems Hutto for his awesome photos, Kathryn Born for her wonderful illustrations, Jennifer Bingham, my copy editor, and Patricia A. Hague, DVM, for being a long-time source of information and supporter of my writing. I'm delighted that you are my technical editor.

Thanks also to Nicholas H. Dodman, DVM, PhD, director of the Behavior Clinic at Tufts University School of Veterinary Medicine; James R. Richards, DVM, director of the Feline Health Center at Cornell University College of Veterinary Medicine; and Jill A. Richardson, DVM, EVP, my veterinary toxicologist.

Behavior specialists: Steve Aiken, Animal Behavior Consultants in Wichita, Kansas; Peter Borchelt PhD, of Animal Behavior Consultant, Brooklyn, New York; Lana Rich of The Catsultants; Pam Johnson-Bennett, author of *Think Like a Cat,* dog trainer Brenda Keller; Karen Pryor, author of *Clicker Training for Cats*; John C. Wright, PhD, professor of Psychology at Mercer University.

Veterinarians: Edward Aycock, DVM, and Judy Johson, DVM, of Lewisville North Animal Clinic; Kelly Gavin, DVM; Johnny D. Hoskins, DVM; Laura LeVan, DVM; Robert J. Munger, DVM, DACVO; Cindy Ragoni, DVM; Bonnie Shope, VMD; Granville C. Wright, DVM; Michele Yasson, DVM, CVA, president of Holistic Veterinary Services in New York.

Rescue: Charlene Denney of Hunt County Humane Society; Louise Holton of Alley Cat Rescue; Mary C. Hill of the Humane Society of Lewisville; Tamara Kreuz-Foehring, author of the *Stray Cat Handbook*; Karen Moore; Kari Winters, California Siamese Cat Rescue; Sondra York, former cat chair of Animal Rescue League; Rachel Querry, Humane Society of the United States.

Breeders: John J. McGongle and Pat Chapman of Caravanserai Turkish Van Cats; Karen Hooker of Pairodoc Turkish Vans; Lee Brooke of Jeminai Turkish Angoras; Lynn Nunn of Coonunnski, Maine Coons; Sally Bahner; Maryjean Ballner, author of *Cat Massage.*

Liz Blackman, owner of 1-800-HELP4PETS; Karen & Cliff Heath; Lauren, Kevin, and Jacquelyn; Allyson Lepinske; Krynda Lorberbaum; Amy D. Shojai, author of *Complete Kitten Care*; Sandra L. Toney, author of *Little Book of Cat Tricks*; Linda Kay Weber; Mary Woodruff.

Publisher's Acknowledgments

We're proud of this book; please send us your comments through our Dummies online registration form located at www.dummies.com/register/.

Some of the people who helped bring this book to market include the following:

Acquisitions, Editorial, and Media Development

Project Editors: Jill Burke and Alissa D. Schwipps

Acquisitions Editor: Natasha Graf

Copy Editor: Jennifer Bingham

Editorial Program Assistant: Holly Gastineau-Grimes

Technical Editor: Patricia A. Hague, DVM

Editorial Manager: Jennifer Ehrlich

Editorial Assistant: Elizabeth Rea

Cover Photo: Index Stock, 23 West 18th Street, 3rd Floor, New York, NY 10011

Cartoons: Rich Tennant, www.the5thwave.com

Production

Project Coordinators: Kristie Rees and Erin Smith

Layout and Graphics: Andrea Dahl, Joyce Haughey, Michael Kruzil, Clint Lahnen, Barry Offringa, Brent Savage, Jacque Schneider, Shae Wilson, Melanee Wolven

Special Art: Kathryn Born. All photographs provided by Weems Smith Hutto.

Proofreaders: Andy Hollandbeck, Carl William Pierce, Brian H. Walls, TECHBOOKS Production Services

Indexer: Aptara

Publishing and Editorial for Consumer Dummies

    Diane Graves Steele, Vice President and Publisher, Consumer Dummies

    Joyce Pepple, Acquisitions Director, Consumer Dummies

    Kristin A. Cocks, Product Development Director, Consumer Dummies

    Michael Spring, Vice President and Publisher, Travel

    Brice Gosnell, Associate Publisher, Travel

    Kelly Regan, Editorial Director, Travel

Publishing for Technology Dummies

    Andy Cummings, Vice President and Publisher, Dummies Technology/General User

Composition Services

    Gerry Fahey, Vice President of Production Services

    Debbie Stailey, Director of Composition Services

Contents at a Glance

Table of Contents

Chapter 11: Cleanliness Is Next to Catliness........163

Chapter 12: I'm Leaving on a Jet Plane:
What Should I Do? 177

Introduction

I remember my first encounter with kittens. Someone moved
away from an apartment complex, abandoning a poor pregnant
cat during a rare Dallas snowstorm. I felt like Prissy in *Gone With
The Wind.* I wanted to yell, "I don't know nothin' 'bout birthin' no
baby cats!" I didn't have a clue what to do for them when they got
here. Mom and all but two of the kittens found homes. Surprisingly,
the two I kept survived their first year and are both still with me
almost 18 years later.

That first year, the only thing I knew about kittens was how to spell
the word. In those early days, I made a lot of mistakes because I
didn't know any better; I let the kittens outside and I fed them the
cheapest food I could find. But the more I discovered about these
amazing creatures, the more I loved them. When I first started fostering kittens, I found out what a difference premium food made in
both their health and in the way the litter boxes smelled. I began
keeping them inside the house for their safety. I stopped declawing
them. Cats became my passion. Before I knew it, people were
coming to me with their kitten questions. Who'd have thought? I
don't want you to make the same mistakes I made. I want you to
have the information I wished I'd had as I raised my first little kittens . . . so I wrote this fun, easy-to-use book.

About This Book

Bookstores' shelves are full of books about kittens. Most of them
provide accurate information about kitten care. But in order to
understand some of them, you almost need a degree in veterinary
medicine. You won't need to keep a medical dictionary sitting next
to you in order to read *Kittens For Dummies.* I've explained everything to you in plain, everyday English. And because kittens are so
much fun to have around, I tried to make this book fun to read as
well.

I'd love you to read this book cover to cover, and if you do, you
and your kitten will benefit. But if you want to pick and choose
information to get you through a particular situation, you'll be able
to find it quickly. You don't have to wade through pages and pages

of text to find out that a saucer of milk could give your kitten the runs so badly he could try out for the Olympic track team. Just a glance at the able of contents will lead you to that section.

I don't bore you with details about those rare diseases that affect only 1 in 10 million kittens here, but you can find out about colds and other diseases that any kitten can catch. I also tell you how to prevent them.

I go over some of the stupid mistakes I've made with my kittens over the years. I'm confessing my mistakes (and the hard-learned mistakes of others), so you don't have to do the same thing. I even include an entire section on how to rescue a kitten in trouble. I talk you through catching, bottle-feeding, and weaning that kitten, then help you find him a new home. You won't find that anywhere else, at least not alongside a comprehensive care guide.

You'll love this book because you can choose which section is most important to you at any particular moment. Look at the table of contents or the index for what interests you, and dive right in. And I try not to repeat myself. So when I talk about how to buy a kitten carrier, for instance, I also list the other places in the book where you can find out about flying with your kitten or how to best protect your kitten when you're driving around town together.

Conventions Used in This Book

To help you navigate through this book, I've set up a few conventions:

- ✔ *Italic* is used for emphasis and to highlight new words or terms that are defined.
- ✔ **Boldfaced** text is used to indicate the action part of numbered steps.
- ✔ Monofont is used for Web addresses.

Kitty elimination is a major part of your kitten's life, so we're not going to get hung up on formality here. When I've spoken to the nationally known behaviorists, they talk about pee and poop instead of urine and feces. I'm going to follow the lead of these experts and talk about pee and poop, too, just like the big boys.

And speaking of boys, I'm equal opportunity here. Behaviorally, boy and girl kittens exhibit similar personality traits after they've been spayed or neutered — especially if they've been altered early in life. Throughout most of the book, everything applies equally to both boys and girls. I alternately refer to your kitten as "he" or "she" and "him" or "her." I even do the same thing when it comes to spaying and neutering, except in the one section where I talk about the specific operation.

What You Don't Have to Read

I've written *Kittens For Dummies* so you don't have to read every single word. I spent a lot of time writing this book, and I'd love for you to peruse every syllable, but if you're in a real hurry, you can skip past

- **Text in sidebars:** The sidebars are the shaded boxes that appear here and there. They share personal stories and observations. You also can find very specific information or technical details about a disease or product. Although the information may be helpful, sidebars aren't necessary reading.

- **Anything with a Technical Stuff icon attached:** This icon indicates detailed medical or technical information that can give you a complete picture but isn't critical to your caring for or understanding kittens.

- **Anything flagged with a The Cat's Meow icon:** This icon tells you about some of the exciting products I've tested in my other life as a cat product reviewer. If you're not interested in buying kitten stuff, you can just keep moving down the page.

- **The stuff on the copyright page:** No kidding. You'll find nothing here of interest unless you're inexplicably enamored by legal language and Library of Congress numbers.

Foolish Assumptions

I assume because you're reading this book that you

- Either have a kitten or you're interested in getting one.
- Want to give your kitten the best care you can.
- Want to have a close relationship with your new furry friend.
- Want to keep your kitten as happy and healthy as you possibly can.
- Want to understand how to communicate with your kitten and understand what she's trying to tell you.

How This Book Is Organized

To make it easy for you to get the poop on owning a baby kitty, *Kittens For Dummies* is divided into six parts. Each part addresses a different aspect of life with a kitten.

Part I: Your Companion for Life

You want to get a kitten, and you have so many decisions to make before you take the plunge! This part helps you sort out what you want and should expect from your future companion. You can figure out whether you want an energetic kitten or an older more laid-back cat. I also help you decide if you'd like a kitten-of-all-breeds or a specific breed. This part tells you where to look for the kitten of your dreams and gives you tips on how to pick out a kitten who's happy and healthy.

Part II: Preparing for and Bringing Home Your Kitten

This part tells you how to prepare your home, family, and other pets for a kitten. I tell you how to introduce her to everyone and what to fill both her food bowl and her litter box with.

Part III: Caring for Your Kitten

Your kitten is home. Now what? From primping to prevention, this part shows you what's involved in the day-to-day care of your kitten. I go over what to do when her tail is dragging and how to kitty-proof your home.

Part IV: Kitten Psychology: Understanding Your Furry Friend

You and your kitten speak different languages. You need to figure out ways to understand the kitty language: Felinese. Your kitten uses her voice, body language, and sometimes peeing outside of the box to get her point across. Part IV helps your kitten understand what you're saying to her and gives you tips on how to translate her actions. You can use your new understanding of her way of thinking to keep her entertained and out of trouble.

Part V: Welcoming the Unplanned Kitten

Thousands of kittens need help. Some are so little they can't do anything for themselves. Others just need a helping paw to get them out of danger before you set them on the path to a new life. In this part, I go over what to do when you end up with an unexpected visitor.

Part VI: The Part of Tens

In this part, I go over the kitten owner's happiest moments along with the scariest. You find out how to deal with the most common emergencies a kitten owner will face. At the opposite end of the spectrum, I give you some tips for entertaining and bonding with your kitten.

Icons Used in This Book

The icons in this book help you find particular kinds of information that may be of use to you:

You see this icon any time I offer you a suggestion to help you take better care of your kitten or make life easier or safer.

This icon appears whenever I provide really important information you won't want to forget

Don't ignore this icon. It tells you when something has the potential to harm your kitten or cause you problems.

This icon flags text that gives you a more complete picture of what I'm talking about, but you can skip over this information unless you're detail minded or need some bathroom reading.

This icon highlights neat products that I've found to be very useful. If you're not interested in getting out your pocketbook, you can skip past this information.

Where to Go from Here

Where you open the book and start reading depends on a number of things:

- ✔ If you're still looking for a kitty companion, head to Chapter 2 to weed through all your options.

- ✔ Chapter 3 helps you with your purchase of a registered kitten, and Chapter 4 gives you advice on how to adopt a kitten with a handicap or one from a shelter.

- ✔ Rescuing a kitten from a dangerous situation is explained in Chapter 8.

- ✔ I discuss what to do when your kitten gets sick and go over steps you can take to keep him healthy in Chapters 9 and 10.

- ✔ You can read about grooming in Chapter 11.

- ✔ You can start checking out behavior issues in Chapter 14.

- ✔ Look in Chapter 17 for information about nursing unweaned kittens.

Anything I haven't mentioned can be found in either the index or the table of contents.

So now you're ready to embark on an adventure called kitten ownership. You'll find a lot of giggles, a few tears, and always a new discovery. Don't worry if you sometimes feel a little lost like I did. For you, I've created this helpful guide.

Part I
Your Companion for Life

The 5th Wave   By Rich Tennant

"Stuart, wake up! The kitten's been grooming your eyebrows again."

In this part . . .

You're thinking about getting a kitten, and you have so many decisions to make! This part helps you decide whether a kitten will even fit into your lifestyle. If you decide you do want a kitten, Part I helps you figure out whether you want a specific breed of kitten or an everybreed. Then I tell you where to get him and even help you decide whether you want to adopt a kitten with a handicap.

Chapter 1

Getting the Lowdown on Owning a Kitten

You're about to enter that wonderful and sometimes chaotic world of kitten ownership. This chapter helps you make those first important decisions about what kind of kitten to get, how to prepare your home for the new arrival, and how to keep him happy and healthy.

Before you do anything else, I recommend that you take the following quiz to help you evaluate your lifestyle and determine whether you're ready to adopt a kitten and whether a kitten would be happy in your home. You may decide to skip the whole kitten caboodle and adopt a mature, well-adjusted cat. Kittens can be high energy and high maintenance, so weigh your options before taking the plunge.

Can You Fit a Kitty into Your Life?

Not everyone's cut out to live with a kitten. If you're not prepared, that little ball of fur can turn into, well, a pain in the cat. Before you head to the shelter or accept a kitten from a friend, stand back and look at your lifestyle objectively. Ask yourself the following questions:

✔ **Am I a neat freak?** If so, a clumsy little kitten knocking over potted plants, tracking litter all over your floors, and leaving balls of fur on your couch cushions may be enough to put you through the roof. Adopt a pet rock instead.

✔ **Do I plan to move soon?** If you may not be able to make arrangements to bring your new kitten with you, wait and adopt a kitten after you're settled in your new place.

✔ **Does my landlord permit pets, and can I afford the pet deposit?** Arrange to pay your pet deposit before you adopt. Some landlords let you break the payment up over time and pay installments with your monthly rent payments. And don't think a kitten is easy to hide. An unauthorized kitten could have you scrambling for a new home when you get caught and kicked to the curb.

✔ **Is my home already crowded with animals, and are my other animals aggressive or territorial?** Crowded pet environments tend to breed behavior problems. If you have aggressive or untrained pets, an innocent kitten may become a midnight snack. On the other paw, kittens make great companions for some older cats and dogs. See Chapter 6 for advice on introducing your new kitten to resident pets.

✔ **Am I ready to take on the financial expense of raising a kitten?** Caring for a cat costs somewhere between $400 and $700 annually for cat food, litter, vet bills, and other expenses.

✔ **Am I having personal problems or going through lifestyle changes like marrying, divorcing, or going off to school?** Even though kittens provide a great deal of comfort when you're going through a stressful time, you may find it impossible to keep him.

✔ **Is anyone in my home allergic to cats?** You can do some things to reduce the dander like vacuuming daily and bathing the cat weekly. Allergic folks can also take shots, but if you're not prepared to make the commitment, you may want to adopt a different kind of pet.

✔ **Do I work long hours or travel a lot?** A kitten can make the house so friendly to come home to, but a kitten at home by himself can't learn manners and tends to tear up the house. It may be better to adopt an older cat or a pair of cats rather than subjecting a kitten to hours and days of loneliness. If you plan on traveling after you get your kitten, check out all your options in Chapter 12.

✔ **Do I have young kids under the age of 6?** Most youngsters under 6 don't fully understand that a kitten is alive and not a toy. If you do have young kids, you may want to wait until they're a little older to adopt a kitten, or consider adopting a mature cat who's used to living with small kids. If you feel your youngster can handle the kitten gently, be sure to teach her respect for the kitten before it arrives (see Chapter 6). Also plan to monitor your child's time with the kitten.

✔ **Do I have time to train and play with my kitten to avoid behavioral problems?** Raising a happy, well-socialized cat with good manners takes work. He needs to be taught what's expected and he needs exercise and entertainment (see Chapter 15). If you don't have the time, your cute little ball of energy can turn into a large out-of-control pain in the neck.

✔ **Am I willing to make time to groom my kitten regularly?** If you have a busy schedule that leaves little time for combing kitty, you may want to consider a shorthaired kitten instead of a longhaired breed such as a Persian. For more information on kitten maintenance, see Chapter 11.

✔ **Can I make the 18-year commitment?** Raising a kitten takes a special person with a real commitment. An inside cat can live 15 to 20 years. That's as long as it takes to raise a child. Ask yourself if you're up to making that kind of commitment.

Forget dog years: What's that in cat years?

Did you know that an inside kitten can live for 15 to 20 years? Forget the old wives' tale that one trip around the sun equals 7 kitty years. The following table shows you how your kitten's years really tick along.

Cat Years	Human Years	Cat Years	Human Years
1	15	12	36
2	24	15	76
5	36	18	88
6	45	21	100

If you feel strongly that a kitten would be a welcome addition to your home, be sure to read Chapters 2, 3, and 4, where I help you weigh your kitten options: indoor versus outdoor, registered versus random bred, longhaired versus short, adopting from a shelter versus responding to an ad and so on.

Keeping Kitten Healthy

A healthy kitten doesn't just happen. As the owner, you need to be proactive, because your kitty can't tell you when she feels sick. You should start as soon as you bring her home — maybe even before. Take the kitten to get checked out within the first week at home; or before you bring her home if you have other cats. If you don't have a vet already, check out Chapter 6.

You need to play voyeur when your kitten poops and pees, feel for lumps and bumps during her monthly exam (see Chapter 10), and watch for signs she's just under the weather. Take her to the vet annually and keep her current on her vaccinations. You can find out about the most common and deadly viruses and their vaccinations in Chapters 9 and 10.

You must make some important decisions about your kitten's health and well-being. One of the most important decisions you can make about your kitten's future is whether to have him (or her) fixed. Just a simple snip as early as 8 weeks old can mean the difference between your boy cat peeing on the wall or properly in the litter box. If you decide not to spay your girl, you may get less sleep because every few weeks she's going to keep you awake all night yowling because she's in heat. And early altering prevents several forms of cancer and other illnesses.

As with kids, kittens occasionally get sick or hurt. They're still young and vulnerable, with immature immune systems. You can find more detailed information on common kitten illnesses in Chapter 9 and about responding in case of emergencies in Chapter 20.

Keeping kitty healthy takes more than vaccinating and worming — you need to exercise him mentally and physically to keep him entertained and out of trouble. I tell you how to wear him out when you're home and while you're away in Chapter 15, so he wants to snooze at the same time you do.

Keeping Kitten Happy

Kittens keep you on your toes and challenge your imagination. You're going to need to put some effort into keeping your new friend safe and entertained. You need to search your home for objects, chemicals, and plants that have the potential to hurt your kitten. You also need to find out the difference between food that nourishes your kitten and something that can harm him. You need to give him things to do and introduce him to the house rules.

Preparing for a warm homecoming

Like a newborn baby coming from the hospital, your kitten needs some accessories to make life easier for him and you. Start your shopping spree by buying a cat carrier so you can bring him home in safety. You can find out about all the cool stuff kittens need in Chapter 5. In Chapter 6 I tell you how to set up a _safe room_ — a small quiet room where he can feel secure as he gets acquainted with your family.

Before you bring your kitten home or as soon as possible afterward, get down on your hands and knees and think like a kitten. Remove everything you can find that the new king of the house can chew, swallow, push over, or get tangled in. Pick up any loose string, loose screws, rubber bands, toxic plants, and so on. Chapter 8 has a long list of dangerous things to watch out for when kitten-proofing your home.

Feeding to keep him fit and trim

Feed your kitten a quality diet. Spending a few extra cents per meal on better food is like collecting dividends on an investment. After all, it keeps your kitten healthier, and that pays off big when she gets older. Find out all about the best foods to feed your kitten in Chapter 7.

Occupying his every waking hour

Kittens aren't as high maintenance as puppies are, but they still need plenty of love, attention, and patience. Taking the time for the right kind of play helps you bond with your kitten. It also makes her less likely to seek out trouble around the house.

Opening Your Home to an Orphan

Few things tug at your heart the way a lost or orphaned kitten does. So I give you the lowdown on what to do when you come across a needy little kitten. In Chapter 16 I tell you what to do and where to turn for help when trying to rescue a weaned kitten, and in Chapter 17 I go over how to raise a bottle baby. I also give you some tips on health and behavioral issues that orphans have in Chapter 18. Finally, in Chapter 19, I tell you what to do with your little friend when he gets big enough to live without your constant attention and help you decide whether you want to keep him or find a new home. Raising an orphan is a lot of work, but the process isn't as complicated as most people think.

Chapter 2

Choosing the Right Kitten for You

In This Chapter

▶ Staying inside or out

▶ Going over the advantages of kitten age

▶ Thinking about cat hair

▶ Choosing a male or a female

▶ Deciding if you want a registered kitten

▶ Going to the right place to get your kitten

▶ Picking a great kitten

*O*ne or two? Longhaired or short? Boy or girl? Random bred or a kitten with a pedigree? Geez, what a lot of decisions to make before you select your first kitten! Lucky for you, this chapter helps you find your perfect match — a kitten whose personality is compatible with the lifestyle of your family. Or maybe you'll decide to adopt two kittens or an older kitten or even a cat. If you decide on a cat, pick up *Cats For Dummies,* Second Edition, by Gina Spadafori (Wiley Publishing, Inc.).

Living as an Innie or an Outie

One of the most important decisions you must make for your kitten is whether he will live as an indoor cat, an outdoor cat, or will come and go as he pleases. Whether your kitten will live inside or out affects how much grooming he requires and which vaccinations you need to keep him updated on. You also want to consider the ordinances in your community concerning cats running loose. And never declaw a kitten who you're going to let outside. Find out about declawing in Chapter 14.

Out and about

Statistics show that outdoor cats live significantly shorter lives than inside cats — the outie lives only 7 years, but inside cats average a whooping 14 to 18 years. Whether he lives outside fulltime or comes and goes at will, an outside cat's life is cut short by diseases, fights, cars, marauding dogs, evil kids, and poisons — not to mention his own curiosity (see Figure 2-1). You can discover all the horrible things that can happen to your kitten outside your home in Chapter 8. (Can you tell I'm against keeping your kitten outside? I had to learn the hard way.)

When I discuss the difficulties faced by outdoor kittens, I'm talking about both full-time and part-time outsiders. They're both exposed to the same risks, just for different lengths of time. However, kittens who live outside exclusively need added help when it comes to extremely cold and extremely hot weather. In the cold winter months, you must provide your kitten with shelter and warmth to prevent frostbite, and in hot weather you need to make sure she has fresh water; otherwise she's at risk of dehydration.

Figure 2-1: If your outside kitten gets into trouble, you may not find out about it until it's too late to help.

Keeping your indoor kitten company — a second kitten

If you don't already have a cat and especially if you work long hours away from home, do your kitten (and yourself) a favor and bring home a two-pack. A single kitten, home alone, can turn your house upside down. When you're at work and the kids are in school, that lone kitten will do what any bored kid would do: think up his own entertainment. It'll likely involve shredding the couch, unrolling the toilet paper, and climbing the curtains. And when you're trying to get a good night's sleep, he'll want to play bite the toes under the cover. A second kitten will give him something to focus on besides that fresh roll of toilet paper and your toes. Instead of stalking your ankles as you walk down the hall, he'll attack his buddy.

Naturally, certain expenses, such as food and vet visits, will double with a second kitten, but your kittens can share the litter box, scratching posts, grooming tools, and toys. A second kitten shouldn't cost that much more.

And never, under any circumstances, let a declawed kitten go out-side without supervision. Because claws are a kitten's first defense, a clawless kitten is a sitting duck (or sitting kitten?) for roaming dogs and predators. Also, he can't climb a tree fast enough to get away.

I used to let my kitties hang out in the neighborhood when they wanted to — before I learned better. I had kitties getting into cat-fights, hit by cars, chased by dogs, trapped in a neighbor's attic, and caught in a garage door mechanism, and I've also lost kittens to feline leukemia. Two of my cats disappeared without a trace. Since I've turned them into inside cats, my vet bills have gone way down, and my cats live a lot longer. Now I'm happily paying vet bills for geriatric cat care.

Serving life on the inside

Being a strictly indoor kitten is no bed of roses either. Without activities to use up her energy and keep her occupied, the inside kitten quickly becomes a royal pain in the litter box: Behavior problems are much more common among indoor cats (see Chapter 14). But don't think you have to suffer just to keep your kitten safe. You can find a lot of fun and practical suggestions in Chapter 15 that help stir up some excitement in a kitten's life and keep her happy and well-adjusted when she's stuck inside.

On the positive side, your inside kitten will develop into a member of the family, preferring people as friends rather than being aloof and obsessed with going outside. Because inside kittens aren't exposed to diseases and other outside dangers, they're healthier and they don't get in as many life-threatening accidents as outside cats.

My kitties get the best of both worlds. They're safe and they still get to enjoy fresh air, thanks to the Cat Fence-In containment system I installed on my fence. You can read all about it in Chapter 15.

How Old Is That Kitten in the Window?

From roughly 6 weeks to 4 months of age, young kittens are cute wads of fur who sleep nearly 20 hours a day and spend the other four hours with the pedal to the floor racing through the house. For the sake of your family and your future kitten, you should ask yourself whether a rambunctious kitten will fit into your lifestyle. You need to make sure you have the time and patience to teach a kitten manners. Your new friend may not completely calm down for years.

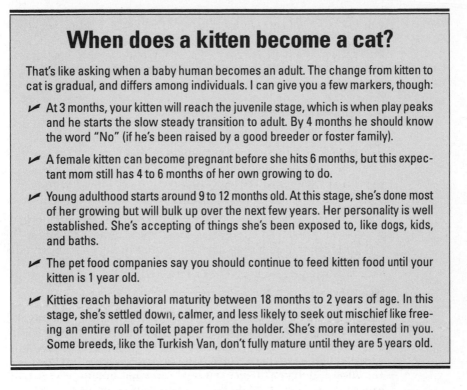

When does a kitten become a cat?

That's like asking when a baby human becomes an adult. The change from kitten to cat is gradual, and differs among individuals. I can give you a few markers, though:

- ✔ At 3 months, your kitten will reach the juvenile stage, which is when play peaks and he starts the slow steady transition to adult. By 4 months he should know the word "No" (if he's been raised by a good breeder or foster family).

- ✔ A female kitten can become pregnant before she hits 6 months, but this expectant mom still has 4 to 6 months of her own growing to do.

- ✔ Young adulthood starts around 9 to 12 months old. At this stage, she's done most of her growing but will bulk up over the next few years. Her personality is well established. She's accepting of things she's been exposed to, like dogs, kids, and baths.

- ✔ The pet food companies say you should continue to feed kitten food until your kitten is 1 year old.

- ✔ Kitties reach behavioral maturity between 18 months to 2 years of age. In this stage, she's settled down, calmer, and less likely to seek out mischief like freeing an entire roll of toilet paper from the holder. She's more interested in you. Some breeds, like the Turkish Van, don't fully mature until they are 5 years old.

Between 4 and 8 months a kitten goes through adolescence. Just like a human kid, he knows the rules, but tests them. These adolescent kittens are still young enough to be fun, but not as much work as the younger kitten.

If you're considering adopting your first kitten and you think a young kitten may have too much energy for you to handle, consider bringing home an older kitten — someone 8 months old or even older. Older kittens tend to have better manners and established litter box habits.

An older kitten will

> ✔ **Have an established personality:** If you have a special personality in mind, you may be happier with an older kitten. Young kittens start out cute and affectionate, but as they get older, their personalities can change. Your lap kitten may develop into an independent cat or a clingy cat who hovers

under your feet all the time. An older kitten comes with a more established personality. Granted, even an older kitten can have mood swings, but if he's a lap kitten at the shelter, he'll probably be a lap cat next year. You won't be disappointed, because he's not likely to change as much as a young kitten can.

✔ **Be less destructive:** Don't expect to be able to keep your Hummels and your Dresden doll on the coffee table with a young kitten in the house. Young kittens can turn today's treasures into Tuesday's trash faster than you can repeat this sentence. Although older kittens still have energy and can get into mischief, you're likely to have fewer headaches than you will with a kitten going through adolescence.

✔ **Be more affectionate:** When a kitten reaches 9 or 10 months old and that wild energy has toned back some, he's more interested in spending time with you. Kittens go through adolescence just like kids. They also go through that, "Don't touch/hold me" stage. After they go through that stage, they're usually more interested in you.

✔ **Adjust faster and require less supervision:** Young kittens need constant supervision, which may be difficult in busy families. If you don't have the time to exercise a kitten and teach him manners, you'll have problems down the road. Your kitten can't figure out how you want him to behave without your help. It could take you months — or even years — before you reach the same comfortable relationship with your young kitten that you could have with an older kitten in just a few days.

✔ **Make better companions for older resident animals:** If you're looking for a buddy for your 14-year-old cat, a young kitten probably wouldn't be old Fluffy's first choice. Kittens can be a pain in the tail for an older cat with creaky bones and arthritis. A pouncing and biting kitten can make even the most tolerant resident pet want to jump ship. Sometimes, resident pets will smack and hurt small kittens out of frustration. However, a 10-month-old kitten won't break if he gets into a couple of short territorial bouts with your cat.

Most kittens can figure out how to get along with almost any cat, but a kitten may not have as promising a career in a home with an older dog. If you're looking for a buddy for Buddy, avoid adopting a kitten altogether and look into an adult cat who's lived in a home with dogs instead. Most rescue groups can give you some background information on *owner release cats* (cats who have lived with families but were surrendered for any number of reasons like moving or allergies).

✔ **Have a better chance of surviving the tight grip of a toddler:** If you have kids under 6, rethink the young kitten thing. Small children often have problems understanding that a small, furry kitten lives, breathes, has feelings, and shouldn't be held by the neck, squeezed, or stepped on. Until the kitten reaches about 6 months, he's fragile and can be injured easily. And remember, a frightened kitten who just wants to get away from his tormentor may bite or scratch your preschooler.

Older kittens make better companions for toddlers because they can handle rough petting and aren't as likely to suffocate when squeezed. They're also more capable of staying out of a toddler's reach. If you want a companion your kid can dress up in doll clothes, adopt an older cat from a rescue shelter. You can find a mature cat used to kids who had to be given up because, for instance, his owners moved and couldn't take him along. For more on picking a compatible cat for your kids to pat, see *Cats For Dummies,* Second Edition, by Gina Spadafori (Wiley Publishing, Inc.).

When can you bring your kitten home?

No reputable breeder will permit you to take your kitten home before she turns 12 weeks old. Some catteries even make you wait until she's 16 weeks.

Be patient. Kittens have a high mortality rate — about 25 percent — from birth defects, parasites, or bacterial or viral infections. If a kitten dies, it'll probably happen before she turns 16 weeks. Also by 16 weeks, your kitten should have had the entire series of viral shots, been wormed, and maybe spayed. She'll have a stronger immunity built up, and you'll save money on medical stuff.

And your kitten needs some training that only other cats can give: Mama cat needs to finish socializing your kitten. And kitty needs to wrestle with her siblings so she learns to play properly. Otherwise, she's more likely to bite you and attack your ankles. Mom will also make sure kitty knows how to flush and put the lid down, or at least the kitten equivalent.

Fluffy or Baldy?

When deciding what type of kitten to get, you may want to consider how much time you have for grooming. Some longhaired kittens, like Persians (pictured in the color insert), must be groomed every day. Others may simply need an occasional comb-through when they're shedding. If you want an indoor/outdoor kitten, you may want to stick with a shorthair, because long hair attracts grass, burrs, and gunk.

The longer the hair, the greater the care

I have to admit that I love to look at well-groomed longhaired kittens. But when you go to cat shows and see the Persians, Birmans, and Norwegian Forest Cats, remember that their owners have spent a lot of time getting them ready. Coats that silky don't happen by accident.

Grooming any longhaired kitten, whether for a cat show or simply to keep the kitten's hair clean and tangle free, takes more time than caring for a shorthair. Just how much longer varies from breed to breed and kitten to kitten. For example, you'll find the longhaired Persian on the high side of the groom-o-meter labeled "labor intensive." A Persian's coat mats in no time at all. So if you're looking at a Persian or a domestic longhair with a Persian-type coat, expect to comb daily — more when he's shedding. Medium-length coats, like those of Balinese and Turkish Angoras, can go a week between combings. For more information about grooming your kitten, read Chapter 11.

If you get a longhaired kitten with fluffy *britches* (you know, the ruffled fur along his bottom and back legs that resemble Victorian underwear), you'll have to keep an eye out for cling-ons after he uses the litter box. *Cling-ons* aren't warlike aliens from *Star Trek;* they're clumps of poop clinging to that long fur. Be prepared to occasionally wipe off your kitten's butt; otherwise, he may do the butt scootin' boogie and use the carpet as toilet paper.

Although you don't need to bathe a longhaired kitten unless he gets into something, you should check him with a comb or pin brush at least once a week for mats. If you don't, the mats will get progressively worse. Eventually, the skin beneath the mat will become irritated and raw, and could develop an infection. If the clumping gets too bad, you may need to take kitty to the groomer or vet to get shaved (see Chapter 11).

In addition to frequent grooming, cats with long coats shed twice yearly — once when they change their wardrobe from summer to winter and once when they put away their fur coats and get out their shorts. Be prepared to bring the vacuum out for a daily de-furring during shedding season.

If you want a longhaired kitten, you'll have to make a commitment to regular grooming and cleaning. Get a kitten with longer hair only if you have time to spare.

Shorter hair means easier care

Short hair fits a kitten's active lifestyle, because most shorthairs don't need much fussing. Although not as striking as some long-haired kittens, shorties make your life much less complicated in the grooming category. And as with the longhairs, shorthaired kittens don't need baths unless they get into something you don't want them to lick off.

Even though shorthaired kitties don't mat, they still shed as much as longhairs; it just looks like less because it's shorter. Under normal circumstances, a quick weekly brushing should cut down on shedding and that hairball projectile vomiting. Learn all about this Olympic event for kitten in Chapters 9 and 11. During seasonal shedding, comb your shorthair a couple of times a week.

Bald is beautiful

You may be able to throw away your comb if you bring home a hair-challenged kitten. But what you save on grooming tools, you'll need to reinvest in sweaters. Be careful: These kitties chill easily. Shedding is a non-issue, and fleas don't care much for kittens without fur coats. However, bald cats, like the Sphynx, and near bald, like the Devon Rex, tend to have greasy skin and need to be bathed every few days. The oil from the kitten's skin stains fabrics the way greasy hair will stain a pillowcase. Bathing isn't that big a deal. After all, just wash them, towel them dry, and put them on the floor. They don't have fur so they don't need to be blow-dried. But do remember to keep them warm! These kittens aren't good candidates if you want an outdoor pet because they're more sensitive to the cold. Too much sun on that unprotected skin isn't good for them either.

Hypoallergenic kittens — Not really

Fel D1 is a protein in the kitten's saliva that causes allergies. When she grooms herself, the protein attaches to cat dander. So, there's no such thing as a hypoallergenic kitten. But if your allergies aren't severe and you would like to have a cat, you may have some options.

✔ **Go girl:** Girl kitties tend to produce a lot less of the Fel D1 protein.

✔ **Get him clipped:** Neutered males make less Fel D1 than intact males.

✔ **Buy an allergy-friendly breed:** Some breeds appear to produce less of the protein including the following:

Cornish, Devon, and Selkirk Rex

Sphynx

Siberian

Just because a kitten produces smaller amounts of the protein doesn't mean your allergies can tolerate her. Lots of these poor kitties are sent to shelters or returned to the breeders by hopeful people who turn out to be too allergic after they get a cute little kitten home. If you're interested in a kitten, ask the breeder if you can spend time in the cattery — the longer the better — before deciding to adopt. Insist on a clause on the contract that allows you to return the kitten if your allergies don't tolerate his presence.

Considering an X or a Y Chromosome

You've probably read that male kittens grow up to be aloof and unfriendly with some nasty personal habits, and girls grow up to be more affectionate. That can certainly be the case if your cat hasn't been neutered or spayed. But if you alter your kitten — especially if you take care of this before she blossoms into puberty — you won't be able to tell the difference. Find out all of the benefits of altering your kitten and about early spay/neuter in Chapter 14. If you're considering buying a registered kitten and want to keep him intact for showing or breeding, you may want to check out the disadvantages of not altering your cat, also described in Chapter 14.

All the cats in my house have been altered. I don't see much differ-ence in their behavior. Unless you don't plan on altering your kitten, the gender just doesn't matter. But if you don't neuter your outdoor kitten or if you neuter him when he's older, he may have more wan-derlust than girls or boys neutered early.

A Random-Bred from the Pound or Registered with Papers and a Crown?

Which is better: a registered kitten with papers or a random-bred kitten who sleeps on your paper? They both have advantages. I love the elegant beauty and dignity of a Maine Coon or a Turkish Van, but I also marvel at the intricacies in the coat of the blended kitten.

Picking a pedigreed kitten

When you buy a purebred kitten, you know to some extent how your new friend will look and behave. For instance, if you want a cat to fetch, get a Maine Coon or a Turkish Van. If you want a kitten you can carry on a conversation with, get a Siamese or an Oriental type. When you buy a registered kitten, you have a good idea of what you're getting in the temperament department (although you do run into exceptions). Persians like to lie around, and Abyssinians will climb the walls. Look over the different breeds in Chapter 3 and see if any of those whiskers tickle your fancy.

Although pedigreed kittens could run up to a $1,000 or more, you can buy a *pet-quality kitten* — a pedigreed kitten whose appearance disqualifies him for show, but who can make a great pet — much cheaper. Because only one or two kittens out of a litter meet the show standard, your breeder should be able to offer you some very nice pet-quality kittens.

Some breeds have a higher tendency for certain health conditions than random-bred cats. You can read about these concerns in Chapter 3.

Is it a boy (:) or girl (i)

Trying to decide whether you're looking at a boy kitten or a girl kitten can be challenging, even for those of us who do it regularly. Lift up the tail and check out those little privates. You'll see the anus, which is easy to spot, and then below that you should see another opening. Comparing the openings of two different cats, you'll see that a boy's part looks like a colon (the punctuation) with two dots. The girl's bottom will resemble an upside down exclamation mark. There will also be a little more distance between the boy's dots because that's where his testicles will be when they descend when he's about 7 weeks old. The following figure helps you tell the difference.

Female   Male

All mixed up: Getting the best of all breeds

You don't have to spend a fortune to get a loyal companion. *Moggies,* or random-bred kittens, make great pets. Granted, they're a little like buying a dime store grab bag: You just don't know what you're going to get until later. But if you're just looking for a companion and you don't need to dictate the personality, a moggy may be just the kitten for you. They're way cheaper than registered kittens, they're just as loving, and you've got an endless selection of colors, patterns, and coat lengths to choose from.

If you plan to adopt a moggy, check your local humane shelter before heading to the pet store (as I explain in the "Picking the Right Place to Pick Out the Pick of the Litter" section later in this chapter). Most humane shelters offer you kittens who are fully vaccinated for rabies and common virals, tested for diseases, and possibly even altered. Shelters are full of healthy random-bred kittens. Plus, you save a life when you adopt one of these little guys.

Picking the Right Place to Pick Out the Pick of the Litter

If your kitten just wanders up to you or you rescue him, then you've got a done deal; you don't need to worry about where to get a great kitten. But if you have to go out and find your new pet, you want to get the happiest, healthiest kitten you can. Don't worry about encountering a shortage of kittens to choose from. At certain times of the year, you can practically pick up a free kitten from a kid giving them away on the street corner, although I don't recommend doing so. (To find out why a free kitten may cost you a boatload, turn to Chapter 4.) But take a look at this list, and you should be able to get just what you want:

✔ **Shelters:** Kittens in shelters definitely need good homes. However, some shelters don't screen or treat their kittens for health problems, so you need to be careful. Also you don't know what the kitten has been exposed to physically or emotionally. On the other hand, some shelters are the opposite, and the kittens have been thoroughly screened. The price of the adoption fee is one indication of the amount of care and screening a kitten has received. But even in the best situation, you're unlikely to receive background information on a shelter kitten (unless a foster home is involved). If you're not looking for a particular breed, really consider adopting from a rescue group. Even if you get a kitten from a no-kill organization, you're definitely saving a life. After all, your kitten will open up room for another.

Talk with the shelter workers or volunteers. They may know the kitten personally and be able to give you some inside information about his personality. You can get more detailed info on shelters in Chapter 4.

✔ **Reputable breeders:** Although you'll pay more for a registered kitten, you should be able to get a well-adjusted and healthy kitten from a breeder. You'll want to screen your breeder well to make sure he's not a kitten mill or backyard breeder (see Chapter 3). Do your homework because some breeds are predisposed to certain medical conditions.

✔ **Newspaper ads:** You can find kittens in the want ads. Some breeders may choose to take out an ad in the local paper. Screen them well. I tell you how to do that in Chapter 4. There's no health guarantee with these random-bred kittens (No telling what the mom cat has been exposed to.) Again, beware the backyard breeder who just likes to make kittens for fun and profit. You need to read about them in Chapter 3.

✔ **Special needs kittens:** If you have enough patience and a big enough heart, you may make a wonderful home for some special kitty, and some relieved shelter workers will be delighted to see you coming. Some disabilities, like deafness, take virtually no extra work on your part. Some may require an ongoing expense. Call any shelter or rescue organization. I'm sure they have a special kitty who's been waiting for someone like you.

✔ **Pet stores:** Avoid buying a kitten from a pet store. These kittens tend to be poorly socialized. I've had pet stores tell me that they get their kittens from good breeders, but no reputable *cattery* (where kittens are bred and raised) would sell a kitten without screening the potential owner personally to see if he will make a suitable home. Unfortunately, these kittens are often the product of *kitten mills,* (where caged queens are kept in horrible conditions and forced to have litter after litter). If you buy a kitten from a pet store, you're encouraging both the store and the kitten mill to continue their shady business practices.

Individuals: You may be offered a kitten from someone who has a litter at home. In Chapter 4, I talk about how much money a free kitten can cost you. Read that before you get a freebie from your neighbor.

Selecting the "Purr"-fect Kitten

Thousands of kittens are available for adoption in your area at any given time. With the staggering number of kittens needing homes, you can find a happy, healthy, and well-adjusted kitten if you just take your time. Out of those thousands, some will be unhealthy; others will have a bad attitude. Hard as it is, try to stand back, look at the kittens objectively, and keep the following ideas in mind:

- Unless you *want* to go into kitten rehab, avoid the grumpy guys or kittens who need a major medical insurance policy.

- Let the kitten pick you. Breeders tell me that sometimes a kitten is attracted to a certain person and will do everything she can in order to go home with that person. All you have to do is walk past a cage and you find that paw tapping you on the shoulder with a face begging for you to take her home. Pay close attention to that kitten — even if she isn't exactly what you had in mind.

- Either sit on the floor and let the kittens come to you, or take the kittens out of the cage one at a time. Handle each individually. After a couple of minutes, the kitten should relax. No matter how cute, if she stays taut while you pet her, she probably won't be comfortable at your home either.

- Look for a kitten who wants to play. Ask the breeder for a teaser toy, something with a little length to it so your fingers aren't right next to the fangs and claws. (If you go to a shelter, bring your own cat toy.) A healthy, well-socialized kitten should bounce and play.

- Listen for a kitten who purrs like a diesel motor. Purring is a pretty good indication that she's responding positively to you.

- Put away any kitten who nips or bites. This kitten may become a chewer or biter when he gets older.

- Don't decide to adopt a kitten until you've seen him use the litter box. He should cover his poop. Kittens cover their business instinctively so other predators and more dominant cats can't find them. A kitten who doesn't cover his poop may abandon proper litter box habits later in life.

✔ If a kitten acts a little shy around you, ask the breeder or foster mother to handle him. If she can't get him to play or he won't let her handle him, take a pass. He may not have been well socialized or handled by people enough. Believe me, you'll be disappointed if you pay $400 for a kitten who doesn't want to have anything to do with you. Don't adopt a wall-flower or wild child hoping he'll change when you get him home. Sadly, a lot of these kittens stay suspicious of people.

✔ While you're on the floor with the kittens, give each one a nose to toe mini-exam. You can find out how to give kitty a once over in Chapter 10.

Especially when buying a registered kitten, take him to your own vet to get him checked out right away. Check for that health guar-antee in the contract. Most breeders will insist you visit the vet within the first week, or you'll forfeit your health guarantee, which usually covers genetic defects. Even if a kitten looks healthy, she could have a heart murmur, parasites, or other problems that you need to know about. You may decide to keep her even if a problem is discovered, but at least you'll go into it with your eyes open. Or the defect could be life threatening, and you may want another kitten or a refund.

No matter where you get your kitten, you need to get her tested for several fatal viruses such as feline leukemia and feline immunodefi-ciency (especially before you introduce her to your other cats). Some breeders and shelters perform the screening before they make their kittens available for adoption, so be sure to ask them whether your kitten has been tested. (Read more about these dis-eases and vaccinations in Chapters 9 and 10.)

Chapter 3
Buying a Registered Kitten

* *

* *

A Persian kitten may be gorgeous, but she'll also be a grand disappointment if you want a low-maintenance kitten to romp with your 10-year-old son. If you're interested in buying a registered kitten, take the time to read this chapter, which helps you match cat breeds with your lifestyle and suggests where to buy a registered pet.

Looking at Purebred Registered Kittens with Pedigrees — Huh?

When you go looking for kittens, you're going to get hit with a lot of cat lingo. People throw around the terms "purebred," "pedigreed," and "registered" without bothering to differentiate what each means. What *you're* looking for is a registered kitten. Take a look at these terms to help you figure out why:

 ✔ **Pedigrees** are family trees, stating lineage going back from three to six generations.

 ✔ **Registries** are organizations that give a written history of the cat breeds in pedigree form. A registry is basically a document repository of the breed's lineage. The three main cat registries in the United States are the Cat Fanciers Association (CFA), The International Cat Association (TICA), and the American

Cat Fanciers Association (ACFA). The actual registration papers are returned from the registry to the kitten's new owner. Between 37 and 56 breeds of cats are recognized by the three main cat registries. Be aware that you can get a cat who's registered in one organization and not in another. Your kitten can also be registered in all three registries.

✓ **A registered kitten** has a documented pedigree in a recognized breed from a cat registry.

✓ **A purebred** cat is a naturally occurring breed of cat who's bloodlines haven't been diluted by other breeds or random-bred cats. Only a few natural breeds like the Turkish Van, Siamese, and Japanese Bobtail can claim to be purebred. A lot of people will use this term incorrectly when they actually mean registered kitten.

The pros

Random-bred kittens, sometimes called mixed-breed kittens or *moggies,* are delightful like a grab bag because you never know what you're getting (see Chapter 2), but pedigreed kittens have a wonderful predictability about them. Unlike moggies, you can pick out a pedigreed kitten with a personality to mesh with your lifestyle.

The cons

Unless you've already chosen a breed and know a breeder, buying a pedigreed kitten is an investment in time and money that takes more work than picking a kitten from a shelter or a friend's litter. You need to figure out the type of cat you want and locate a trustworthy breeder. You should also be prepared to lay down more green stuff on a registered kitten than you would on a random-bred kitten.

Understanding What's Behind that Pedigreed Price Tag

When you buy a pedigreed kitten, expect to plop down somewhere between $350 and $750 for a *pet-quality* kitten — a healthy kitten who doesn't meet the appearance standards to be shown. For instance, he may have the wrong color eyes or a kink in his tail. If you've got your heart set on a show-quality kitten, expect to pay between $750 and $2000 — or even more depending on the breed and the bloodlines.

At those prices, the breeders are raking in the dough, right? Wrong! Breeders, at least the ones who do it right, make almost nothing on kitten sales. The price of the kitten covers the fee for *stud services* (the fee charged by the male's owner), any emergency medical expenses for the queen and the kittens, and a host of other costs.

Kittens from a reputable breeder may be expensive, but they're worth the extra cash. After all, you're getting a robust kitten with a health guarantee who's been bred to get the best disposition possible. Mom and Dad have been screened to attempt to rule out genetic defects. In this case, money *can* buy peace of mind.

Matching Your Lifestyle with a Breed of Kitten

One breed of kitten behaves differently from another and has different grooming needs. Look at the pace of your life and decide what kind of kitten fits in. Some breeds rock around the clock; others will clock their hours contentedly away in your lap. Don't get a pedal-to-the-metal Abyssinian to be a lap cat for your 80-year-old grandmother.

While every breed has a distinctive personality that typifies its cats, every kitten is an individual (just like a kid). Some could be more temperamental than others. Make sure you and your kitten have the right chemistry.

Table 3-1 lists the most popular and the more unique breeds and what they're like — what they look like, how active they are, how much they talk, how big they get, and how much grooming time they require to keep them looking their best. Review the table and pick a few breeds that have characteristics you're looking for. Then, after you narrow your choices to a few breeds that both appeal to you *and* fit your family's lifestyle, find out all you can about the breeds. After all, you may have this kitten for 20 years. He needs to blend into your household.

The best place to find out more about a breed is at a cat show. There you can take a peek at how big the kitten may get and what he'll look like when he's grown. You can talk to breeders about the quirks of each breed. (Unfortunately you can't hold or pet the kittens.) You can also research breeds online at http://cfainc.org or www.tica.org.

Note: Different cats go by different names in the various registries. The names below came from Cat Fanciers Association.

Table 3-1   Popular Cat Breeds and Characteristics

Breed	Physical Description	Activity Level	Vocal Level	Social Style	Adult Size	Grooming Needs	Other
Abyssinian/ Somali	Lithe, but muscular body; ticked tabby (like a cougar)	Extremely active, playful	Not chatty	Likes interactive play, inquisitive, too busy to be a lap cat but likes to hang out with people	Medium	Aby's close lying coat only needs seasonal or occasional hand grooming; Somali's medium length coat needs monthly brushing	
American Shorthair	Muscular, thick body; at least 80 coat colors and patterns	Calm	Not chatty	Very affectionate, wants to be beside you	Medium to large	Short, close-lying coat needs hand grooming every week	
Birman	Stocky but elongated body; pointed coat with white feet, deep blue eyes	Active, busy, and curious	Not chatty	Very affectionate, wants to be with you, but not on your lap	Large	Silky semi-long non-matting fur, weekly brushing	
Burmese	Cobby, solid, muscular cat	Moderately active	Very chatty with a soft voice	Lap cat	Medium	Close lying coat Hand groom when you pet	Doglike personality, likes to fetch

Breed	Physical Description	Activity Level	Vocal Level	Social Style	Adult Size	Grooming Needs	Other
Cornish Rex/ Devon Rex	Cornish body is compact, refined; Devon body is greyhound-like	Active likes to fetch	Very chatty	Lap cat	Medium	Both need frequent baths; Cornish has very short non-shedding coat that needs hand grooming; Devon has longer loose curls	
Egyptian Mau	Medium length, muscular body, distinctspot pattern and banded tail	Very active	Very chatty	Lap cat	Medium	Short close-lying coat, hand comb monthly	
Maine Coon	Well-muscled	Moderately active	Soft voice	Very affectionate, good with kids and dogs	Large	Long, shaggy coat needs grooming every few days	Called the gentle giant; sometimes prone to hip dysplasia
Manx	Compact, solidly muscled	Moderately active	Not chatty	Affectionate	Medium to large	Longhair or shorthair with thick double coat; both types require daily brushing	Make sure litter habits are solid especially with tailless or stumptailed

(continued)

Table 3-1 (continued)

Breed	Physical Description	Activity Level	Vocal Level	Social Style	Adult Size	Grooming Needs	Other
Norwegian Forest Cat	Solidly muscled, large boned; comes in every coat pattern and color except color point	Moderately active	Chatty	Affectionate, but not a lap cat	Large	Long double coat with dense undercoat	Likes to be up high
Ocicat	Solid body, very powerful and muscular, cream coat with dark or light brown spots and markings	Very active, athletic	Varies, some are chatty, some aren't	Lap cat	Moderately large	Close lying coat needs only seasonal grooming	
Persian/ Exotic Persian/ Himalayan	Cobby body, massive head; Himalayans have points and blue eyes	Not active	Not chatty	Affectionate	Large	Exotic Persian's short dense coat needs brushing daily, others require combing several times a day	Prone to eye and sinus problems
Ragdoll	Large, heavily boned	Moderately active	Not chatty	Lap cat	Large	Moderately long coat with wooly undercoat needs daily combing	
Russian Blue	Fine-boned, long, and firmly muscled; coat only comes in blue with silver tipping	Moderately active	Not chatty	Affectionate, but not a lap cat	Medium	Plush double coat needs hand grooming every few days	

Breed	Physical Description	Activity Level	Vocal Level	Social Style	Adult Size	Grooming Needs	Other
Scottish Fold	Short, round, well-padded body and folded ears	Moderately active	Not chatty	Affectionate, gets along with kids and dogs, wants to be with you, not on you	Medium	Double-coated; short coat needs weekly combing; long coat needs combing twice a week	Breed has occasional problem with the tail stiffening
Selkirk Rex	Heavy boned, muscular body	Moderately active	Not chatty	Not a lap cat but enjoys people	Large	Long or short non-matting curly coat; both coat types need monthly bath instead of combing, overbrushing can reduce curly appearance	
Siamese/ Oriental	Long, lean body and delicately boned; Siamese have lighter bodies with points on face, ears, legs, and tail, have sapphire eyes; Orientals come in most colors and patterns except pointed, have green eyes	Very active	Extremely chatty	Lap cats, good with kids	Small to medium	Close lying coat only needs seasonal combing	

(continued)

Table 3-1 *(continued)*

Breed	Physical Description	Activity Level	Vocal Level	Social Style	Adult Size	Grooming Needs	Other
Siberian	Muscular	Active	Chatty	Likes people, doglike	Medium to medium large	Semi-longhair, needs combing twice weekly	
Sphynx	Barrel-chested and muscular, but naked-looking cat with large ears	Very active	Somewhat chatty	Lap cat	Medium	Hairless, has oily skin, must be bathed every few days	Feels like suede, and warm to the touch like a hot water bottle
Tonkinese	Muscular, but balanced and proportioned; blue-green or aqua eyes	Active	Carries on conversations	Shoulder cat	Medium	Fine, close-lying coat needs seasonal combing	
Turkish Angora	Long and fine boned	Very active	Moderately chatty	Affectionate	Medium	Non-matting semi-longhair, comb weekly to monthly	
Turkish Van	Massive, strong, wide bodied	Very active, loves to fetch	Fairly chatty	Affectionate, but not a lap cat	Large	Semi-longhair, non-matting coat, comb weekly	Swims when pools of water available; smart

Defining Colors and Patterns

You're going to start hearing words like tabby and calico. These aren't breeds; they're coat patterns. When you talk to breeders, they're going to be throwing these phrases around. Knowing what colors and patterns these terms represent can help you visualize what your future kitten may look like. You'll also hear about eye color.

Looking at patterns

In the wild, a cat's survival depends on his ability to disappear into his background. Invisibility protects him from larger predators and gives him an edge when stalking mice and lizards. His tabby stripes, mimicking the colors of rocks and bark around him, perfectly blend him into his environment.

But because survival no longer depends on concealment, the feline repertoire of markings has expanded. Colors that wouldn't do well in the wild have become popular for pets.

Like breed names, terms for coat patterns vary depending on the country, the breed, or the association your cat's registered in. Some of the most common words you may hear include

- **Solid:** This kitten has only one color whether it be white, gray, black, brown, cream, or smoke. You won't find any pattern in the coat. A solid cat can have a small locket of white on his chest or stomach.

- **Bi-color:** This term describes a kitten who's about one-third to two-thirds white with distinctive patches of another color on the head and torso.

- **Tabby:** All tabbies have eye make up (Cleopatra copied it), an M-shaped marking above each eye, and *ticking* (when a single hair has several bands of color). The most common types of tabby are

  - **Mackerel tabby:** The stereotypical tiger striped kitty, this is nature's finest camouflage and the most common tabby pattern. Ticked hairs alternate with solid hairs to form stripes that run like ribs down his sides, preferably unbroken and evenly spaced. These extend from a line down his back creating the effect of a fish's skeleton. He has stripes on his legs and tail with finer lines on his face.

- **Classic tabby:** This style of tabby usually has broader stripes than a mackerel tabby with a bull's-eye or swirl on his side. He also has face, leg, and tail stripes.

- **Ticked or agouti tabby:** The ticking is evenly distributed over his entire body without stripes or spots. It resembles a deer's coat. The Abyssinian is the prime example.

- **Spotted tabby:** Ticking forms spots or rosettes along his sides with striping on the face, legs, and tail.

✔ **Points:** He has a pale body with darker legs, tail, and ears. Pointed cats always have blue eyes. This marking is most associated with the Siamese.

✔ **Van:** A white cat with color restricted to the head and tail. A van pattern is a bi-color cat.

✔ **Calico:** A white cat with patches of red and black. Calicos are almost always females. Male calicos can't reproduce.

✔ **Tortoiseshell or tortie:** A black cat with patches of red. Torties are also usually female.

✔ **Tuxedo:** A black cat with white markings on the feet, chest, and stomach.

The beauty's in the eye color

A kitten's eyes open when he's between 7 and 14 days old. At first, every kitten has blue eyes. At about 1 month old, his eyes begin to change color. Usually, his eyes settle into their new and permanent color by about 3 months. However, the color may continue to intensify until as he matures.

A kitten's eye color is a gift of nature. Those hypnotic tones run the color spectrum from lemony amber to iridescent green to ice blue, and vary from kitten to kitten. Some kittens even have odd eyes; each eye is a different color, for instance an amber and a blue or a yellow and a green. Your kitten's eye color is genetically related to his coat color.

Locating a Registered Kitten

You won't have to look very far to find registered kittens. But you may need to do some legwork to find a healthy, well-adjusted one.

Being wary of pet store "purebreds"

Buying a kitten from a pet store is risky. Because you can't screen the breeder, you have no idea of the conditions the kitten was raised in or whether he's litter trained. Worst of all, the kittens usually come from *kitten mills,* which are large, high-profit catteries where the poor mama kitties are confined to squalid cages and bred over and over until they're physically worn out. If a cat has problems giving birth, too bad — this poor mama won't get a late-night trip to the emergency clinic. They don't care about breed standards, either, so the kittens could have all kinds of genetic defects that show up later in life. The pet store often charges you as much as a show-quality kitten would run from a reputable breeder. Sometimes the registration papers are even questionable. If you buy a kitten from a pet store, the store profits, the kitten mills profit, and you and the mama cats are the ones who pay for it.

However, some pet stores, like PetsMart and Petco, provide cage space inside their stores for humane societies or purebred rescues to hold adopt-a-pets. The store doesn't profit from the adoptions, which are solely between the family getting the kitten and the rescue organization. Everyone, especially the kitten, wins. I use this method to find homes for my foster kittens. You can find out about adopt-a-pets in Chapter 4 and purebred rescue at the end of this chapter.

Buying directly from a breeder

Instead of buying a kitten from a middleman like a pet store, you're better off going straight to the source and buying from a reputable breeder (and I stress the word *reputable*).

Finding a reputable breeder

Here are a few ways to get in touch with a local breeder:

- ✔ **Attend cat shows.** You can get to know some breeders and learn about the breeds of kittens you're most interested in all at the same time.

- ✔ **Call cat registries.** They may not give you the name of an individual breeder, but you can ask for the name of the breed council and breed club secretaries. These contacts can give you the names of reputable breeders in your area. Cat registries can also tell you when and where local cat shows will be held. (I suggest a few reputable registries you may want to contact in the "Cat registry contacts" sidebar in this chapter.)

When you call the cat registries ask them to refer you to an Approved Cattery or a Cattery of Excellence (more about catteries later in this section). These breeders have been through voluntary inspections by a licensed vet who evaluates the sanitation and living conditions. The breeder must be re-approved yearly to keep these designations.

✔ **Read cat magazines and peruse local newspaper ads.** Cat magazines have a large list of kitten ads categorized by breed. This is a good starting place to find a breeder in your area. You may find a very good breeder through the newspaper, but screen carefully. Keep reading to find out how to do that. The paper's a favorite advertising outlet for dangerous backyard breeders (BYB).

✔ **Surf the Internet.** Breed clubs and catteries often have Web sites with information about the cats and catteries. One of the best Internet sources is the Fanciers Breeder Referral List at www.breedlist.com, which provides breed standards, articles, lists, and registries and gives you links to clubs and advertising breeders. When you find a breeder you like, be prepared to screen her. I give you some tips on how to do this in the "Screening a breeder" section later in this chapter.

Cat registry contacts

Conveniently, you can find breeders in the same place you find cats of every breed, color, and coat style — a cat show. And you can find cat shows by checking the entertainment section of your local paper, surfing the Web, subscribing to magazines like *Cat Fancy*, or contacting cat registries such as

✔ **Cat Fanciers Association (CFA):** The world's largest cat registry, CFA has been around for nearly 100 years and recognizes 37 championship breeds. It sponsors over 350 shows a year. Contact CFA to find out about shows in your area by calling 732-528-9797 or checking out the Web site at www.cfainc.org.

✔ **The International Cat Association (TICA):** Established in 1979, TICA sponsors 350 shows annually and recognizes 56 breeds. You can find TICA cat shows on the Internet at www.tica.org or contact the association at 956-428-8046.

✔ **American Cat Fanciers Association (ACFA):** This registry was formed in 1955. It recognizes 49 breeds and holds over 50 cat shows annually. Look at the ACFA site at www.acfacat.com or call 417-725-1530.

Screening a breeder

Buying a kitten from a breeder is a little like dating. If you listen to your mother, you won't commit your life to the first or only person you ever date, and if you listen to me, you won't necessarily buy a kitten from the first breeder you meet. You need to ask questions first and buy later.

The breeder-owner relationship is a long-term relationship. Most breeders want to stay in contact with the kitten buyers for the life of the kitten. That could last 20 years. So look for a breeder who not only has good-natured kittens, but whom you like and get along with.

Be careful of backyard breeders (BYBs). These people may love their cats and kittens, but aren't real picky about the genetics of the cats they use, so you could wind up with a kitten with all kinds of health and behavior problems. They often sell the kittens way too early — at 5 or 6 weeks of age — and also the kittens may not have interacted much with people. If you're lucky, your kitten may get one set of shots. BYB prices can be cut-rate or they may be extremely expensive.

To avoid buying from a BYB, screen, screen, screen. Take a look at some questions you should ask each breeder to help you determine if his practices are on the up and up:

- ✔ **How much do your kittens cost and what does that include?** You can expect to pay up to $750 for a *pet-quality kitten* — a healthy kitten who doesn't meet the show standards and can't be bred. For that kind of price you should receive a fully immunized and wormed kitten. Ask who gave the shots. Many breeders give their own inoculations but can give the name of the manufacturer and lot number of the vaccine. The kitten may or may not be microchipped or altered. With a pet-quality kitten you won't be allow to breed him or her. The selling breeder will either fix the kitten before you get her or not transfer the registration papers until you show proof that you've fixed her.

- ✔ **Do you have a health guarantee? How do you handle genetic problems?** A reputable cattery will take a cat back if she develops genetic problems, even years after the purchase. Make sure to take the kitten to the vet within a few days of buying her to be checked out.

✔ **Will I have full ownership of my kitten? What are your contract restrictions?** Make sure you actually own your kitten when money changes hands. Some breeders maintain partial ownership in the contract.

✔ **Where do you register your kittens?** They should answer with one of the main U.S. registries like CFA, TICA, or ACFA. I recommend you stick with the big three. Some of the smaller registries just issue papers. A legitimate registry will hold shows.

✔ **What are the health problems associated with this breed? What issues have your cats experienced? Has your cattery had feline infectious peritonitis (FIP)?** If the breeder says the breed doesn't have problems, take a second look. Most breeds have at least minor health concerns. For instance, flat-faced Persians can have breathing and tear duct problems, Maine Coons sometimes have hip dysplasia, and Scottish Folds can develop arthritis. That doesn't mean your kitten will. But you want to know whether these problems run in your kitten's lines. FIP, a fatal disease that could take years to show up, can be a problem in the close quarters of catteries. Find out about FIP in Chapter 9.

✔ **What breeds do you raise?** Make sure the kitten is a real breed before you buy him. A lady I know bought a "purebred calico" with bogus papers. Calico describes a coat pattern, not a breed of cat recognized by a registry. Do your homework. If the breeder claims to be having a hard time finding her records or the paperwork seems disorganized, look for another breeder.

✔ **Can I have some references?** Get the names of kitten adopters from several years ago and also recent sales. Contact them to find out if they've had any problems either with the kitten or the breeder. Ask about the kitten's disposition and health (and the breeder's, too). Talk to the breeder's vet. If the breeder is conscientious, the vet will sing his praises like crazy. If the vet declines any information, his silence is very telling.

Inspecting the cattery

When you're done with your phone screening, ask to visit the *cattery*. That's a place where pedigreed cats are bred and raised. Red flags should shoot up if the breeder says no. The breeder could be hiding something from you. If he agrees to show you around, keep the following checklist in mind:

✔ Make sure the kittens are raised *underfoot,* which means they live in a home-type environment with a lot of human contact and affection — not kept in cages.

✔ Ask to look at the *sire* and the *queen,* (dad and mom). They should be friendly and outgoing. Kittens learn a lot about how to behave from mom.

✔ Pay attention to the way the breeder treats the kittens and how they respond to him. They shouldn't run away frightened when he enters the room; they should be happy to see him.

✔ Check for sanitary conditions:

  • The kittens shouldn't be overcrowded.

  • Litter boxes should be relatively clean, not overflowing with last week's poop. This afternoon's poop is okay.

  • Food and water dishes should be clean.

Hopefully, you can sit down on the floor and let the kittens wander up to you, so you can choose the happiest, healthiest one of the bunch. Check out Chapter 2 for more advice on how to pick out a healthy, well-adjusted kitten.

If you feel uneasy about the breeder or the conditions at the cattery, keep shopping. You don't want to enter into a long-term relationship with someone who makes you uncomfortable.

The screener becomes the screened

A responsible breeder should care about whom she sells a kitten to. She probably will ask *you* a battery of questions, so come prepared to

✔ Sign a contract promising not to declaw the kitten and to return the kitten (or cat) to the breeder if you can't keep him. Most breeders are against declawing. Find out why in Chapter 14.

✔ Make a commitment to keep in touch for the life of the kitten.

Knowing what to do if you must buy sight unseen

If you can't visit the breeder, make sure his cattery is an inspected one. I discuss this in the "Finding a reputable breeder" section earlier in the chapter. Ask other breeders if they've bought cats from the breeder. Get the contact information for other kitten buyers.

The only time I bought a pedigreed Turkish Van kitten, I purchased unknowingly from a BYB across the country. The kitten arrived with a bad case of ear mites, an ear infection, and little previous human interaction.

Performing a "purebred" rescue

If you don't need the papers or you'd like to rescue a kitten but have your heart set on a certain personality, purebred rescue may be the way to go. Volunteers from these organizations comb through the shelters and retrieve the cats and kittens who fit the recognized breed standards. They also pick up kittens from owners who are moving, redecorating, or have developed allergies. While reputable breeders have a clause in the contract requiring the buyer to return the kitten should he no longer want him, many buyers ignore the stipulation and simply give up the kitten to the pound.

In many cases, you won't actually know whether the kitten is really registered or a good imitation, but these groups know breed standards like the backs of their paws. They don't declare a kitten registered unless they have the papers to back it up. Surprisingly, a great many kittens do come packing pedigrees and registrations. Like all other rescues, these kittens and cats will come to you already altered so you won't have any litters in your (or your kitten's) future.

You can expect to pay between $100 and $150 for a purebred rescue. Although what is included varies from group to group, the adoption fee will most likely include spay/neuter, feline leukemia virus test, worming, and vaccinations. You can find a purebred rescue organization in your area at www.fanciers.com/rescue.html or www.felinerescue.net.

Chapter 4

Adopting a Random-Bred or Special Needs Kitten

A dopting a random-bred kitten (or *moggy*) isn't as complicated as buying a registered kitten. You can find so many needy kittens to choose from that the hardest part may be narrowing all your choices down to just one kitten (or two). This chapter gives you some tips on where to look for your new family member. I also go over how to pick out a well-adjusted and healthy random-bred kitten and let you in on the potential problems with "free" kittens.

While most people look for the best and healthiest kitten available, you may want to take that extra step and adopt one of the many special needs kittens with handicaps. They make wonderful pets who require very little additional care. You can save a life and gain a loyal companion in the deal.

When you go to pick out your kitten, bring the whole family. Adopting a kitten is a family decision. Even the 7-year-old should be there so you can see how she interacts with the kitten.

Thinking about Adopting a Random-Bred Kitten?

Whether you call your new friend a plain tabby kitten, random-bred, a domestic longhair or shorthair, household pet, or (my favorite) a moggy, he's still a kitten with unknown heritage. But a kitten doesn't need a pedigree to be a loving companion. A moggy can provide you with companionship and endless hours of amusement even if his ancestors didn't ride over on the Mayflower.

The pros

The greatest reason to adopt a random-bred kitten is to save a life. Bringing home a kitten, even from a no-kill shelter, frees up space for another kitten. Other benefits include

- Moggies are often healthier and have fewer of the genetic defects than certain breeds of cats because of the vast gene pool.
- You can choose from hundreds of combinations of colorful coat patterns and any length and density of fur. You can also choose among different eye colors.
- Even when you adopt a kitten from a humane society, you pay less than you would pay for a pedigreed kitten.
- You can adopt kittens from groups that have already neutered and fully vaccinated the kitten.

The cons

The positives of adopting a random-bred kitten outweigh the negatives, but keep these potential downsides in mind:

- If you adopt a random-bred kitten, you won't have the predictable appearance that you get when you buy a kitten of a specific breed.
- The kitten's future disposition is more of a mystery than it is with a registered kitten.
- Many times you aren't privy to the kitten's family and health history; for example he may have inherited heart disease or hip dysplasia from his mom or dad.
- In many cases, you don't know what kind of diseases the kitten's been exposed to, by neighborhood cats or at a shelter.

Locating a moggy

Kittens in need of a home seem to be everywhere, especially in the springtime. You take a bigger risk by adopting from some sources than others. In this section, I provide advice on which kitten outlets are usually safe and which you should be wary of. Regardless of where you get your kitten, be sure to give him the quick physical examination I talk about in Chapter 10 to make sure he's healthy.

Adopting from shelters and rescue organizations

An animal shelter is one of the most convenient places to find kittens. You should have a number of litters to choose from representing many colors, coat patterns, and dispositions. If one kitten doesn't connect with you, the one in the next cage may. I like to divide shelters into three categories:

- ✔ **City or municipal shelters (or pounds):** Cities or counties run these shelters and take in kittens from the streets, kittens their owners gave up (often called *owner release* kittens), and confiscated kittens. Sometimes cities contract the operations of the shelter to nonprofit humane societies. How much they charge to adopt a pet depends on the city; you may get a cheap kitten with frills and no strings attached. Others may require prepayment for rabies shots, spaying/neutering, and microchipping (see Chapter 10).

  Although a few cities have no-kill shelters, kittens in most municipal shelters are in danger of being put to sleep in a matter of days. So, if you adopt a kitten from one of these shelters, you're definitely rescuing him from certain death.

  These kittens may have been exposed to all kinds diseases, because publicly funded shelters must take any cat, including cats with highly contagious diseases. Even a kitten who appears healthy could develop an upper respiratory infection or worse after he gets a home.

  Take your shelter kitten to the vet as soon as possible. (On the way home would be best, especially if you have other cats.) Have her checked for parasites and tested for feline leukemia virus (FeLV) and feline immunodeficiency virus (FIV). You can get all the details on these diseases and parasites in Chapter 9.

- ✔ **Rescue organization with a shelter:** Usually nonprofit groups run these shelters and take in kittens brought in by individuals who find or rescue them from the streets. They usually charge an adoption fee significantly higher than many city shelters because the kitten has often been altered and may have received shots, worming, blood tests, or microchipping. Because these groups either have a vet on staff or receive a greatly reduced rate from area vets, your adoption fee will probably cost less than the combined price of the procedures if you paid for them separately at a vet's office. You should have fewer health problems with these kittens than you would with pound kittens, but the kitten's condition depends on the quality of the shelter. Because of limited space, these shelters either have to euthanize unadopted cats or turn cats away when the facility is full.

Most rescue shelters either neuter your kitten before putting him up for adoption or require that you have it done when he turns 6 months old. They ask you a lot of questions to make sure your home is suitable. For example, if you rent, the shelter may ask you to show proof that you've prepaid your pet deposit.

✔ **Volunteer rescue organizations using foster homes:** These nonprofit organizations are run by volunteers, and they take in owner release kittens and kittens pulled from pounds and other rescues, but they house the animals in volunteer foster homes instead of at a central shelter. This is my favorite way to put a kitten up for adoption, because the kittens have lived in a family setting as opposed to living in a cage while awaiting adoption. The foster parent should be able to tell you if the kitten gets along with kids, dogs, uses the litter box properly, or anything else you may want to know before you welcome the little guy into your home. Also, a foster home is a less stressful environment for the kitten. Because these groups have so few foster homes, you may not find the selection you would at a city or larger nonprofit shelter. The kitten should already be altered or the shelter will provide a voucher so you can have him neutered. Testing and shots are often included. Expect to go through a stringent screening process. As with any adoption situation, give the kitten's eyes, ears, and nose a good once over to make sure he hasn't picked up anything while in foster care.

Fostered kittens usually go home healthy, but occasionally a sick kitten slips through the cracks. You can increase your chances of picking out a healthy kitten by reading Chapter 2.

Before you go to the shelter, call and ask these questions:

✔ **What's your adoption fee and what does it include?** That way you know whether you need to pay an additional amount for shots or neutering after you adopt the kitten.

✔ **Do you have any background information on your kittens?** You may be able to find out why his family surrendered him or where he was found.

✔ **Do you have a shelter or do volunteers foster the kittens in homes? If your kittens live at a shelter, do they stay in cages or are they allowed to play in an open environment?** Foster homes and open catteries make for better-adjusted kittens and usually offer better information about what the kitten will be like in a home environment.

✔ **What kind of handling do your kittens get?** Look for facilities where the volunteers handle and socialize the kittens opposed to leaving them in cages until they get adopted.

✔ **Do you have a room where I can get acquainted with the kitten before I can adopt him?** A quiet room with no other cats around can help you get to know the kitten's real personality.

✔ **Are you a no-kill shelter, or do you euthanize healthy kittens after a number of days?** I know many people who find it comforting to save a kitten from certain death following the loss of a beloved pet. If this is important to you, you may want to go where you can give a kitten a last-minute stay of execution.

Taking a chance on a free kitten or stray

No doubt you've seen those tempting newspaper ads for free kittens or driven past a family giving kittens away in a parking lot. You may even have a friend or neighbor trying to find homes for a litter of kittens. You may find it hard to resist those big green or amber eyes. But you know the saying, "There's no such thing as a free kitten." Or is that a free lunch?

If you take a kitten from someone who hasn't bothered to spay his cat, you're just encouraging him to continue to let his cat reproduce. And the expenses you run up after you bring home a "free" kitten may end up costing you more than the adoption fee you'd pay a shelter. To prove my point, I called vet clinics all over the country to find out how much a free kitten really costs. The absolute cheapest "take-home price" I found was $197 for a girl and $152 for a male, but the average price for basic care and testing was $335 females and $290 males.

That little orphan who shows up at your doorstep or that you snatch out of the jaws of death on a busy street undoubtedly needs some kind of medical assistance. For example, Nixie, my Tonkinese-mix, was 8 weeks old and weighed less than a pound when I rescued her in rural South Texas. She had worms, ringworm, ear mites, and a badly abscessed paw. Just treating her immediate problems cost $175. I had to shell out even more to have her spayed later.

The bottom line: You're going to pay for a kitten, one way or another.

And even after the initial veterinary care, you still have to pay for monthly flea care, annual shots, occasional medical services, food, and cat litter. After you add together the initial expenses and the yearly upkeep, your "free" kitten could cost you between $400 and $600 a year. So even if you do get a free kitten (with everything already done), expect expenses later on.

To save money, you can sometimes adopt a kitten you found: Some rescue groups let you adopt the kitten through the organization, which means you pay an adoption fee but the kitten receives basic screening (if they do this), shots, and spay/neuter from their clinic or designated vet. You pay $50 to $100 to adopt the kitten, which is a pretty good deal. Contact your city's animal control to get a list of local rescue societies. If you can't find a group that agrees to do that, ask if you can get a certificate for a reduced spay/neuter. Turn to Chapter 14 for more suggestions on getting your kitten altered at a low cost.

Avoiding pet store purchases

Too many pet stores still sell "oops kittens" from irresponsible people who continually allow their unspayed cats to roam and get pregnant. These kittens often come with most of the same problems I described in the "Taking a chance on a free kitten or stray" section earlier in this chapter. For instance, these kittens usually have had few or no shots, and mom's been outside exposed to who-knows-what.

My advice: Find a pet store with an adopt-a-pet program. These stores have abandoned the sale of kittens and puppies, instead opting to offer space where rescue organizations can display kittens for adoption. Many of these kittens live with foster families until they find what rescuers call a "forever home." You should find a good selection of adoptable kittens during weekends at most PetsMart and Petco stores.

Caring for Special Needs Kittens

While you're at the shelter you may run across a sight that tugs at your heart: a kitten with a handicap. You don't need to ignore the kitten in that cage to be polite. Unlike humans, kittens don't dwell on their misfortunes. Kittens don't become depressed over the loss of a leg, sight, or hearing. They just get on with their lives and figure out how to cope. So if a kitten who doesn't have all his facilities tugs at your heart, don't be afraid to take a second look. The one thing a handicapped kitten simply can't do is go outside unsupervised. He'll need a little extra consideration after he gets to his new home. But you may be surprised by how self-sufficient *handicats* (cats with disabilities) are. Keep reading to find out more about coping with the different problems.

Loving an amputee

Amputee kittens seem to be able to land on all four feet — or rather all three. Although you don't see it every time you go to a shelter, you may occasionally see a kitten who's one leg short of a full set. Or you may happen across an injured kitten and decide to adopt him. You can feel comfortable that these kittens are still rewarding pets: With a few exceptions, you won't find any difference between a kitten with three legs (a *tripod*), and one with four.

An amputee can be more expensive than an ordinary kitten. If you find the injured kitten yourself, you wind up footing the hospital expense. If you adopt an injured kitten from a shelter, it may ask you to make a donation toward the kitten's medical bills in addition to paying the adoption fee.

Even immediately following his surgery, a tripod kitten doesn't need to be carried around. He's got to build up his other muscles and figure out how to compensate for his amputated leg. It may be hard, but let him discover how to get around on his own.

Of course, the kitten needs some time to adjust. Take a look at this list to discover a few things you *can* do to help:

- ✔ A kitten who's lost his front leg has problems landing from jumps, especially if he's jumping down from a high perch. If he likes a special high place, place a stool or bench nearby so he can get up and down more easily.

- ✔ Your kitten now needs to relearn simple tasks like using the litter box. He's got to figure out how to balance, cover his business, and turn on only three legs. He may step in his poop until he figures things out, so be sure to give him frequent footbaths.

- ✔ If he's lost a front leg, he needs permanent help grooming the eye and ear on that side. Clean out his ear and wipe out his eye regularly.

Never let your tripod

- ✔ **Outside without supervision.** Whether he's missing a front or a back leg, he can't climb a tree as quickly as a four-footed kitten. He's more vulnerable to predators and dogs. If something manages to catch your three-legger, he doesn't have all of his claws for protection. Also, his internal organs are more vulnerable at the amputation site because he doesn't have his shoulder to shield them.

✔ **Get overweight.** Not only is it harder for a fat tripod to get around, all that added bulk stresses his joints, putting him at risk of arthritis.

✔ **Get lazy.** He needs exercise. If you adopt him immediately following his surgery, remember to make sure he gets a little gentle exercise to build up his muscles.

Loving a blind kitty

Don't just pass up a blind kitten. These kittens can do just about anything their sighted counterparts can do, even catch flies. They have such acute senses that they act like any other kitten. Because they can't see things that frighten sighted kittens, they are fearless. Don't be surprised if, within a week of coming home, your blind kitten is scaling a 6-foot cat tree in a single bound.

Blind kittens, at least the ones I've met, have been quite friendly. If you take a blind kitten home, she may hide until she completely adjusts to her new surroundings. But after she's more comfortable, she's likely to be underfoot most of the time.

These kittens don't like being picked up or carried around because it disorients them. However, your kitten may enjoy sleeping next to you while you watch TV.

If you adopt a blind kitten, bring her home and start her out in the safe room I describe in Chapter 6. That way, she can establish her own little territory before being introduced to the rest of the house. You also need to kitty-proof the house even more than you would with a sighted kitten. Get down on your hands and knees and see what kind of mischief she could get into. Make sure every little crevice is blocked and install childproof locks on the cabinets. (Discover more about kitty-proofing your home in Chapter 8.) Take a look at the following list for some more tips to help your new kitten adjust to her surroundings:

✔ Keep your toilet lid closed. Blind kittens are extremely inquisitive. You don't want your kitten climbing inside and drowning.

✔ Never rearrange the furniture, and don't move the kitten's food bowl or litter box. Blind kittens memorize the layout of the house by marking it with their scent glands — the friendly facial pheromones not the gross peepee kind.

✔ If she occasionally bumps into things, pad the legs of the furniture to protect her head.

✔ Don't leave stuff lying around that she can bang into.

> ✔ As with other handicapped kittens, never let a blind kitten outside without supervision. Even with her heightened senses, she's no match for a predator.
>
> ✔ Blind kittens like to play just as much as any other kitten. If your kitten can find the toys, playing games is easier for her. Toys with bells, squeakers, and crinkles make it possible for her to run after her playthings. Make sure she plays in an open area so she doesn't slam into anything.

Your blind kitten can bring you a lot of joy. I even know one visually challenged cat who intimidates some of the other family cats. With her heightened senses, a blind kitten often fits right in with everyone else in your house.

Caring for a deaf kitten

Like other kittens with difficulties, deaf kittens make great pets. They start adapting to their deficiency when they're very young. For example, deaf kittens keep track of what's going on around them by feeling vibrations. So the kitten may not hear the door open when you come home, but she can feel it and comes running to greet you just the same. When she greets you, her voice may be louder than most kittens because she can't hear herself. A small deaf kitten may sound very yowl-y.

Deafness in kittens occurs most often in white kittens with either blue eyes or odd eyes. Not all white kittens are deaf. And odd-eyed kittens usually have at least some hearing on the side with the green or yellow eye (if they have a green or yellow eye, that is). Deafness can also happen because of an injury or a birth defect. Like humans, a kitten can be deaf in either or both ears, and each ear can suffer a partial loss of hearing.

Communicating with your deaf kitten can be a big challenge. But with a little practice using hand and facial signals, it shouldn't take *too* long. Although it depends on the kitten, most start grasping what your facial and hand signals mean during their first week with you. Remember, you have to be consistent with your message. Don't let something be wrong one moment and okay the next.

The most important lessons and problems are

> ✔ **Come:** The most important command. In an emergency you don't want to have to chase your kitten down. An Angora breeder I know taught her deaf kitten to come when she wiggled her forefinger in the "come here" sign. To train your deaf kitten to come

1. **Wiggle your finger.**

   The kitten sees something moving and comes over to check it out. This trick only works when the kitten is looking at you. You could also lead her to you using a laser pointer or a flashlight and then offer a reward. Another method to get your kitten's attention is clapping your hands (if she's close enough to see the motion).

2. **Immediately put the kitten on your lap and pet her.**

   If you want, you can add a lick of baby food as a reward for coming. That way she associates good things with the signal.

✔ **No:** When the kitten gets into something she shouldn't, a *gentle* tap to the top of the head, nose, or even the paw — along with a stern look — gets your point across. Kittens begin to understand facial expressions very quickly, but the busier she is, the more perseverance it will take to teach her "No." Water guns work well to enforce the no command, too, especially when you teach kittens not to jump on tables and countertops.

Because you communicate with your hands, never strike your deaf kitten. Hitting doesn't work with any cat. Your kitten simply begins to fear you and your hands.

Because deaf kittens are sensitive to touch and learn to communicate using vibrations, try humming to your kitten when she's sleeping on your lap. She feels like she's close to her purring mother again. Remember, though, that when she's sleeping she can be easily startled. You can wake her calmly by patting a cushion or tapping on a wood floor. Or you can attract her attention by getting down on her level and waving your hand.

Because deaf kittens startle easily when sleeping, families with mischievous or rambunctious kids don't make an ideal home. When startled out of a sound sleep, a kitten may bite. However, a Turkish Angora breeder tells me that her deaf kittens are great around well-behaved kids because they can't hear the shrieking and screaming that frightens most kittens.

Probably the most nerve-wracking moment in owning a deaf kitten comes when you can't find her. Scream as you may, she doesn't come. When this happens, remind yourself that hearing kittens don't necessarily always come when you call them, either. Don't worry. Eventually your kitten will come out to use the litter box or eat. Take a look at the following list for a few tricks that can help you keep tabs in your kitten:

✔ Just like hearing kittens, the deaf kitty will find cozy hiding places. Make a point of finding your kitten's favorite spots.

✔ Providing she's not too well hidden, you may be able to attract her attention by opening a can of really stinky cat food. If she's in a place where she can smell it, she may come check it out.

✔ Put a collar with a bell on her so you can hear her when she's moving around the house.

Try to keep tabs on your kitten so you know she's safe, and always be careful that she doesn't sneak out when you leave the house. Deaf kittens are fearless. They can't hear things that would warn a normal kitten to stay out of the way like a car horn, a person shouting, or a barking dog.

Overall, deaf kittens make wonderful pets. They adapt to new homes as easily as hearing kittens do. Unlike her hearing counterpart, a deaf kitten doesn't usually hide when she arrives at her new home. And when you have company or a party, she parties right along with you because she isn't afraid of the noise.

Part II
Preparing for and Bringing Home Your Kitten

The 5th Wave   By Rich Tennant

"I asked you to buy three things for the kitten to play with, so you bought a ball, a cello, and a microscope. I think your performance expectations for this kitten are a tad high."

In this part . . .

Your kitten will quickly become another full-fledged member of the family, so you want him to be comfortable. This part tells you what kind of supplies to buy when he first moves in. And to start your kitten off on the right paw, Part II gives you tips on how to introduce him to everyone in the family — whether they have two feet or four. I also explain how feeding your kitten a good diet ensures him a long, happy, and healthy life.

Chapter 5

Making Your Kitten Comfy

. . . .

In This Chapter

▶ Picking the right litter box

▶ Sifting through litter options

▶ Getting the lowdown on scoops

▶ Finding the best food and water bowl

▶ Choosing a carrier

▶ Buying a bed

▶ Sorting out scratching posts

▶ Getting the best collar

▶ Selecting safe cat toys

. . . .

A collection of diapers, bottles, and a crib greet the new baby coming home from the hospital. And just like a new baby, your new kitten needs some stuff to help make him feel comfortable in his new surroundings. You need to look for a cat box, litter to put in it, and scoops for poop. You need to buy food and water bowls. Your kitten needs a carrier to ride home in, a comfy bed, a scratching post, and toys that he can use safely.

In the old days, you had to buy pet supplies at the pet store (except for cat food). Not any more. You can shop for your kitten at pet super stores, discount centers, and grocery stores — even via the Internet or a pet supply catalog. For really unique or off-the-wall items, check out cat specialty boutiques or cat shows.

Shopping for a kitten can be like shopping for a new baby: so many cute things. But just because a cat product is cute or smells good to you doesn't mean your kitten will like it. Some kitten products look cute, but pose a hidden danger. Others work just fine for dogs or puppies, but don't specifically fill your kitten's needs. Still others are perfect for the kitten, but the upkeep may be too labor-intensive for you.

When buying any kind of kitten accessories, evaluate these products the way you would a baby's items:

✔ Think safety first

✔ Determine whether kitty will use it

✔ Decide how much upkeep it requires

Consider each item from both the kitten's perspective and yours. You'll find store shelves lined with kitten stuff. But don't worry; I'll help you wade through all the options.

Getting the Lowdown on Litter Boxes

For you, the litter box may rank in importance just below your deodorant; something to keep things smelling fresh that you don't spend much time thinking about. But the litter pan and cat litter are two of the most important things in your kitten's life — after his food, of course.

Your kitten has a list of desirable features that have absolutely nothing to do with what you want. He wants plenty of room to move around and dig in, and he wants a clean toilet just like you do. Like kittens, litter boxes come in all shapes, sizes, and price ranges. You can find many varieties of boxes, including hooded, automated, sifting, self-cleaning, and even plain ol' plastic open litter boxes.

Take into account the size of kitty you're adopting before you choose this important piece of apparatus. A Maine Coon or a bruiser of a random breed will soon outgrow the standard covered litter box.

If you decide to use clumping litter, avoid boxes with sharp edges or indentations in the bottom where pee can pool. Those channels make it almost impossible to pick up those clumps sticking to the corners and edges without breaking them. Left behind, those broken pieces will eventually begin to stink. Rounded corners and flat bottoms help cut down on Smelly Box Syndrome and makes scooping easier. For more on clumping litter look at the "Checking Out Litter Options" section, later in this chapter.

Some kittens don't like to poop in the same box they pee in. After your kitten pees in the pan to mark it, he may not want to poop in it and spoil his scent. So you may need to invest in two litter boxes, even if you have only one kitten. If you put a second box too close to the original box, the kitten may just consider it another pee box. Keep it across the room.

Hooded or covered boxes

People like hooded litter boxes. Hoods reduce the amount of litter the kitten tracks or kicks outside the box. They also hold in odors and prevent your delicate human eyes from having to watch your kitten use the bathroom. These points translate into disadvantages for your kitten. A covered pan holding in odors may force your kitten to hold his breath while he potties. And if you can't watch him use the box, you won't see him strain to pee or find bloody poop. Another problem is that big cats in little covered boxes can't turn around to cover their poop. That's why you often see cats scratching the area around the box instead of inside. Later, your cat may just decide that getting into that tiny box is too much trouble and go in front of it.

However, covered boxes can provide your kitten with a sense of potty protection if he suffers from prying eyes or harassment from other pets or children. And they do help keep litter inside the box while your kitten's digging to China. These boxes usually cost somewhere between $10 and $20.

Automated litter boxes

Do you want a litter box that cleans itself? It'll cost you. Automated litter boxes don't come cheap. Plus, you must use a premium litter with them, otherwise the clumps will break up, and the box won't be properly cleaned. Two of the most popular of these types of boxes, Purrforma Plus and LitterMaid, use rakes to scoop up the waste. Shortly after the cat uses the box, the rake magically sweeps across the litter, dumping the poop and clumps into a storage area. (Purrforma gives you a covered box option.) Remember, because an automated box requires electricity, you need to keep it close to a power outlet (some can be fed batteries, instead).

The manufacturer recommends the LitterMaid for kittens over 6 months of age. However, if you want the advantage of the self-cleaning box, keep it turned off and then switch it when you're present, to empty the receptacle. The kitten gets used to the box in safety, and you still have the advantage of a box that scoops itself. Automatic litter boxes, like the one in Figure 5-1, are perfect for kittens who are finicky about using a dirty litter box.

Figure 5-1: The automated LitterMaid Self-Cleaning Litter Box makes owning a kitten even more wonderful.

Sifting and self-cleaning boxes

Non-automated self-cleaning boxes work with clumping litter. These boxes come with an assortment of ingenious ways of reducing your work. You can roll some of these enclosed boxes to maneuver the clumps into a waste drawer. Other boxes incorporate sifters into the box design, which eliminates the need for a litter scoop. Pour the used litter through the sifter or lift the sifter from the bottom of the box. The sifter catches the yucky stuff. Although these boxes save time, the ones that require you to pour litter from one pan to another stir up a lot of dust. But because they don't require a power outlet, you can have many of the advantages of an automatic box anywhere in the house. They run between $20 and $40.

Plain plastic open litter pans

If you don't want to invest in an automated box, I recommend the plain low-tech open box, because your kitten will probably prefer it. You'll like it too, because at about $10, this litter box is the cheapest. Because these boxes are open, you won't have to worry about your kitten being hemmed in when she gets older. These boxes are so cheap that every few months you can toss them rather than having to scrub down an icky pan. When your kitten is little, start out with low sides that she can climb inside easily. The next time you throw it out, buy a bigger one with higher sides.

Checking Out Litter Options

Because the domestic kitten has his ancestral roots planted in the desert, she has a natural attraction to sand, especially when it comes to her toilet. To cats, coarse litters and pellets feel like walking barefooted on a rocky beach. Studies have shown that a cat prefers fine-grained clumping litters because they're softer against her sensitive paws.

If you can find out what kind of litter your kitten's been using, get a bag of that. If you're not crazy about it, for whatever reason, find a litter you think she may like and blend it with the familiar stuff. But switch gradually. Sudden changes in her litter could inspire your little feline friend to leave evidence of her displeasure just south of her box.

People and kittens have different priorities in determining the best litter. We humans look for odor control, a low amount of dust and tracking, and an affordable price. Kitten priorities are more basic. They want to know two things: Does it stink? Does it feel good against my paws?

In most situations, you're the boss. You're going to tell your kitten what she must eat, what shots she need, and if she can go outside. However, you must defer to her desires when it comes to cat litter.

Sniffing out scented litter

Kitty litter contains odor-control additives from perfumes to charcoal. Although scents may make the box smell better to you, they don't win any awards from your kitten. Kittens are concerned about odor, but in a different way than you are.

A kitten's nose is at least 100 times more sensitive than a human nose, so imagine how strong even a mild fragrance smells. If your kitten misses her mark, behaviorists suggest that you should probably switch to unscented litter. Peeing outside the litter box is the number one behavior problem in cats, and scented litters are the number one reason, which is why I strongly recommend against using them. I discuss kitten litter box behavior in more detail in Chapter 14.

If you need something to control the odor, clean the box more often or, as a last resort, buy litters with charcoal additives.

Getting the right kitty litter

Cat litter is a highly personal choice for the kitten who poops in it and for you (because you get to clean the box). It comes in a wide variety of forms and textures (see Figure 5-2). Today cats may find their box full of everything from

- Traditional clay
- Clumping clay
- Corn or wheat
- Paper pellets
- Wood pellets
- Silica gel crystals

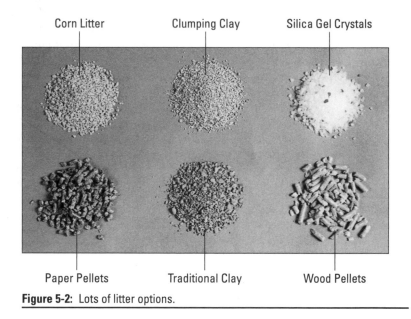

Corn Litter   Clumping Clay   Silica Gel Crystals

Paper Pellets   Traditional Clay   Wood Pellets

Figure 5-2: Lots of litter options.

Your kitten should enjoy using her box. You should be able to giggle as you watch her dig and play in the litter. If she just jumps in, tends to her business, and then jumps out immediately, you've got a problem brewing. Consider switching to a brand or style of litter that makes the litter box more enjoyable — while keeping her safety in mind.

Litter elevates kitties from pest to pet

In 1948, a Michigan woman asked Ed Lowe to find a litter for her cat's toilet. Like most people, she kept a sand pile next to her house for her kitty box, but a thick layer of ice covered it. She'd tried fireplace ashes. Unfortunately, that caused sooty paw prints all over the house. Lowe gave her kiln-dried clay granules that he'd been trying to sell to chicken farmers as nesting material. The farmers didn't go for it, but Mrs. Draper loved it. Lowe figured that other cat owners would be just as excited, so he packaged Kitty Litter in small bags that he sold for 65 cents.

Because the cats' bathroom was simplified, their popularity skyrocketed. In 2003, 73 million Americans owned cats.

Traditional clay saves the day

Traditional clay litter costs the least and demands the most work from you. Poop and wet litter should be scooped daily. Change the litter once or twice weekly and give the box a good rinsing. Buy clay litter just about anywhere. It comes in scented and unscented varieties and tends to be a little dusty. A 10-pound bag of litter costs between $2 and $3.

Clumping clay for your clumping needs

Clumping clay litter forms into a hard ball when it comes in contact with liquids — like kitten pee. This makes maintaining the litter box a breeze. Just scoop everything solid daily and add fresh litter. About once a month, you should dump all the litter and replace with clean litter. You can buy the clumping litter in low-tracking formulas, scented, and unscented. You pay between $7 and $10 for a 14-pound box.

Some preliminary research has associated the dust from both traditional and clumping clay with feline asthma. In other studies, scented litters have been associated with human asthma. Although the research is far from conclusive, I avoid the clay litters altogether even though neither my cats nor I have asthma.

Clumping clay litter can potentially harm kittens. Because kittens haven't mastered the art of graceful peeing, they sometimes sprinkle their feet or step in a wet clump. If a kitten licks litter away from her paws, she could ingest enough litter to form a mass in her digestive tract. That mass could block her intestines, in which case you find yourself with a very sick baby and an outrageous vet bill. Manufacturers say that no scientific evidence supports this claim, but I've watched my kittens groom away clay clumps and prefer to err on the side of caution. If you want to use a clay clumping litter, wait until your kitten is 6 months old. She's more coordinated about her potty procedures, and her larger body can tolerate tiny amounts of ingested litter. You can still safely get the advantages of a clumping litter by using an alternative clumping litter.

Corn flakes and wheat flakes: Not just for breakfast anymore

Now that the United States has almost 75 million feline pets, many living strictly inside, a lot of clay litter ends up in landfills. American ingenuity has adapted by turning biodegradable grain into cat litter.

Crumbled corn, corncob flakes, and wheat litters all have many of the advantages of clumping clay without the hazards. If kitty swallows any of the natural clumping product, it simply passes through the digestive tract and winds up in the litter box again. These litters are soft against kitty's paws and don't need perfumes to mask odors. Another huge advantage is that grain litters don't contain clay dust. The crumbled corn World's Best Cat Litter clumps hard enough for easy scooping boxes. Plus you can flush these products because they're biodegradable. Don't let the level of the wheat litter get too low; you'll have to chisel it from the floor of the litter box. (Remember the flour glue you made in elementary school?) You'll find the grain-based litters at the high end of the cost meter; a 14-pound bag runs between $8 and $17.

Got allergies? My kitten pals use the crumbled corn litter because they like it, it's the only alternative litter I've found that works in automatic boxes, and it doesn't have clay dust or scent to aggravate my allergies.

Paper and wood in the litter box? Pawsitively!

I keep a copy of the newspaper in the bathroom for a little light reading. Kittens can find paper in their bathrooms, too. They may find that the newspaper *is* their bathroom. Paper and wood litters come in

- ✔ Granules
- ✔ Shreds
- ✔ Pellets

These litters weigh less and are easier to handle than their clay counterparts. Besides the obvious ecological benefits, you can safely flush what sticks to kitty's stools. They control pee odors fairly well. Because they don't coat the poop like the finer litters, poop smells until it dries out. It should be scooped daily and the box changed weekly.

The granules are rough on the paws. These litters are a little more difficult to find than the clay litters. Usually you must get them at pet specialty store and you'll pay $7 to $10 for 20 pounds.

Silica gel isn't for your hair

The silica gel litter is a mixed blessing. In a single-kitten home, one bag almost completely negates pee odor for a month, but the same stinky poop is a problem, just like with pelleted litters. Some shapes track everywhere, and the stuff is pricey. Expect to pay between $13 and $18 for 8 pounds.

I found one of my 4-week old foster kittens with a bead stuck to his nose. I removed it, but it did raise concerns of a choking or blockage hazard in small kittens. One woman told me that she removed the litter from her home after a visiting toddler mistook it for candy.

Looking into Scoops

Now that you have your litter box and your litter, you need to consider the litter scoops. Can you dig it?

In the old days, people used fry strainers to clean the box. Cooking utensils still work, but now you have a wider choice of scoops. Just find the right one for your box and the type of litter you've chosen. Look for a sturdy scoop that's designed for your litter.

Believe it or not, scooping clumping litter is an art. First, don't use a flimsy plastic scoop. It breaks up the clump. Those stray and broken clumps stay behind stinking up even in a freshly scooped box.

When buying litter scoops, make sure you buy the right one for the job. Some people use several types of litter in their homes: clumping, beads, and wood. You can use the same scoop on all the types if you get a scoop with large slots.

If you use pellets or silica gel litters, you need a scoop with wider openings. Pellets and gels won't flow through the scoops designed for traditional litter.

Discovering Kitten Dinnerware

Next to you, your kitten has two loves that his life revolves around: the litter box and the food and water bowls. Because kittens are such unique creatures, they have special needs even when it comes to dishes. When purchasing eating utensils, remember that cats are not just small dogs. Look for dishes with these qualities:

- ✔ Wash well and stand up to hot water
- ✔ Made of anything but plastic
- ✔ Durable
- ✔ Shallow eating surface

Look for a dish able to withstand high temperatures in the dishwashers to kill bacteria. A kitty dish must also be able to withstand a little abuse. Bowls made of steel, pottery, or stoneware should do the job.

Plastic bowls come in lots of cute designs, and they're cheap and virtually indestructible. In the long run, however, cheap could cost you a great deal more than a pottery bowl. Plastic bowls accumulate little scratches that harbor a collection of feline acne-causing bacteria. For more on feline acne, see Chapter 9.

Regardless of the type of bowl you use, keep your kitten's dishes and dining area clean. Pick up canned food when he finishes dinner, and clean up crumbs. Wash your kitten's bowls after every meal.

Buy a dish that is shallow and wide. For canned food, the bowl should be no more than 1½ inches deep, like a saucer. A dish for dry food can be 2½ inches deep but the bowl should be kept relatively full. Pass up deep bowls or bowls with small diameters like dog bowls.

Why a dog bowl is not a cat bowl

Kittens have very sensitive whiskers. Some experts believe that kittens can even scent with them. Cats hate to soil those elegant feelers or bang them against the bowl whenever they take a bite. Always feed your kitten from a very shallow bowl or even a saucer.

Have you ever been to a friend's house and watched the cat drinking from the toilet? I bet if you sneaked a peek at the water bowl, you found a plastic one. Kitties prefer toilet water to their plastic bowl because the water stays cooler and fresher. Sometimes, the minerals in the water react with the plastic bowl to create a film over his reservoir. Look for durable water bowl materials that keep the water cool.

As with the food dish, give your kitten an ample water bowl made of ceramic, glass, or stainless steel. You don't need to look for shallow drinking bowls! A deep stainless steel dog drinking bowl won't insult your kitten.

Getting Carried Away: The Right Kitten Carrier

A kitten is like a baby. When your child rides in the car, you strap him in the backseat in his safety seat because you want him to be in the safest place possible. Your kitten needs to travel safely, too. Always keep him in his carrier and strapped in the backseat. Sadly, many people involved in automobile accidents lose cats because they escape through broken windows. So strap the seat belt around the carrier handle so the carrier doesn't go flying through the air if you slam on the brakes.

Before you buy a carrier, think about where your kitten will travel. For more information about traveling with kittens, read Chapter 12. Consider your lifestyle and where you'll take your kitten.

Soft-sided carrier

You can use soft carriers for trips around town or when taking kitty on a plane. When shopping for a soft-sided carrier, make sure you get one with sufficient ventilation and a support that prevents the top from sagging down on the kitten. Also look for seatbelt straps for in-town use. Carry it like a shoulder purse. How does the strap feel? How about the carrying handle? Is the carrier bulky? Can it be washed in case your kitten has an accident? If you plan to fly with your kitten, look for either a light carrier or one with wheels. Struggling with a heavy carrier along with your luggage in an airport terminal wears you out. Make sure the carrier is airline approved and that it has pockets for important travel documents.

Carrying on about the carrier

If your kitten only sees her carrier when you take her to the vet, you're probably going to have to play hide-and-seek when you need to take her somewhere. Then after you find her, you get to shove your suddenly eight-legged kitten through the miniscule opening. Neither game is much fun for you or the kitten. Try to make her like her carrier and train her to go to it. In case of fire or other emergency, per-suading her to get into her carrier could be a lifesaver.

Get her used to her carrier by putting it out in the middle of the room and leaving it open. Put a towel inside to make lounging comfortable. Don't make her look at the carrier. Just set it down and go about your business. Her curiosity soon gets the best of her, and she checks it out. You may even occasionally put a treat inside. When you see her hanging out inside, close the door for a few seconds, praise her, and give her a treat. You can even tease her with a cat toy through the air openings.

After she's comfortable with her carrier, teach her to go inside on command. Let her see you toss a treat into the back of the carrier and say in a cheerful voice, "Kennel." When she's got "Kennel" down, take her for a ride around the block. When you're done, don't put the carrier away. Let her get used to seeing it so she doesn't associate it with trips to the vet. Find out how to buy a carrier in Chapter 5.

I like the SturdiBag, which is very light, doesn't collapse on the kitten, and has seat belt straps. This carrier is perfect if you plan to take your kitten on a plane ride with you (see Chapter 12). Check it out at www.sturdiproducts.com.

Hardshell carriers

The hard carrier that you buy depends on your situation. Do you plan on shipping your kitten cross-country for breeding or only driving him around town? Do you have enough storage space in your home or do you need a carrier that can be stored in a cranny around the apartment?

If you plan on shipping your kitten, buy an airline-approved carrier, which requires that your cat have room to lie down, stand up, and turn around. Such a carrier also must have room to fit a litter box and food and water dishes that mount inside the door.

Any carrier needs plenty of ventilation, but should still be sturdy. Try the locking mechanism. Also you should be able to open it without difficulty, but it shouldn't spring when bumped. How does the carrier feel when you hold it by the handle? It should feel comfortable. Remember, when your kitten's grown, he's going to add another 8 to 13 pounds to the total weight. Does the carrier scratch your leg when you walk? Examine the bolts. Are they made of a material that will hold the carrier together in case of an accident? If you have limited storage space, look for the newer styles that collapse down to a few inches when not in use. Carriers run from $10 up, depending on where you buy them.

Bedding Down for a Cat Nap

Trying to decide what kind of bed to get your kitten and where to put it may require the skills of a cat psychic. Some kitties love a formal cat bed, while others prefer to sleep dangling precariously from the staircase banister. The length of your kitten's fur may help you determine what kind of bed to purchase. All kittens like to sleep in the sunlight, but longhaired kittens usually stay warmer than those with short hair. On the human side of the equation, look for a machine washable and dryer-safe bed. If you buy one that requires hand washing, expect to regret it on washday.

Beds come in many shapes and colors, from pads of polyester fleece to convincing faux mink.

Cat mats

Kittens love the feel of mats made from faux lambskin, and will often dance from paw to paw with eyes closed in ecstasy before curling up for a nap. These mats require little care. Most pads can be machine washed and tossed into the dryer. Check the washing label before you buy. You'll find that mats protect furniture from accumulations of cat hair. If Fluffy sleeps on the left side of the velour sofa, a cat mat will collect much of the fur that ordinarily becomes trapped in the material fibers. When guests leave, they may not have to use as many adhesive sheets from hair roller to remove kitten fur from their behinds. Slide the mat inside your kitten's carrier for travel and for trips to the clinic. Smelling of home, the mat provides comfort and familiarity.

Cup and hooded beds

Shorthaired kittens tend to prefer cup or enclosed beds because they hold more warmth than open beds. They make great hiding places and provide security for your kitten. On the negative side, cleaning them is somewhat difficult. Look for beds stuffed with polyester batting because they require the least amount of care.

Although the foam core beds look great on the shelf, you have to wash the cover and foam core separately. Most foam forms must be hand washed and air dried. Avoid beds with pine or cedar stuffing because cats dislike the smell.

Kitten hammocks

Most kittens enjoy hammock-style beds that raise them off the ground. These beds conform to the individual kitten — wrapping around her like a mama cat. She not only feels secure in the hammock, but also owns a 360-degree view of her world, a life-saving necessity in the wild. Most hammocks are easy to care for; simply remove them from their supports and throw them in the washer. You may find that this low-maintenance sleeping place suits both you and your kitten.

Window perches

Like humans, kittens need something to stimulate them, keep their minds occupied, and their little bodies out of mischief. Because a kitten can't do crosswords or jog, give him a place that interests him. From his little window to world, he can see birds and watch the neighborhood kids play. Window perches are inexpensive, most are relatively easy to install, and they give kitty something to occupy his mind.

Cardboard boxes

Kittens have simple needs: Your new kitten's bed need not set you back even a dime. Given a choice between an expensive bed and a cardboard box, your baby may very well jump into the box and snooze away. The cost — free. When the box gets yucky, replace it. Drop a towel or old baby blanket inside, and you have a bed fit for a king on a pauper's budget.

Finding a Scratcher for Scratch-Along Cassidy

Although you may think that a scratching post is just another toy, I believe it's an important behavioral tool. Scratching is a natural part of kitten behavior. Your kitten scratches to

- ✔ Mark her territory
- ✔ Exercise her muscles
- ✔ Sharpen her claws

If a tree isn't handy, kitty looks for the next best thing — your furniture. Scratching posts help protect your décor and your sanity. When considering cat scratchers you have several options:

- ✔ Cat trees or scratching posts
- ✔ Scratching pads
- ✔ Logs

The most important thing to consider when buying cat furniture is that it must be heavy enough to support climbing and stretching. Don't buy a little $10 scratching post and expect it to do the trick. If his post tips while he's using it, the kitten will go straight to the sofa because it doesn't move when he gives it a vigorous scratching. Even upscale cat furniture costs a lot less than most couches do.

Look for a post at least 30-inches high with a heavy, stable base. Make sure it doesn't wobble when you put pressure against it. Examine how the covering is attached. Does it have staples that can work their way out and be swallowed by your kitten?

Fortunately, kittens can't resist the feel of inexpensive cardboard scratchers. Cardboard may remind them of tree bark, and it stimulates the paw. The packet of accompanying catnip doesn't hurt, either. Some scratchers lean at a 45-degree angle for an upper body workout, and this is fine with kittens, who love the angles.

Kittens usually avoid the scratchers that hang on doorknobs; they prefer to scratch things that don't move.

Although buying a solid scratching post can set you back a bit financially, if you're handy with a drill satisfying your kitten's need to stretch and claw need not break your bank. Cut or buy a stout log or two with bark still attached. Mount it to a two-foot square piece of plywood. You can even bolt one log horizontally and one vertically to satisfy kitty's need for isometric exercises.

Collaring Your Kitten

The purchase of the collar is filled with contradictions. You hopefully plan to keep your kitten inside, so theoretically, you shouldn't need one. Unfortunately, you can't prevent every unexpected event. The plumber may accidentally hold the door open for too long and let kitty out while he lugs a handful of tools into your house. Or your kids may carelessly leave the door ajar. Because kitty can't talk, a collar with an identification tag may be her only chance of making it home. But cats can become tangled in brush, so the collar needs to have a safety latch that pops free if she struggles against something. After this, she's free and safe, but she has no ID.

However, a collar works well in tandem with a microchip that your veterinarian can inject just beneath the skin between the shoulder blades. Even if he loses his collar, a microchip provides a code that can return the kitten home. (For more information on the microchip, turn to Chapter 10.)

Don't put a dog collar on a cat. Dog collars don't have safety releases. And *never* put a choke chain on a cat. That's a tragedy waiting to happen. Even an elasticized collar can strangle a cat if he's hanging by it. Only purchase a collar with a quick release latch that you have personally tested.

Toying with Your Kitten's Affections

Like a toddler, every kitten should have lots of toys. You can find hundreds of toys for your kitten, and if you're like me, you want them all. Take the time to inspect every toy for safety. Think baby. Be wary of anything with child-safety warnings about

- Parts small enough to swallow
- Dangling parts like string

If something can hurt a child, it can hurt your kitten. Remove any tiny hazards like sewn-on eyes, bells, or other small pieces. Also cut away string and yarn that kitty can chew off.

Don't let your kitten play with anything string related unless you're there to supervise. String in an unsupervised kitten's paws could cause a disaster. Innocent as string may seem, swallowed string or yarn can bunch up a kitten's intestines into an accordion and then slice them like a knife. You don't want to see that vet bill! If you find your kitten with a string hanging out of her mouth or bottom, take her to the vet immediately. Do not try to pull it out yourself! You could seriously injure her. Find out more about what string can do in Chapter 8.

Chapter 6

Welcome Home, Kitty!

. . . .

. . . .

*I*t's a big day for your family. The new kitten's coming home. You're ready to throw a welcome home party so everyone can meet your new family member. Everyone's having a happy time — everyone but the kitten.

She has no idea what's going on and that you're making all this commotion in her honor. All she knows is that mom's not there to protect her from the chaos and noise. She can't play with her brothers and sisters. And those nice people who used to put the food out have disappeared, too. In addition, everything smells wrong. Millions of people are milling around, and it's sooooo noisy. Her whole world changed. To her, it's right out of *The Twilight Zone*.

In this chapter, I provide advice that will help you give your new addition a homecoming she can appreciate. Take a few minutes to plan her arrival, and later she'll love you for it.

Planning Kitty's Arrival

Before you bring your kitten home, be sure to do the following:

> ✔ **Make an appointment with your vet.** The vet will check her over for fleas, parasites, and diseases. If you don't have a vet, see the "Paging Dr. Dolittle" sidebar in this chapter for advice. If you have other cats, be sure a vet checks out the new kitten

before she enters your home. If you don't have other cats, you can bring the kitten home and then take her to the vet for a checkup, testing, and vaccinations within the next week. Check out Chapter 10 for more info about shots.

✓ **Kitty-proof your home.** Get down at kitten eye-level and pick up anything small enough for a kitten to swallow, like paperclips or nuts and bolts. Get rid of all your poisonous plants or put them out of your kitten's reach. Spray your electrical cords with bitter apple. Flip to Chapter 8 for more advice on kitten-proofing your home.

✓ **Teach your young children how to handle a kitten safely.** I tell you how in the "Coaching Kids to Care for Kitties" section later in this chapter.

✓ **Gather the appropriate kitty necessities.** Among these is a carrier (see Chapter 5), which you'll use to transport the kitten to the vet and then home.

✓ **Prepare a safe room.** I tell you all you need to know in the following section.

Preparing a safe room

Set up a warm, quiet nest in a small room where the kitten can get acclimated for a week or so. While locking her in a room alone may seem to you like a punishment, it's a sanctuary to her. Cats are territorial creatures, so this little room of her own will help her feel comfortable and at home. She can get acquainted with her own space before she's thrust into your hectic daily routine. From her safe room, she can adjust to the sights, sounds, and smells in her new home.

Don't pick a room where your present cat and dog like to hang out. That will just foster resentment among your pets. Instead, chose a small room that sees little or no traffic like a guest bathroom.

You'll want to furnish her room with the following items, which I discuss in Chapters 5 and 7:

✓ **Food and water bowls:** Shallow bowls made of steel, pottery, or stoneware work best.

✓ **Litter box and cat litter:** Place the litter box against the wall opposite her eatery. You don't eat in the bathroom, do you?

✓ **Bed or something soft to lie on:** You can even give her a cardboard box with a towel or sheet placed inside.

✔ **Scratching post or cardboard scratching pad:** An inexpensive corrugated cardboard pad will satisfy her scratching needs.

✔ **Toys:** Give her balls with bells inside. You'll know when you hear the bells that she's feeling comfortable enough to play.

Paging Dr. Dolittle

If at all possible, find a vet before you bring your kitten home, or soon afterward. Here are some ways you can find out about vets in your area:

✔ **Ask friends, neighbors, or coworkers for recommendations:** If you adopt a kitten from a local breeder or rescue society, ask for the name of its vet.

✔ **Contact the American Animal Hospital Association:** Check out www.healthy pet.com or call 800-883-6301 to find accredited animal clinics around the country.

✔ **Contact your state's veterinarian association:** They won't give specific recommendations, but they'll tell you about vets in your area. Check for prior complaints about a local vet with the veterinary state board and the Better Business Bureau (www.bbb.org).

After you get recommendations, call the clinics. Do you keep getting a busy signal? Are you placed on hold for long periods of time? An occasional busy signal happens, but if you don't get through after calling several times, you can assume they may be too busy to give your kitten the quality of attention he requires. Once you have them on the phone, here are some questions to ask:

✔ **What are your hours?** Are they open weekends or evenings? Be sure the clinic's hours work with your schedule.

✔ **Is this a cats-only practice?** Do you want to go to a cats-only vet or a general practice? In a cats-only clinic, your cat won't be stressed by barking dogs. But such a place isn't as convenient if you need to take your dog to the vet at the same time.

✔ **What do you charge for exams and shots?** Ask how often they recommend vaccinations and about payment arrangements.

✔ **Are your vets on call after hours, or do you refer clients to an emergency clinic?** It's important to know where and how far away you'll have to take your kitten if he gets sick after hours.

After you've narrowed down your choices, visit the clinic(s) you're considering and check out the cleanliness of the facility, friendliness of the staff (to both customers and their pets), and any other factor that's important to you. You may even want to find out such details as whether they perform sterile surgery with masks, gowns, and gloves.

Make sure her safe room is actually *safe*. Remove anything sharp and anything she can break, swallow, or chew on that can hurt her. (Check out Chapter 8 to find out what objects can hurt your kitten.) Keep her room warm; kittens are more susceptible to the cold than adult cats are because they don't have thick coats to keep them warm.

Timing her entrance

Unless you unexpectedly rescue the kitten, try to schedule her arrival at the start of your weekend, so you have plenty of time to help her adjust to her new surroundings. However, try to bring her home while the kids are still at school or when you know a lot of people won't be at the house. Doing so gives her a chance to get used to her new home while her surroundings are relatively calm.

Also, holidays are hectic, with people coming and going and making lots of noise — all of which most kittens hate. If you want to give a kitten as a gift, give a stuffed animal and an IOU or a kitten carrier with the promise to adopt one. Kittens need to be kept quiet and calm while they're adapting to a new home, which is usually an impossible feat during a hectic celebration or holiday.

Coming Home

From a little kitten's perspective, everything is big and scary. That's why it's important to bring your new kitten into a calm environment — her safe room.

Surviving the drive

When you do bring your kitten home or to the vet, never let her run loose in the car. She may hide near the pedals or do something that may cause an accident. Not only could you be hurt, but she could also escape through a broken window or suffer injury. Take the same care you would with your kid. Always keep your kitten in a carrier strapped into the backseat. If the carrier doesn't have a seat belt strap, wrap the seat belt around the handle. Don't risk losing your kitten — or putting your own life in danger — just because you don't want to hear her cry.

Finding sanctuary in The Porcelain Refuge

When your kitten arrives home, take him right to his safe room. Open the carrier door and step aside to ease his apprehension. Don't drag him from the carrier — he'll come out when he's ready, so let him check out his surroundings at his own pace. He may even wait until you've left the room before venturing out.

Keep your kitten in his room for the first day. Let him get accustomed to his corner of the world. He may have been outgoing at the breeder's house, but don't be surprised if he suddenly hides behind the toilet in this strange place — adjusting may take him a few weeks.

Your kitten will likely miss mom and her siblings and may cry when alone. If he's lonely, one or all of three of the following products may comfort him:

- **Bach Flower Essence Rescue Remedy:** A few drops orally help keep your kitten calm safely and naturally.

- **SnuggleKitties:** Different from stuffed animals, SnuggleKitties have a battery-powered heartbeat. This makes the kitten feel as if he's snuggled up to a real live cat. If you don't want to buy a SnuggleKitty, take just enough of the insides out of a stuffed animal to insert a ticking clock, and then sew the animal back together.

- **Feliway:** Spray this comforting facial pheromone in the bedding area. The pheromones emit a comforting scent made specifically for your furry feline. Or ask the person you adopted her from if she has a towel or toy that smells familiar to your kitten.

Check on your kitten every few hours and take time to play with her and talk to her. If she lets you, pick her up. The more gentle attention you give her, the quicker she will bond with you.

Let the kids go in the kitten's room one at a time and sit on the floor for a few minutes at a time; make sure they're quiet (see the "Coaching Kids to Care for Kitties" section for more information about teaching your kids how to handle the kitten). Don't let other animals enter the room!

If you find your kitten rubbing her face against cabinets or furniture, you know she's starting to feel at home — this is how she marks her territory. Find out more about what this means in Chapter 13.

Seeing the sites

After the first 24 hours, watch how the kitten acts in her safe room. If she's walking around confidently with her tail up and her ears forward checking things out, open the door and offer her a short supervised excursion. Lock up the other pets and keep the kids quiet. While she's checking out the landscape on her big adventure, don't let her wander out of your eyeshot. She won't remember where she left her litter box. So when you see her sniffing around, pick her up, rush her back to her room, and place her in her litter box, pronto.

When you open the door, your kitten may simply stare at you as if to say, "Have you lost your mind?" Forcing a timid kitten out into the house will just make her more withdrawn. Instead, let her explore the household at her own pace.

When your kitten seems more confident and knows where her litter box is, you can let her out for longer periods. Continue to keep an eye out to make sure she doesn't get into trouble. Check out Chapter 8 for the lowdown on what you should look out for. Always put her in her safe room when you leave the house or go to bed, though, even after she's gotten comfortable in her new surroundings.

Coaching Kids to Care for Kitties

It's only natural for children to want to hold the kitten the minute their new pet comes through the door. But rather than looking forward to childish affection with great anticipation, the kitten sees the child, even a toddler, as a giant alien. Little kids may even be scarier than older ones because of their erratic movements, and their high-pitched voices that seem to carry at 150 decibels.

To get off on the right paw and create a loving bond between kid and kitten, your kid may need coaching before you bring a kitten home. Some ideas you should teach your kids before the kitten arrives are

- How to act around the kitten (quiet and calm)
- How to properly pick up and hold a kitten
- What appropriate play with a kitten looks like
- When to leave the kitten alone
- How to interpret a kitten's body language (flip to Chapter 13 to read all about what your kitten's telling you)

Teaching kids respect through empathy

From their mother, kittens have to learn not to bite hard or hurt their siblings and to keep their claws in when they play. They learn these things by practicing on each other. You can teach your kids similar lessons about appropriate play (which I cover in detail in Chapter 15).

First, have your kids get down on their hands and knees and place their faces about six inches from the floor, playing "kitten." That helps them see the world — and how scary it can be — from a kitten's perspective. Let them see how frightening their jumping and running can look from a kitten's view by having one child remain on his hands and knees while another jumps and runs nearby.

Kids can experiment by petting and stroking a stuffed animal. When they practice with a plush toy, have them sit on the floor, as they will do with the real kitten. Show them the difference between gentle stroking, patting, and hitting. Kittens love being stroked or scratched under the chin, between the ears, and at the base of the tail — this may even cause "elevator butt." Be sure to supervise these practice sessions.

Instructing kids how to handle kitties

Although kids and kittens just go together, children don't instinctively know how to treat a kitten. They're going to need you to teach them how to act around the kitty and to supervise until they're kitty competent.

Petting the kitten

Teach your kids that the kitty will want to be with them only if they touch him gently. Kittens don't like being patted. Teach them to stroke the kitty softly from the head down the back, and to never grab his ears or tail or poke at his eyes. Also teach them that although puppies like to have their bellies rubbed, kittens hate it. The belly is a kitten's most vulnerable place. Without a great deal of trust, the kitten will likely interpret it as a threat and scratch or bite to get away. If kitty struggles, let her go. If she's not manhandled, she'll soon decide she wants someone to love on her. Be patient until then.

Make kids understand that poking and punching hurts and that you won't permit teasing the kitten. If they disobey, put the kitten up immediately. Be ready to remove the kitten from the child's hands should he or she get too rough.

Never leave preschoolers alone with a kitten. A friend told me that when her kid was little, the youngster thought the kitten needed to be dried in the clothes dryer. You never know what may happen if you turn your back.

To make your kitten more comfortable with the children, you can spray Feliway on the kids' pants legs, socks, or shoes. Only do this to clothing that won't be damaged by the slight alcohol content of Feliway.

Getting to know the kitten

After your kitten gets settled into his safe room, let the kids go in one at a time and visit for a short while. Have each child sit on the floor, and remind him or her that kittens prefer soft voices. If the kid becomes loud or boisterous, send him or her out. Next, show the child how to hold the kitten and gently stroke her (see the sections "Petting the kitten" and "Holding the kitten" in this chapter).

Once the kitten leaves her safe room to explore, have the kids sit quietly on the floor. Offer the kids and the kitten some incentive to be good, and entice the kitten to interact with the kids. Offering a blob of turkey baby food on a spoon will help them bond. Make sure the baby food doesn't have onion in it or it could make the kitten sick. Read about that in Chapter 7. This reinforcement gives your kitten positive vibes about hanging around these kids. Another lesson to teach your children: They must keep their hands and fingers away from the kitten's mouth.

Playing with the kitten

As the kitten becomes more comfortable with your family, you can begin to show the kids how to use toys to play with him. Pheasant feathers make an excellent first cat toy for a toddler because kittens just can't resist them, and even if the kid gets a little rough, the feathers won't hurt the kitty. Teach older children not to let the kitten play with their hands — if they do, they create a bad habit for the kitten that's hard to break. A three-pound kitten pouncing on their hands may be funny, but at 12 pounds, it hurts. Instead, give the kids a Kitten Mitten or pheasant feather for well-supervised rough play. These are just two of the fun kitten toys discussed in Chapters 15 and 21.

Make sure that the kitten has some place where he can climb to get away from the kids. When the kitten hovers just out of reach or hides, you know the playing has gotten out of hand. Most kittens would rather stay out of a toddler's way than scratch him. If the kitten can't get away, he will defend himself by hissing, scratching, or biting. Understand, however, that in this situation, the kitten isn't the one who needs a timeout. Discover more about what kitten body language means in Chapter 13.

Keep an eye on your kids when they're playing with the kitten (for their sake *and* the kitten's sake). You don't have to be the one watching every moment. Your older kids, if they're responsible, can supervise. However, you should be nearby just in case.

Enforce an on-the-floor rule. If the little one wants to play with the kitty, she must sit on the floor. After she sits, hand her a feather or give her some baby food. Don't allow her to walk around holding the kitten — she may drop him. If you are firm with your kids early on, they'll learn to respect the kitten. If kids break the rules, put the kitten in the safe room. No more playing.

Just like toddlers, kittens tire easily. Explain to the children that their new companion needs timeouts for naps, too. As the kitten grows older, playtime can increase.

Holding the kitten

If you want your kitten to bond with a child, you must teach the child to pick her up and hold her properly. The kitten will struggle if she feels she's in danger of being dropped, and she may scratch your child out of fear. To avoid this, teach your child

- ✔ Not to pick up the kitten by the back of his neck.
- ✔ To pick him up with one hand under the kitten's chest, behind his front legs.

 ✔ To put her other hand under the kitten's bottom.

 ✔ To hold the kitten close to her chest (see Figure 6-1).

Figure 6-1: Older children can help teach their younger siblings how to hold the new kitten properly.

Coming Together with Other Animals

Most homes today house more than one type of pet. So odds are that your kitten will need to learn to get along with other cats, dogs, and maybe a guinea pig or two.

The following sections provide suggestions that can make your kitten's transition into his new home less stressful for him and your other pets.

Meeting the other cats

Life is getting ready to change for your resident cat. He's been the pet baby in the family. Now you're getting another baby.

On the big day, without ceremony, bring the kitten into the house, go straight to his safe room, and close the door. Immediately give your resident cat a treat so he associates good things with the presence of the kitten.

Your resident cat will realize very quickly that the house is abuzz with a new smell — another cat. He may stare at the bathroom door or growl or hiss, but you're better off ignoring his strange behavior. If you respond, whether sympathetically or reproachfully, you teach him that his behavior gets a reaction, and he'll keep doing it.

Let the cats play footsie through the crack under the bathroom door. They'll get used to each other's scents before they come into contact.

 When you begin letting the new kitten out on short excursions, place the resident cat in the safe room and feed him or give him a treat. Let him associate the kitten's scent in the room with food — a positive connotation. Once the kitten's few minutes have expired, swap the animals back to their regular stations.

Within a few days to a week, the kitten should walk around confidently, checking things out. At this point, put the kitten in his carrier and set it down in a room with the resident cat. The senior cat will likely act indignant, staring threateningly, hissing, and maybe even growling. The kitten will likely return the honors. Pet the elder and tell him how good he is. Give him a treat. Then put the kitten up. Later in the day or the following day, repeat the performance for a longer period.

When the senior cat begins to ignore the kitten, open the carrier door and let them meet face to face. Don't pet or show affection to the kitten while the older cat is around. Praise and pet your resident kitty for being good and accepting. Then, give them separate bowls and feed them across from each other. This reinforces the pleasant association with the kitten's presence. After they're finished with their snacks, send the youngster back to her room. If it doesn't go this well, then put the kitten away and try again later.

 Don't leave them alone together until you're convinced they're friends. I feel comfortable leaving them alone once they start grooming each other.

After your cat and kitten get used to each other, keep the following do's and don'ts involving your resident cat in mind to help foster a friendly relationship:

- ✔ **Don't yell at him if he hisses at the kitten.** That just reinforces that this upstart is trouble.

- ✔ **Don't ever put them together and let them fight it out.** Someone's going to get hurt.

- ✔ **Do give him even more attention than he's been getting.**

- ✔ **Don't lavish attention on the kitten in the senior cat's presence.** Quite the reverse, praise the *resident cat* and pet him when the kitten is around.

- ✔ **Don't change his schedule around.** Feed him and change or scoop his box at the usual time, if you have one.

- ✔ **Do get the new kitten his own litter box and food and water bowls.**

Getting along like cats and dogs

You've heard the saying, "Cats are from Venus, Dogs are from Mars," right? Just like the kitten thinks we're giant aliens, he thinks dogs are aliens with no manners. Dogs are pack animals. On the other paw, cats in the wild are solitary and territorial. The kitten finally believes the house is home when a big smelly dog trots up, sticks his nose in the kitten's butt, and says, "Hi, I'm Fido. And you are . . .?"

The confused pup can't understand that in Felinese, he's just made a huge faux paw. He really can't grasp why this strange creature just gave him a bloody nose. When the kitten's ready to be friends, he'll turn around and offer his rear end for the dog to sniff. In animal language, "Wanna smell my butt?" is a compliment. To sniff out more about kitten behavior, check Part IV.

If you're concerned about how your dog will react to the kitten, try using pheromone therapy such as Comfort Zone with D.A.P. This product works like a plug-in air freshener. It mimics a natural reassuring pheromone produced by female dogs when nursing. Use it in the room where the dog normally hangs out. It takes two weeks for this product to have an effect on dogs, so plan ahead.

Now it's time to introduce the kitten to the dog. This could be tricky because many dogs look at kittens as prey. At the very least, make sure your dog responds to the Stay and Leave it! commands discussed in the "School isn't just for kids" sidebar in this chapter.

It's important to introduce the dog to the kitten's smell first. Your dog has no doubt smelled the kitten under the safe room door. As with the resident cat, they may have played with each other under the door. And during the time the kitten has been isolated in her safe room, the dog smelled your hands after you played with the kitten. He's even detected Eau de Kitty in the living room after the kitten's been exploring.

School isn't just for kids

Obedience is a must when introducing the kitten to your dog. Like the kids, the dog must learn it's never acceptable to harass or torment the kitten. Obedience training is preferable, especially if your dog is large, but if you haven't had a chance to take him through classes, you can give him a remedial course that teaches him two important commands:

- ✔ **Stay.** Have the dog sit, with a leash attached to his collar that is stretched across the ground. Then give him the hand signal using the flat of your right hand, palm facing the dog with your fingers pointed up. Move your hand toward his face stopping right in front of his nose without actually touching him. Say, "Stay." Then walk to the end of the leash. If he gets up, sternly say, "No!" and move him back to where he was. Once again, give the command and make the hand signal. If he stays, even for just a moment, praise him. Each time you do this, make him stay for a few seconds more. When you can move to the end of the leash, get a longer leash. Continue practicing this command until he stays for 30 seconds to a minute.

- ✔ **Leave it!** This means, "Leave it alone. Ignore it." When the dog is on lead, put a piece of food that he likes on the floor and walk past it so it's within reach of his mouth. When he reaches for it, put your foot over the treat. At the moment he glances away even slightly, say, "Yes!" and hand him a treat from your pocket. When he gets to the point that you can drop the treat on the floor and he doesn't pay attention to it, add the command, "Leave it!" Once you say, "Leave it," don't allow him to touch it. Only give him treats from your pocket. Practice this for five minutes at a time every day until the dog thoroughly understands the concept — this will probably take at least a couple of weeks. When he understands this command, try it with the kitten in the carrier or behind a baby gate, teaching him to leave the kitten alone. When he becomes proficient with the kitten, gradually replace enthusiastic praise for the treat.

When your kitten strolls comfortably around the house, make the dog spend some time in the kitten's safe room and put the kitten in the dog's crate, so they get used to each other's scents. Then switch them.

When the dog doesn't appear obsessed by the kitten smell, he's ready for the big introduction. First, fill your pocket with a load of your dog's favorite treat. Then put the dog on a leash and let the kitten in the room (see Figure 6-2). When the kitten enters the room, give the dog a treat. You want him to associate good things with the kitten's presence. If the kitten decides to get the heck outta Dodge and sprint for her safe room, let her. They don't have to become best friends in one night.

Figure 6-2: Use a leash to restrain your dog when he meets the kitten for the first time.

When your dog and kitten seem to be a little more comfortable around each other, feed them — the mega-doggie reward. Either put the kitten's food on the counter or feed them at opposite ends of the kitchen with the dog on a leash. He'll begin to associate the kitten's presence with being fed. But don't let your dog eat the kitten's food.

Never allow your dog to charge the kitten, even in play. On the other paw, don't let the kitten attack the dog, either. Believe it or not, the dog could suffer a pretty nasty eye injury. Until they're comfortable together, keep the dog on a leash and out of kitten's reach.

Also, don't yell at the dog as he's lunging at the kitten. It's too late for an effective correction at that point. You need to correct him while he's thinking about chasing the kitten. Watch his body language. If his eyes are glued to the kitten and you observe his muscles becoming tenser and tenser, he's likely to pounce soon. Give him a correction or disapproval now, while he's building up to his attack, because this is when he'll make the strongest connection between your correction and his (almost) deed. This is a good time for the "Leave it!" command (see the "School isn't just for kids" sidebar in this chapter).

Give Fido lots of attention, especially when he starts making contact with the kitten. Until they're one big happy family, don't pet the kitten in front of the dog. Keep the visits brief at first, and gradually lengthen them. Praise the dog when he's friendly to the kitten and give him treats when he ignores her. Continue to keep him on a leash until he pays no attention to the kitten after she has entered the room.

When the time comes to let them meet unrestrained nose-to-nose, make sure the kitten has several escape routes and high hiding places that she can easily reach to get away from the dog.

How long it takes for the dog and kitten to get along depends on the dog's breed, how well trained he is, and whether or not he's been around cats much. Be aware that some hunting dogs, like terriers and greyhounds, will instinctively go after a kitten because she scurries around just like prey.

Someday soon you may look up and, to your delight, find the two of them curled up together catching a nap. Be aware, however, that just rubbing up against a dog sprayed with some types of doggie flea treatments could be fatal to your kitten. Instead protect the dog with a cat-safe spot-on or flea spray, like Adams Fleas and Tick Spray (www.farnam.com).

Survival of the smallest

When it comes to introducing your kitten to the smaller pets in your home, I have just three words: Don't do it. You have a curious and excitable kitten with plenty of time on his paws. He likely wants to get into everything, especially that hamster cage or fish bowl. You know what they call hamsters in cat language? Dinner. It's just not practical to expect animals living at opposite ends of the food chain to coexist peacefully. Sure, you've seen some TV shows where a cat and a mouse or a cat and a bird live lovingly together. Your kitten will love your guinea pig or parakeet, too. He'll love the way they taste. After all, in a wild setting, your kitten would be hunting them.

Make sure your critters live in kitty-proof enclosures; turn their room into a cat-free zone unless you're around to supervise all the time. Even if a critter lives in a safe shelter, if he sees a kitten hovering outside his cage staring at his every move, the poor little thing may have a nervous breakdown. If the kitten is ever permitted in the same room, put a box or house in the cage where the small pet can go inside to escape the ever-present eye of the kitten.

Chapter 7

Providing a Meal Fit for a Kitten King

....

....

The ideal diet for your kitten is actually a mouse. It comes in all-natural meal-sized portions, fresh, with no unnecessary additives like fillers, dyes, and preservatives. Unfortunately, the same can't be said of most pet food.

In this chapter you discover the difference between a high-quality diet and inferior food. I tell you which ingredients are good for your kitten and which aren't. Also, a lot of things that people eat can hurt your kitten; I warn you about those, too.

Sniffing Out Quality Cuisine

The old saying, "Garbage in, garbage out," definitely applies to a kitten's diet. When you put gosh-awful, smelly, cheap food in his bowl, what you find in the litter box will make your eyes water. Poop, of course, is a byproduct of what your kitten eats. Poor quality food equals nasty stink.

And cheap kitten food usually doesn't provide your kitten with the balance of vitamins and nutrients he needs to stay healthy. Your kitten can get a whole myriad of diseases and ailments because of vitamin and mineral deficiencies caused by the wrong kind of food or a low-quality food. And cheap kitten food also tends to use unhealthy additives. Problems caused by inferior food can include feline lower urinary tract disease and obesity.

Your kitten needs more protein, taurine, fats, and vitamins than an adult cat. So feed him a high-quality diet specially formulated for kittens. Premium kitten food helps keep your kitten healthier and happier, because it tends to cause fewer urinary tract problems. If you feed your kitten a high-quality food, you can actually see the difference; his coat shines, and he feels more energetic. My favorite kitten foods are Nutro Max Cat Kitten Food, Dick Van Patten's Natural Balance Ultra Premium Cat Food, or Iams Kitten Food. If you want to know which food is the best, compare the labels and keep the following tips in mind:

- ✔ Only consider a brand that has the words "Complete and balanced for kittens" or "for all life stages" on the label. That tells you that this food complies with Association of Animal Feed Control Officials (AAFCO) requirements for a complete diet. It should also state that it meets the requirements of the AAFCO, preferably by animal-feeding trials.

- ✔ Check out the order of the ingredients:

  - The first ingredients listed should be specific sources of protein like chicken, turkey, or beef instead of ambiguous words like meat or even poultry meal. Just because the company lists poultry or poultry meal first doesn't mean it's a good choice.

  - Pay attention to what follows, too. The first ingredient may be poultry, but if filler cereals like corn meal, brewer's rice, and corn gluten follow, the combination of the grains may exceed the meat content. Because kittens can't digest the grain, all that extra junk will make you gag when it comes out the back end. It just passes through his system to make *bigger* smelly poop. He has to eat more to feel full. If you find a food with grain listed as the first or second ingredient, feed it to a cow.

  - Make sure the food contains an absolute minimum of .04 percent *taurine,* an essential amino acid required by kitties. (I won't feed canned food with less than .07 percent taurine or dry food with less than .16 percent taurine.) If your kitten goes for too long with too little taurine, she could suffer permanent blindness or a life-threatening condition called *cardiomyopathy,* a thickening of the muscles of the heart.

> ## Vegetarian kittens
>
> A vegan lifestyle is becoming increasingly popular, and so is turning pets into vegetarians. Don't let anyone talk you into it: Putting your kitten on a vegetarian diet is cruel. The FDA says there's no such thing as a good vegetarian cat diet.
>
> Unlike dogs, cats can't adjust to a low-protein diet. If your kitten is deprived of animal protein, his body will just rob its own tissue to satisfy its need. Some companies claim to make all-vegetable supplements to balance a vegetable-based diet, but there haven't been long-term or controlled studies to prove their safety. Besides that, no feeding trials have tested the palatability of the food.
>
> Living a human vegan lifestyle takes a lot of resolve. If you feel so strongly about it that you need your pet to reflect your ethical belief, consider getting a bunny, a hamster, or a horse; something that doesn't need meat.

  ✔ Look for the brands that tout human-quality ingredients. Otherwise you could be feeding your kitten meat from dead or diseased animals. Don't let anyone convince you that it doesn't matter. Of course it does.

  ✔ Avoid kitten food with preservatives such as BHA, BHT, and ethoxyquin. Instead look for food that uses Vitamin E — tocopherol — or Vitamin C — citric acid — as preservatives. Avoid foods with dyes (if for no other reason, kitty ralph full of food coloring will do a dye job on your carpet) and sugar (your kitten's body isn't designed to break down sugars or carbohydrates).

If you're feeding your kitten quality food, you shouldn't need to give her supplements unless your vet recommends it. You can cause a number of health conditions with overdoses of vitamins and minerals. Overdoses are more common than deficiencies.

Dishing Up Dinner

Your kitten's dinner comes in all shapes and forms. Buy it in a bag, a can, a pouch, or fix it yourself (I discuss homemade and raw diets in the "What's cookin'?" sidebar in this chapter), but be sure to feed him what he's used to for a few days after you bring him home. Making the switch too quickly can cause a real stink.

A matter of taste

Just as your kitten has different nutritional needs than you do, she also perceives flavors differently, through her other senses. The combination of smell and taste give her the interpretation of flavor. If something smells yummy to her, she'll probably eat it. If it smells bad or spoiled, she puts up her nose and walks away, which is why a kitten with a cold quits eating. For more on kitty colds check out Chapters 9 and 10. Even with a sensitive nose on the job, she doesn't taste every flavor you do. She can taste sour, salty, and bitter, but doesn't respond to sweet things, probably because cats can't metabolize carbohydrates.

Kittens are also sensitive to the temperature of their food. They prefer their food to be warm, about 98 degrees — the body temperature of a mouse. Cold food is perceived as food that's been lying around for a while, and long dead. So if you've refrigerated leftover canned food, warm it in the microwave on thaw before you give it to him. Make sure you place it in a microwave-safe dish before you heat it up, though.

Keeping it familiar for a few days

Ask your kitten's breeder or foster parent what he fed her. You should feed that for the first few days and then switch gradually. If you change right away, you'll have to clean runny poop for a few days. I describe how to make the sustenance switch in the next section.

What type of food you feed him depends on your lifestyle, budget, and schedule. Talk to your vet about what she recommends. Feed her a diet formulated especially for kittens or labeled appropriate for all life stages, and your kitten should be happy and healthy.

Making the switch

After feeding your kitten a familiar diet for a few days, switch to the new food gradually. You'll also want to use this technique when she moves to adult cat food (most kitties are ready at about 9 months).

Switch foods by adding a quarter of the new food to his old favorite. After a few days, feed half and half. In a couple more days you can increase to three quarters new food. In two or three more days, he'll be eating his new food only.

Cats establish their eating habits when they're young. If you don't want a finicky eater later, rotate several flavors and brands. This will keep your kitten from developing a preference for a single flavor of cat food. Believe it or not, switching foods can also help prevent future food allergies and deficiencies. Kittens develop sensitivity to grains and dyes after repeated exposures.

Weighing your options

The three most popular food forms are wet, semi-wet, and dry. But be warned: Quality within each form varies, so check the label on each can, pouch, or bag to make sure it includes the quality ingredients I suggest in the "Sniffing Out Quality Cuisine" section earlier in this chapter.

   ✔ **Wet:** Canned or pouched food is the most expensive and most tasty of the traditional options. Wet food has fewer fillers and preservatives than dry or semi-moist, making it the healthiest option. It does require some upkeep though: After 20 minutes, toss it or refrigerate the leftovers. If you leave wet food sitting out, expect a crop of bacteria and bugs.

What's cookin'?

If you have the time to research and prepare the right diet, then cooking your kitten's dinner may be rewarding. But because cats' have such specific nutritional needs, it's difficult, time-consuming, and costly to prepare dinner with the proper balance of healthy stuff. It takes a long-term commitment to prepare your kitten's food. If you run out of an ingredient, you can't just blow it off. Leaving out ingredients could saddle your kitten with heart or eye problems. On the positive side, you can rest easy knowing he's chowing down on high-quality meat and passing on fillers and preservatives.

Some people swear by raw meat diets, but by itself it doesn't make a balanced diet. Raw meat is packed full of nutrients, but like any homemade diet, is difficult to balance. And your kitten could catch toxoplasmosis, parasites, and other bacteria from an uncooked diet. On the other hand, people who believe in raw food for cats, swear by the health benefits because the nutrients and enzymes aren't cooked away.

If you decide on a raw food diet, look into some of the freeze-dried diets. The freeze-drying process reduces the amount of bacteria and organisms and contains added vitamins for a more complete diet. Animal Food Services offers a freeze-dried diet. You can get more information by calling 800-743-0322.

Discuss it with your vet before you take this task on. She may have some recipes that are safe and healthy. Also make sure your vet monitors your kitten closely.

Wet food contains roughly 75 percent water, about the same percentage found in a mouse. This is important because kittens, being desert creatures, get the moisture they need through their prey. If your kitten doesn't drink as much as he should, wet canned food is a good choice.

If your kitten eats a strictly wet food diet, there's nothing to wear down the tartar, so his teeth should be brushed regularly (see Chapter 11) and examined annually by a vet.

✔ **Semi-moist:** Kittens usually prefer semi-moist to dry food. Like dry food, semi-moist can be free-fed (see the section "Deciding How Often to Ring the Dinner Bell" later in this chapter). Cost-wise, it runs between canned and dry kitten food. Manufacturers combine meat and meat byproducts with cereals, grains, and preservatives. It contains about 35 percent moisture. Unfortunately, it has none of the health benefits of either dry or canned. It's high in preservatives and additives, doesn't have enough moisture to be beneficial, and it's not good for the teeth.

✔ **Dry:** Kitten food in a bag costs less than other types and doesn't spoil when it sits out unless you add water. Dry food can be free-fed, which is convenient. And the crunchy bits help "brush" your kitten's teeth, reducing tartar build up. My kittens tell me dry food isn't as tasty as canned, and it usually has a lot more fillers and preservatives than canned food, but it is more convenient especially if you don't know when you'll be able to get home to feed the kitten. Its moisture content is between 6 and 10 percent, which could be a problem if your kitten is prone to bladder infections.

Some people mix wet and dry food together. That may make the wet food go farther, but remember you're compromising the dental benefit of the dry. This mixture will spoil, so don't leave it down for longer than you would canned food.

Deciding How Often to Ring the Dinner Bell

Your kitten does most of her growing in her first 6 months. She should reach her full size between 8 and 12 months. For now, you have a real live eating machine on your hands. While your kitten's still little, let her eat as much as she wants. Many experts recommend that you free-feed kittens semi-wet or dry food and let them nibble all day long. Most kittens will quit eating when they feel full.

Kittens have little bitty stomachs and prefer to graze and nibble up to 20 times a day. If you free-feed, make sure your kitten gets enough exercise. I free feed and offer a morning and evening canned snack.

If you feed canned food, dish some out for your 8-week-old kitten at least four times a day. Kittens like routine, so try to feed yours at the same time every day. Pick up any uneaten food after 15 or 20 minutes. When your kitten's 4 months old, you can drop the feedings down to three times a day. After he's 6 months old, cut back to two or three times a day. Watch his waistline. If you think he's looking a little thin, throw in an extra meal.

Your kitten's body should look like an hourglass when you look at her from above. When you rub her side you should be able to feel her ribs but not see them. From above, a fat kitten will have lost the definition around her midsection, and you won't be able to feel her ribs. However, if you can actually see the ribs, she's too thin.

Treating His Tummy

An occasional treat doesn't hurt your kitten as long as she's otherwise eating a balanced diet. Choose goodies that don't have sugars. Licks of turkey baby food (onion-free), dried liver, or small pieces of cooked chicken or turkey are healthy treats. They're also inspiring rewards when training your kitten. My kittens like Kitty Kaviar, which is an all-natural fish treat (www.kittykaviar.com), and Halo Liv-a-Littles whole beef or chicken treats (www.halopets.com).

Treats and other foods to avoid include

- ✔ **Tuna:** Yes, tuna. Not only is it bad for your kitten, it's addictive. Kittens love tuna so much that they may actually refuse to eat a regular diet. Sadly, tuna is the equivalent of kitty cocaine. In the wild, cats don't catch fish. No matter whether the tuna you feed is cooked, raw, or canned, it will cause very serious deficiencies if fed more than occasionally.

- ✔ **Dog food:** Even if your kitten and your dog get along like brother and sister, don't feed them the same food. Kittens are meat eaters whereas dogs are omnivores; they can eat meat or vegetables. Dog food doesn't have enough protein and taurine for a kitten's needs.

- ✔ **Food with onions or onion powder:** These foods can cause hemolytic anemia, which ruptures the red blood cells. It could eventually lead to kidney failure.

✔ **Milk:** After kittens are weaned, they lose the ability to digest milk. Milk products may make cleaning the litter box an adventure in nasal torture for you. If your kitten likes milk, try milk treat drinks, which are lower in lactose. You can buy them at your local pet supply store.

✔ **Bones:** Cooked bones can splinter and puncture your kitten's bowels or intestines or become lodged and create a blockage.

✔ **Grapes or raisins:** The American Society for the Prevention of Cruelty to Animals (ASPCA) Animal Poison Control doesn't recommend even letting kittens play with grapes or raisins because the juice can cause kidney failure.

✔ **Alcoholic beverages:** You may consider an alcoholic drink a treat after a long day, but kittens and cocktails don't mix. Drunk kittens may sound funny, but they could suffer from alcohol poisoning, slip into a coma, and die. Not very funny at all, is it?

Don't Forget the Water!

You learned in elementary school that water is life, and animals can't live without it. Kittens are no exception.

Kittens have their evolutionary roots (tails?) in the desert sands of Africa. Because of this, the kitten's body is extremely efficient when it comes to water. A kitten's body is about 73 percent water — about the same amount of moisture contained in canned kitten food. Water makes the machinery of the kitten body run: It regulates his body temperature and helps him digest food.

Your kitten loses water every time he goes to the bathroom or exhales. He needs to replace what he looses. Make sure he has access to fresh, clean water all the time. Change his water daily. (If he tends to dribble his kibble in the water dish, move the water three or four feet away from the food.) He needs to drink more if he eats dry food. If he eats canned food, the moisture in the food helps replenish his supply. The more he drinks, the less likely he is to develop bladder crystals.

Part III
Caring for Your Kitten

The 5th Wave   By Rich Tennant

THIS WEEK ON THE CAT CHANNEL

IT'S A 10-HOUR, 3-DAY 5-PART SERIES ON FELINE URINARY PROBLEMS. WANNA WATCH?

In this part . . .

Now that you have a kitten living with you, you probably want to know how to keep him healthy and safe. This part tells you about the innocent-looking things in your home that could hurt your kitten, so you can move or remove them. Because your kitten can't tell you when he's feeling bad, I go over the most common illnesses your kitten will face, how to recognize them, and what to do if he does get sick. I also give you tips on preventative care and grooming. And when the time comes to go on a trip, I tell you how to travel with him or how to find someone to care for him if he has to stay behind.

There's no doubt about it — kittens are c-u-t-e cute! But, like most pets, kittens require a lot of TLC. Make sure you're ready to make the long-term commitment before you invite a kitten into your home (see Chapter 1).

A *queen* (or mother cat) can produce one litter with several fathers. The kittens may all have different colors and body styles, resulting in several different looks.

It's important for a litter to stay together until the kittens are at least 12 weeks old, so they can learn social skills, such as how to play properly and use the litter box, from each other and their mother.

Consider adopting two kittens — they'll help keep each other exercised and out of trouble.

Remember when you bring home your kitten that, like these adorable random-bred kittens, he is used to sleeping with his mother and littermates. He'll be lonely at first, but soon he'll learn that you are his source of companionship.

Keep your kitten safe by transporting him home and to the vet in a comfortable carrier (see Chapter 5).

Keep it clean when it comes to litter. Scoop the scat daily, if posslble, and replace the litter every month.

Quality food helps keep your kitten's coat shiny and gives her more energy (see Chapter 7). Never let her eat Fido's food, which doesn't meet a kitten's nutritional requirements!

At 4 weeks, this orphan is ready to be weaned. If you rescue a kitten, be sure to feed her a milk replacement formulated for kittens, not milk from the fridge (see Chapter 19).

Despite popular belief, cats and dogs *can* live under one roof, especially if you adjust them to this lifestyle gradually over a few days (see Chapter 6).

Introduce the new kitten to your resident cat slowly (see Chapter 6). It's likely they'll become fast friends.

Kittens often get themselves into potentially dangerous predicaments. Keep a close eye on your little buddy, especially as he explores his new home.

Kittens are known for their good grooming habits and seldom need baths, but be sure to bathe them if they get into something stinky or gooey (see Chapter 11).

String makes a fun kitten toy, but monitor your kitten's play to make sure he doesn't swallow it or strangle on it.

Check kitten toys carefully for bells or pieces that could come loose and choke your kitten.

Kittens love to climb and scratch! Give your kitten a sturdy cat scratcher and she'll be less inspired to tear up your furniture.

Nobody says you can't teach a kitten new tricks (see Chapter 15). With a little practice, you can even teach her to kiss on command.

A kitten sleeps 70 to 80 percent of the day. But be ready to entertain him for the rest of his day, or your kitten may resort to clawing the furniture and carpets to pass the time (see Chapter 14).

Groucho enjoys the view from his window perch. Hang a bird feeder outside the window to entertain your kitten for hours.

Give your kitten a taste of the great outdoors, literally, by planting a cat grass container garden in your home. Fill it with grasses and herbs such as oat, wheat, rye, barley, and blue grass, as well as catnip and catmint, which your kitten can hide in and munch on.

Keep a long pheasant feather on hand and keep your kitten pouncing and playing for hours.

When playtime is over, give your kitten a cozy place to catch a catnap.

Nicknamed the Gentle Giant because of his gentle disposition, the Maine Coon is America's native longhaired cat. Maine Coons get along well with kids and dogs.

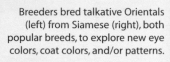

Breeders bred talkative Orientals (left) from Siamese (right), both popular breeds, to explore new eye colors, coat colors, and/or patterns.

Persians are the most popular breed of cat in the world. But be prepared for a workout: Their long coats, which come in a variety of colors and patterns, need daily combing to prevent tangles and mats.

Chapter 8

Out of Harm's Way: Ensuring Your Kitten's Safety

- -

In This Chapter

▶ Warning signs your kitten may be injured

▶ Understanding outside dangers

▶ Removing indoor hazards

- -

Curiosity killed the cat, you've always heard. And unfortunately, this old adage can be all too true. Put a kitten in a room that's 100 percent kitty-proofed, and she'll still get into trouble. In this chapter, you can find out about all the hazards your furry kitten friend faces outside and inside your home. You can also discover how to keep your kitten as safe as possible.

Being Prepared for Emergencies

Unless you live a charmed life, you'll eventually face an emergency with your kitten. She may be injured in an accident or fall ill, but navigating your way though a kitten emergency with happy results will be due, in part, to planning ahead.

Recognizing signs your kitten is hurt or injured

Sometimes it's hard to tell what's wrong with your kitten. If your kitten is weak and listless, is shaking as if having a seizure, won't eat, or is unconscious and won't wake up, she's a very sick little kitty.

Take your kitten to the vet right away if she

✔ Bleeds or has bloody pee or poop

✔ Has repeated diarrhea or vomits more than a couple of times in an hour or continues to poop and puke over several hours

✔ Shows difficulty breathing or walking

✔ Drools or her breath smells different

✔ Has painful peeing or goes outside the box

✔ Is dehydrated

To find out whether your kitten's dehydrated, pull up on her skin. If it stays tented or takes more than a second or two to return to the muscle, she's dehydrated. She needs to see a vet.

When in doubt, contact your vet or emergency clinic for advice.

Having information on hand

If you don't have a family vet, at least find a nearby clinic in case you need to get there quickly. And because kitten accidents always seem to happen after your clinic has closed for the evening, know the location of the closest 24-hour animal hospital. Don't just know the address; know how to get there. You don't want to have to try to read a map when your kitten has a broken leg.

Also, keep emergency phone numbers in a convenient place. (Look at the cheat sheet in the front of the book for the number to the ASPCA Animal Poison Control Center.) Keep a first aid kit in a convenient place. (For what to put in a first aid kit, turn to Chapter 20.)

Ensuring Safety Outside: It's a Jungle Out There

Outside the safety of your front door, adventure mingled with danger awaits your kitten. If you're afraid that forcing him to stay inside will cheat him of the joy of living, think again. If you let him go outside unattended, you may deprive him of life altogether.

An outdoor cat lives an average of only 4 to 7 years compared to 15 to 16 years for an inside cat. For cats, the great out-of-doors isn't so great.

Losing the auto race

By far, the car ranks as the top outdoor-kitten killer. It doesn't matter whether you live in the city or a rural area — cars kill. Don't give your kitten too much credit for reasoning. She doesn't know what a car is and can't keep herself safe. Do the math on a 3-pound kitten versus a 1000-pound car. It's a demolition derby she can't possibly win.

Avoiding antifreeze: The deadly drink

Antifreeze offers kittens an enticing, yet deadly, treat. As little as a teaspoon can be fatal to an average-sized adult cat; much less can kill a kitten. Experts used to believe that ethylene glycol, the active ingredient used in most coolants, had a sweet flavor and animals liked it. Now they think that it's the only water around, so pets drink it regardless of how it tastes. A couple of licks can cause an excruciating death.

Your kitten will suffer irreversible kidney damage in as few as 12 hours after drinking antifreeze. Unfortunately, if you don't get her to the vet within 4 to 8 hours, she may not make it. Early symptoms include vomiting, lethargy, and lack of coordination. Antifreeze isn't just a cold-weather danger. In the spring and summer, people drain their radiators or the engines boil over when other water sources have dried up.

Protect your car with a safer antifreeze containing propylene glycol like Sierra by Old World Industries or Prestone Low Tox Antifreeze Coolant. Although these products cost a few dollars more, your kitten and the neighborhood cats are worth it. If your mechanic doesn't sell an alternative antifreeze, insist that he get it or supply your own. Also, store all automotive products, including oil and gasoline, where your kitten can't get to them.

Having a good time in the engine

The car doesn't even have to be moving along the street to cause problems. Your kitten could crawl up into a warm engine to get out of the weather. When the engine turns over, the blade catches her. If she survives, she can suffer devastating cuts or even broken bones from the powerfully rotating fan blade. One vet told me he treated a stray kitten who crawled up into an engine and hitched a 45-minute ride. The kitten received serious burns to his paw pads, but he lived. The family kept him, and now he's an indoor cat.

Garages aren't a kitten's best friend

You may not think the garage holds so many kitten perils, but it can be a deathtrap. Check out why you need to protect your kitten from the garage in this section.

Steering clear of deadly garage doors

Although automatic garage door openers have a built-in safety, kittens are too small to trigger it. A garage door crushed Ebony, a friend's black kitten, when he ambled into the garage as the device lowered the door down to the floor. Even an unautomated door can cause painful injuries if a kitten should walk across it while the door closes. I confess, when Chani was 7 months old, she was walking on the open garage door as it closed, and she got her paw caught in the mechanism, nearly ripping off her pad. Her paw was saved, but many kittens wind up dead.

Avoiding heat exhaustion

A curious kitten investigating an open garage may find herself imprisoned and at risk of heat stroke, asphyxiation, or kidney damage during hot weather or hypothermia in extreme cold. Even if the cat is not confined for an extended period, she could get into toxic chemicals.

Before I bought my cat fence (to find out more about cat fences, turn to Chapter 15), my kitten Wretched investigated a neighbor's open garage and became trapped in the attic. It took me three days to find him and two more days to get him out. We had to cut a hole in the eaves (and pay for the repair) to free him. I lucked out. Many kittens aren't discovered until it's too late.

Avoiding unfriendly people and animals

Not everyone can like you, right? The same goes for your kitten. In this section, I tell you about what can happen in your 'hood when your kitten meets up with not-so-nice people and pets.

Fighting off Fido, Fluffy, and Flower the skunk

Wandering dogs pose another huge threat to small kittens. Although an adult cat can outrun a dog in a short sprint, a kitten stands almost no chance, especially over a long distance. Under no circumstances should you let a declawed kitten outside unsupervised. A declawed kitten simply can't climb fast enough to get away from a threat.

And as civilization encroaches more and more on rural area, wild predators are becoming a common threat to outdoor cats. Urban and suburban predators go after kittens because they're easy prey; kittens are snack food to coyotes, who just pick them up and run. Skunks and kittens can tangle, and you may have to face a rabies problem.

Any outdoor kitten can fall victim to unneutered cats roaming the neighborhood. If your unspayed girl goes outside, she'll become pregnant, contributing to the problem of cat overpopulation. And if your boy hangs out down the street, he may find himself in the fighting ring with the neighborhood tom. Even a 5-month-old girl can wind up in a family way and an 8-month-old boy can father an entire community of kittens in one night.

Tomcats beat up anything they can't mate with, especially during breeding season — spring, summer, and fall. Even if your cat's been fixed, he can still become a victim of the neighborhood bully. And if he happens to win the fight, he still loses, because cats have some pretty nasty bacteria in their mouths. So left untreated, a cat bite will almost always result in an abscess requiring medical attention: Antibiotics, anesthesia, and the incision will cost you an easy $125. This doesn't count the bills and the heartbreak that you'll suffer if your kitten catches feline leukemia (FeLV), feline immunodeficiency virus (FIV), feline infectious peritonitis (FIP), or rabies from a bite. (To find out more about these diseases and their inoculations, read Chapters 9 and 10.)

If that doesn't convince you to keep him inside, then maybe the ticks, fleas, and ear mites that hitch a ride into your home will. Fleas can cause allergic dermatitis and anemia in kittens, and they're not a lot of fun from the human perspective either.

The neighbor who hates kitties

You probably live in a nice, safe neighborhood, so you don't worry about kitten abuse. You should. Just because you love your kitten, doesn't mean your neighbor does. Every day, animal control centers across the country receive calls from people threatening to shoot kittens just because they're walking on the car, pooping in the garden, or making noise at night. My husband saved a little black stray, Sally, after we heard a neighbor threaten to shoot her because she cried outside his window all night.

Unexplained disappearances increase around days observed by cults. Any kitten can become a victim of cult sacrifice, but especially at risk are those who are black, white, black and white, or dark torties. Many animal shelters and humane groups refuse to adopt out black cats around Halloween.

Eating lilies will have 'em pushing up daisies

If you love greenery, you're going to eventually find your favorite potted plant with missing or gnawed leaves. And this may be more of a problem than you think, because many houseplants are toxic.

A lot of the most popular flowers can be as deadly to your kitten as a sip of antifreeze.

I found this out the hard way. The day I received a birthday flower arrangement, Oliver, my 6-month-old foster kitten, jumped on the counter and proceeded to gnaw on a Stargazer lily. Fortunately, I saw him and rushed him to the vet. After two days on an intravenous drip, he recovered with no lasting effects. But I guarantee that there will never be another lily in my house. If I hadn't witnessed Oliver's crime, I'd have been burying him instead of tossing out my birthday gift.

Oliver isn't unusual. Left to their own devices, most bored kittens will chew on plants to pass the time. Even if it doesn't it doesn't kill your kitten, nibbling on the wrong foliage can cause burns to his mouth and throat.

Protect your kitten by knowing which plants are safe and which ones are dangerous. Take a look at Table 8-1 for the lowdown on poisonous plants.

Table 8-1	Plants to Avoid
Plants	*Effects*
Azalea, rhododendron, lily-of-the-valley, foxglove, milkweeds, yew, mistletoe	These plants are very toxic to the heart
Lilies (Easter, Day, Japanese, Show, Asian, Tiger, Stargazer, and so on). Avoid anything in the lily family.	Licking or chewing on any part of a true lily will kill your kitten
Castor Beans	Seeds contain ricin, one of the most toxic substances on earth
Cycad, Sago, or Zamia palms	Cause liver failure
Autumn Crocus	Causes kidney and liver failure, bone marrow suppression, and bloody diarrhea

Plants	Effects
Oleander	So highly toxic that small amounts can be deadly even to humans
Peace lily and calla lily (aren't true lilies), philodendrons, pothos, shefflera, dieffenbachia	These can cause mouth pain, drooling, vomiting, and loss of appetite
Mushrooms and toadstools (Assume any wild mushroom is poisonous)	Can cause liver, heart or central nervous system failure
Onions	Onions can cause kidney failure and hemolytic anemia, which ruptures the red blood cells. To find out more about why you shouldn't add it to your kitten's food, look at Chapter 7

If your kitten has been grazing, he may get the runs, vomit, have difficulty breathing, or act differently — for instance, by hiding under the bed or not eating. Don't delay; take him to the vet right away.

Remove all toxic plants from his reach. You can replace them with a safe choice — see the sidebar "Safe plants" in this chapter for more on this topic. If you have a less-than-green thumb, consider silk plants as a viable alternative.

If you absolutely can't part with your hazardous plants, Sticky Paws for Plants is a great deterrent for keeping your cat out of your decorative foliage. It's a series of plastic strips coated with an adhesive that you crisscross along the top of the pot. It takes a lot of the fun out of playing in the plants. (Find a retailer near you at www.sticky paws.com.) You can also discourage chewing by spraying the most accessible leaves and stems with bitter apple or pepper juice.

Instead of fighting kitty hall, why not cater to your kitten's natural instincts? Many behaviorists believe the best way to protect both your kitten and your plants is to give kitty a little garden all his own. You can plant a cat garden in just seconds, using kits available from any pet retailer. Even if you have only a marginally green thumb, you can grow greenery that your cat can safely munch on. Cat grass kits come in a variety of forms, from ready-to-munch sprouts to a bag of seeds. Cats can safely eat wheat grass, barley grass, oat grass, rye grass, bluegrass, and, of course, catnip. If you want to plant the seeds in your own soil, make sure the dirt comes from a bag. Your parasite-free kitten could get worms from neighborhood cats who have pooped in your garden.

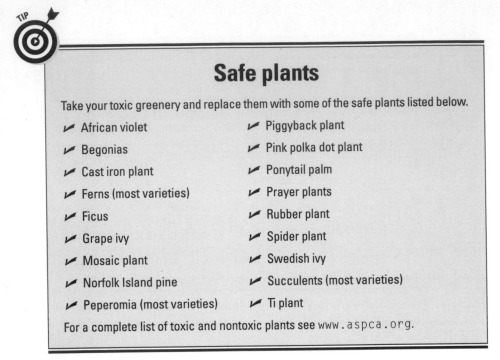

Safe plants

Take your toxic greenery and replace them with some of the safe plants listed below.

- African violet
- Begonias
- Cast iron plant
- Ferns (most varieties)
- Ficus
- Grape ivy
- Mosaic plant
- Norfolk Island pine
- Peperomia (most varieties)

- Piggyback plant
- Pink polka dot plant
- Ponytail palm
- Prayer plants
- Rubber plant
- Spider plant
- Swedish ivy
- Succulents (most varieties)
- Ti plant

For a complete list of toxic and nontoxic plants see www.aspca.org.

Don't be tempted to buy a flat of grass from the nursery unless it is organically grown. Most growers use potentially harmful pesticides and fertilizers.

Understanding the Perils of an Indoor Kitten

Okay, life for an outdoor kitten can be rough, but those on the inside don't always live in a bed of catnip, either. Unfortunately, indoor kittens tend to have more behavioral issues than outdoor kittens. Housebound kittens need things to do and see. A restless kitten will fill his time by scratching the furniture, eating plants, or climbing the curtains. Kittens need activities and toys to stimulate their predatory tendencies; things that make them run and chase and jump. They also need to be kept safe and secure, and this section gives you some pointers on how to do that.

Because your kitten will likely spend all or most of her time inside, you need to find the dangers hidden around your house. Try getting down on your hands and knees and looking at things from kitty's perspective. When you're lower to the floor, you can find things you can't see when you're standing up. Combine good prevention with an eye in the back of your head, and you and your kitten will have many happy years together.

Even though knickknacks may not pose a hazard to your kitten, your kitten poses a hazard to your knickknacks. And broken china could be swallowed and cause choking. Forget the Dresden dolls and the Hummels on the coffee table. Replace them with something less valuable and not as fragile: Catnip mice should work nicely.

Looking out for things your kitten may swallow

Unfortunately, kittens have a bad habit of swallowing things that weren't intended for swallowing. So be sure to pick up any tiny objects you find on the floor. Anything that could choke a baby could harm your cat. Even if it doesn't choke him, it could lodge in his intestines.

In some ways, power cords and string act alive. They wiggle and do everything that decent prey should. They practically beg your kitten to play. So don't leave any string lying out where he can get to it.

Your kitten can't spit things out of his mouth because of the barbs on his tongue. After string makes it into the back of the mouth, it goes all the way through (hopefully). However, if the tinsel or string stops moving, it can create an accordion effect that literally saws a hole in the intestines. Peritonitis follows, and if not treated quickly, death.

Look out for these things around your house that could cause your kitten to choke, strangle, suffocate, or electrocute:

- ✔ Balloon strings
- ✔ Bells from cat toys
- ✔ Bones from cooked or baked poultry
- ✔ Buttons
- ✔ Cooking string and dental floss
- ✔ Dangle toys separated from the pole
- ✔ Electrical cords and holiday lights
- ✔ Fishhooks, fishing line, and other tackle

- Game pieces and marbles
- Grocery bags with handles
- Paper clips, rubber bands, and staples
- Pennies
- Tacks, nails, screws, small washers, and nuts
- Thread, yarn, and sewing pins
- Tree tinsel (icicles) and garland string

Because your kitten can be electrocuted, choked, or strangled, keep an eye-out so dangerous stringy objects aren't anywhere near where he plays. Spray lights or power cords in the areas he can reach easily with bitter apple (available at most pet supply stores), which leaves a nasty taste in his mouth.

Ribbon, string, and yarn can also become wrapped around your kitten's throat and choke him. Don't forget to cut up those plastic holders that come with six-packs of beer and soft drinks. Kittens can poke their head through then get tangled in another object in panic. Don't forget to check his collar every few weeks. Kittens grow so fast that you may have to let it out a notch or two.

I use Cord Short'ner by Safety 1st, which is a circular contraption that you can wrap wires and curtain cords around to get them out of kitty's reach. Buy it at most home improvement warehouses.

Medicines your kitten can't take

If your kitten seems sick, don't reach into your medicine cabinet for a human remedy without getting an okay from your vet. Even drugs that are relatively safe for a dog can kill a kitten because her metabolism differs so radically.

Remember, any medicine is potentially toxic! Three factors determine the dosage: concentration, quantity, and the size of the cat. Is the concentration of the potentially toxic substance 1 percent or 95 percent? Is the amount that the kitten ingested one or two licks or 10 teaspoons? Is the kitten tiny or large?

Don't leave medications unsupervised on countertops or nightstands. And always make sure not to confuse your medication or another pet's pills with your kitten's meds. Take a look at the following list of potentially toxic substances to keep away from your kitten:

- **Advil:** Ibuprofen can cause renal failure and coma, depending on dose. Cats are thought to be twice as sensitive than dogs are to ibuprofen.

- **Antidepressants:** Keep all antidepressants out of your kitten's reach. Some vets will prescribe specific antidepressants to control behavior problems, but only in minute doses. Antidepressants can affect the heart rate and cause seizures or tremors.

- **Aspirin:** Therapeutic doses prescribed by vets are usually safe; however, too much aspirin or aspirin given too frequently can cause an overdose and even death.

- **Calcipotriene:** Calcipotriene is used in psoriasis creams, lotions, and shampoos. Even a small taste can cause kidney failure in kittens.

- **Local anesthetics:** Lidocaine, benzocaine, dibucaine, and other anesthetics are sometimes found in sunburn sprays and topical pain relievers; they can cause liver failure and deprive the body of oxygen.

- **Ma huang/pseudoephedrine/ephedrine:** These substances are found in both diet pills and decongestants. They can cause hyperactivity, increased heart rate, seizures, and even death.

- **Other pain relievers:** Naproxen, nabumetone, indomethacin, diclofenac, carprofen, piroxicam, and so on. These can all be dangerous, even in small amounts.

- **Pepto Bismol and other anti-diarrheal products:** These can contain a form of aspirin. If too much is given or if it's given too frequently, your kitten could get very sick. You may see constipation, lack of coordination, and severe lethargy. Never give your kitten these products unless your vet tells you to.

- **Tylenol:** Also known as acetaminophen, it deprives oxygen to tissue, causing gums to turn blue or dark brown; it also causes liver failure. There is no safe dose of acetaminophen for cats or kittens.

Steering clear of harmful chemicals

Although kittens live up to their reputation as self-cleaning pets, they certainly don't contribute to a self-cleaning house. Quite the contrary, your kitten's presence around the house means you simply must pick up the sponge or the mop more frequently. So you can expect to have more cleaning products lying around after you get a kitten.

Don't expect your new friend to instinctively know which products will hurt her and which ones won't. That's your job. Kittens are so sensitive to chemicals that even the strong smell of some cleaners can make them nauseous. Products that may be mildly irritating to us can be corrosive or burn a cat and they can cause kitty to retain fluid in his lungs. Use cleaners and disinfectants according to instructions. Don't let the word "natural" lull you into a false sense of safety. Remember that tobacco and arsenic are also naturally occurring.

For most cleaning around the house, I like a peroxide-based product called Tuff Oxi. It works great on grease and pet odors. I even use it in the kitten rooms. You can order it at 310-574-3252.

Before having your carpets cleaned, find out what kind of chemical the company plans to use. Check with your vet to see if the chemicals are cat safe, and always make sure floors and carpets are completely dry before letting your kitty walk on them. Even when using disinfectants like pine cleaners make certain the surface has been well rinsed and then thoroughly dried before giving your kitten access to it. These chemicals can be absorbed through the kitten's paw pads.

Many cleaning products contain acids or alkali that could severely injure your kitten. Again, think toddler and use your common sense. If the label says, "Keep out of reach of children," or "Wear eye protection," it can hurt your kitten. Keep dangerous cleaners tightly closed and out of his reach. Watch out for cleaning products like

- Anti-rust compounds
- Automobile battery fluid
- Bleaches
- Drain openers
- Gun barrel cleaners
- Metal cleaners
- Mildew removers
- Painting removal products
- Pool sanitizers
- Rust and ink stain removers
- Toilet bowl cleaners

You may not have ever heard of cationic detergents, but I bet you have some in your house. Cationic detergents, containing strong acids like hydrochloric acid, can be found in fabric softeners, some potpourri oils, germicides, disinfectants, and sanitizers. Unfortunately, the "safe" cleaner or "non-toxic" liquid potpourri could have these ingredients in them without having to mention them on the label: Manufacturers don't have to list them. Either memorize the types of products I just listed, call the toll-free customer service line on the label, or ask your local human poison control if the product contains more than 1 percent cationic detergent.

You also need to watch out for several common household items:

- ✔ **Batteries:** All kinds of batteries, from hearing aid to car batteries, can cause deep burns.

- ✔ **Fertilizer:** Check with manufacturers to see how long you need to keep the kitten off your grass after applying fertilizer. Store all fertilizers in a safe, secure area.

- ✔ **Glowing necklaces:** If your kitten bites through one of these, he'll foam at the mouth like a rabid dog because of the taste. Although your kitten should be okay, seeing him frothing like that may scare you to death. Take him to a vet if the liquid gets in his eyes.

- ✔ **Mothballs:** Kittens are very sensitive to some of the ingredients in mothballs. Veterinary treatment is always needed.

- ✔ **Silica gel packets:** Silica gel packets are found in shoeboxes, medicine bottles, and even some cat litters. (To discover more about silica gel cat box litter, flip to Chapter 5.) If your kitten eats silica gel, it may cause mild stomach upset. Call your vet if he eats silica gel from medicine or supplement bottles — they may have absorbed some of the medicine from the pills.

Watching out for pesticides

Pesticides are just one more thing to worry about. Even pest control products sold for use on pets can hurt or kill a kitten. Keep all chemicals, powders, traps, and baits out of kitty's reach. Try non-toxic options like glue traps or rodent live traps.

Even if you don't use pesticides, snacking on poisoned prey can still endanger your kitten. When the kitten eats a poisoned mouse, she gets a dose of the toxin as well. She can also be poisoned by walking through powder and licking it off her paws, or even by absorbing it through her paw pads.

What to do if kitty eats a poisoned mouse

Commercial rat baits come in three varieties: one type causes uncontrolled bleeding, one affects the central nervous system, and one causes kidney failure.

If your kitten has been exposed to rat or mouse bait, tell the clinic what kind it was. Identifying the chemical helps the vet know how to treat your kitten. Anticoagulant rodent bait responds to Vitamin K_1 treatment (usually given for 30 days or more). If you have any questions, call your veterinarian or the National Pesticide Telecommunications Network (800-858-7378). They can refer you to a company that uses some of the least toxic or organic pest control methods.

Ask your exterminator what chemicals he uses and request an information sheet. Insist on anticoagulant poisons because they have an antidote. Place pesticides in areas that are inaccessible to your kitten, promptly remove dead rodents, and try to curb your kitten's hunting habits. See the sidebar "What to do if kitty eats a poisoned mouse," in this chapter, for more information.

And remember that you need to be careful when fighting fleas, because all flea fighters are not created equal. Never use any flea- or tick-control products labeled for dogs on your kitten. Many dog flea-control products contain a synthetic pyrethrum insecticide called permethrin. This ingredient is so toxic that if your kitten rubs up against or sleeps with a dog treated with permethrin, he could suffer a lethal reaction. Your best strategy: Only use kitten-safe products on the family dog. Check with your veterinarian for flea and tick product recommendations for your kitten.

Be careful with natural remedies, too: A little citrus product will kill fleas, but concentrated citrus oils can burn your kitten's skin, and make him very sick.

And finally, never set off a bug bomb in a house with a pet inside. Even if you've locked your kitten in another room, the air conditioner will circulate toxic mist to his refuge in just a short time. Take kitty to a friend's house or even put him in a carrier outside under a tree if the weather isn't too hot. Air the fumes out of the house before bringing your kitten back inside.

Keeping your furniture and appliances kitten friendly

Kittens love to hide. If there's a door and he's not supposed to get there, that's where he wants to go. Many an inquisitive kitten died by sneaking past the door of a home appliance.

Clothes dryers attract kittens like crazy. If your kitten sees the door is open, he'll seize the opportunity to hide, especially if he can lie on a load of freshly dried clothes. Unfortunately, most of us start the dryer without checking. Now that you have a kitten, you need to look inside *every* time you turn on the dryer. Someone I know failed to look and heard the ka-thunk ka-thunk. She immediately opened the door and found her Snowshoe kitten. Dazed and dizzy, Ling Ling staggered around for a few minutes, but she survived. Another friend didn't stop the machine in time. Her kitten, Sunshine, had already broken his back.

Always visually inspect the dryer before turning it on. Test the damp clothes with a few punches as added insurance.

The kitchen is another kitten minefield. When your kitten gets big enough, he can jump on a searing hot stove element and burn himself, so never leave a stove unattended. Also, don't forget to give the oven and broiler a quick glance before you close the door. At the building supply warehouse you can buy a stove guard intended to keep kids (and kittens) away from pot handles.

Use the same approach when you operate the dishwasher. Kittens can sneak into the dishwasher and drown. Even look in the refrigerator before you close the door.

Installing childproofing products

Although some accidents with appliances are freak occurrences, a little caution could save your kitten's life. Because kittens and small children have so much in common, the same products can protect them both. Check out the baby section of your home improvement center. Use childproof latches to keep nosey little whiskers from checking out cabinets that may contain trash and other unhealthy things. Most of the kitten (kid) safety products cost under $4. I like the Safety 1st products (800-723-3065; www.djgusa.com).

No room offers your kitten complete sanctuary from danger. Keep the toilet seat and lid closed: A kitten climbing on the open commode could fall in or be crushed by the lid and seat slamming down on him. Your ironing board could tip over, crushing the kitten when its legs fold. And be careful when using your reclining chairs — you could crush your kitten when the chair reclines.

Teaching his name

You know the saying: Dogs come when you call them. Cats take a message, and they may get back with you. People who believe that simply haven't learned the right way to call their cat. Although you may find it easier to train a dog to come, when you've taught your kitten to come to his name, you've really accomplished something. Coming to you on command could save his life. If he accidentally escapes the house, you stand a much better chance of getting him back if you've trained him to come when you call. There are three rules to teaching a kitten to come to his name:

✔ **He needs short name.** A champion Persian with a name longer than his fur needs one shortened to one or two syllables that are easy for him to understand like Sam, Sammy, Bogie, or Groucho.

✔ **Use the same name every time you call him.** Your kitten may have a number of names, but when you want him to come to you, you need to be consistent. Don't call him Rudy and Buster and Buddy and Kitty and Precious. You know whom you're talking to, but the kitten doesn't. Stick with only one name.

✔ **Make sure something pleasant happens whenever you call him.** Don't call him, then give him a bath, medicate him, or drop him in a carrier to go to the vet. That teaches him that bad things happen when he hears that word. Instead, give him a treat, feed, him or play a game he really likes. Never use his name with discipline.

Chapter 9

Recognizing Common Illnesses and Diseases

Kittens are more delicate than cats. At some point during that first 9 months of your kitten's life, you may notice that he isn't looking his best — maybe he has bloody poop or is sneezing. It may be nothing. Then again, these symptoms may indicate an illness that demands the immediate attention of you and your vet.

Kitty colds and diarrhea are most likely to be the issues that come up. Even those shouldn't be taken lightly, as kittens dehydrate quickly. But you could be facing more serious concerns, perhaps even life-threatening ones. But don't worry too much! Between ever-improving preventive medicine and advanced care, your kitten stands an excellent chance of living a long, happy life with you.

Catching Kitten Colds

Your poor little kitten feels under the weather: She's got a fever, goo in her eyes, gunk coming from her nose, and she refuses to eat. Your vet will probably tell you that your kitten has an upper respiratory infection (URI). In other words, she caught a cold. She has most likely caught one of two common kitty viruses: feline calicivirus (FCV) or feline herpesvirus (FHV).

What causes those darn kitten colds

Those two viruses cause 80 to 90 percent of kitten URIs. In adult cats, these colds aren't much more than an uncomfortable inconvenience, but because kittens are so small and fragile, these viruses can be fatal. Unvaccinated kittens are in the highest risk group, so make sure your kitten gets those shots. To find out more about how these vaccinations can save you and your kitten grief, turn to Chapter 10.

Just like human colds, kitten colds must run their course. But they're also very contagious, so if you have other cats, lock the sick kitten in a bathroom. It doesn't take much for your kitten to share her cold: a sneeze, a drink out of a water bowl, a shared litter box. *You* can even pass the germs around when you pet her; so always wash your hands after handling her. The symptoms can last between 7 and 14 days, but you may want to keep your sick kitten sequestered from the rest of your cats for 21 days.

How you can tell if kitten has a cold

If your kitten exhibits any of the following symptoms, she may have a cold:

- Runny, snotty nose, gooey eyes
- Excessive sneezing
- No energy
- Loss of appetite
- Sores or ulcers on the tongue, mouth, and even the nose
- Limping from joint pain

Dealing with dehydration

The younger the kitten is, the less body mass he has, and the more quickly he can dehydrate. Check to see how dehydrated your kitten has become by tenting his fur. Pull the skin at the scruff of the neck out and see how long it takes to move back in place. The skin of a well-hydrated kitten should spring back almost immediately. Skin that remains tented indicates that your kitten requires fluids from a vet injected under the skin. If the fur returns sluggishly, give him unflavored Pedialyte by mouth with a dropper or syringe and keep an eye on him. If he's squirting watery poop down the back of his legs, get him to the vet — along with a gift of runny poop in a zip-up plastic bag. Discover other ways to test for dehydration in Chapter 18.

If your kitten's feeling too bad, she may not be drinking enough to replace the water she loses, and she may need to have some fluids injected under her skin by a vet (see the "Dealing with dehydration" sidebar in this chapter). If left untreated, kittens can die from a secondary infection, lack of nutrition, or dehydration.

What to do for a kitten with a cold

So you know for certain your kitten has a cold. Here are ways to treat the poor little creature.

Chicken soup is m-m-m good

Your mom recommends chicken soup for colds. I do too. When my fully weaned kittens refuse to eat, I give them low-sodium diluted chicken broth or unflavored Pedialyte. I also force feed a special canned food called Hill's Prescription Canine/Feline a/d through a syringe. (Get the a/d and the syringe from your vet.)

Feeding a reluctant patient

When I have a kitten who won't eat, I buy Hill's a/d (a tasty food with the consistency of baby food formulated for sick kitties) from the vet. I always keep a couple of extra cans on hand in case of emergencies. Ask your vet for a syringe that works for feeding your kitten and how much and how often you should feed her.

To feed the kitten

1. **Hold him in your arms with his rump against your stomach.**

   That way he can't back out of your grasp.

2. **Insert the syringe tip in from the side of his mouth in the gap between the canines (fangs) and his molars.**

   Don't go straight in from the front because you could force the food or fluid down his throat and choke him.

3. **Press slowly; only give the kitten a tiny bit. He needs time to swallow it.**

   I find it easiest to manage the plunger with my thumb.

Don't continue to reuse the syringe when the rubber plunger dries out. You will no longer be able to push the plunger gently, and when it finally does give, you may shoot too much food into kitty's mouth, choking him.

Clearing up the goo

To break up that heavy-duty sinus congestion, I set up a vaporizer with some Vicks Vapo-Steam. Also saline nasal drops (straight saline with no decongestant or antihistamines) can help loosen up pasty crud caking up a kitten's nose. Use the drops three or four times a day with normal congestion (if you can get them up his tiny little nostrils). A kitten who is mouth-breathing can take drops up to six times a day. Put one drop in each nostril and then get out of the way. When he sneezes, it's *snot* going to be a pretty sight. The hard part is holding him still long enough to get the drops up his nose. Even a sickly 3-pound kitten can have the strength of the Terminator when fighting off a nasal invasion. The nose drops really help, though, so don't give up.

Getting the Skinny on Skin Problems

Your kitten's skin is her largest organ. Remember that the skin can tell you when something's amiss. Run your fingers through your kitten's fur to check for scabs and bumps.

Acne: Not just for teenagers

You probably never thought you'd hear your kitten complaining about her complexion. Kitten acne results from contact with bacteria — usually from plastic or dirty bowls. Plastic scratches easily. Those little scratches harbor bacteria that even hot water from the dishwasher can't reach. Your kitten rubs his chin against the plastic bowl, and next thing you know, he's got zits. Acne can also develop if your kitten doesn't groom very well or if she has allergies. Kittens with acne look like they have fleas on their chin. These flea-like lesions are actually (yuck) blackheads. In more severe cases, you may see reddened pimples, other crusty developments, and hair loss.

When blackheads appear on your kitten's chin, throw out all of the plastic bowls and replace them with ceramic or steel bowls (see Chapter 5), and wash his dishes daily in hot water.

Back when Chani was a kitten, she got those crusty blackheads on her chin. My vet gave me an acne shampoo to scrub her chin with and told me to toss the plastic food dishes. The shampoo didn't help — but then I got more of it on me than I did on her chin! However, shortly after I threw her plastic bowls out, the acne went away.

TIP

Put a warm, moist cloth against the kitten's chin to open the pores, and then clean it with hydrogen peroxide. Don't pick at or squeeze any of the sores, and don't use human acne medicine because it can poison your kitten. (Read more about human products that can hurt your kitten in Chapter 8.) If you don't notice an improvement in a week, see your vet. Her acne may have become infected and need antibiotics.

Ring around the ringworm

Despite its name, ringworm isn't a worm at all, but a fungus related to human athlete's foot that (usually) causes hair loss in a circular pattern (see Figure 9-1). Unlike other parasites, the ringworm just stays on top of the skin and affects the hair and hair follicles.

Figure 9-1: Ringworm, although contagious, isn't the end of the world.

The great news is that within two to four months of catching it your kitten should build up immunity to ringworm. Persians and Himalayans seem to be more susceptible than other breeds.

WARNING!

Make sure to wash your hands well after handling a kitten with ringworm. Early in my fostering career, I actually gave my foster kitten, Seryi, ringworm. I'd handled several other cats at an adopt-a-pet. Soon I developed a perfect little red ring on my belly. So don't be surprised if you get ringworm. Remember that *you* can use an over-the-counter fungal treatment, but your kitten can't. He'll just groom it off of his fur, and it could make him very sick. Contact your vet about treatment. You can treat your kitten's ringworms with

- ✔ A series of dips or shampoos
- ✔ Antifungal solution and ointments

    ✔ Oral medications

    ✔ The homeopathic remedy tellurium

Wash your kitten's bedding with bleach and vacuum his favorite hangouts.

Talking about Tummy Trouble

Tummy trouble is one of the most common and serious kitten health problems. A kitten may have a problem with the squirts, he may be plugged up, or he may have stuff coming up the wrong way.

Diarrhea and vomiting can turn from an inconvenience to life-threatening dehydration quickly. If you notice that your kitten is having repeated occurrences, don't waste time — get him to a vet. See the section "Knowing When to Take a Kitten to the Vet Immediately" later in this chapter for more info.

Coughing up info on hairballs

Your kitten likes to keep herself clean. She spends hours removing loose hair from her coat with that amazing barbed tongue. Unfortunately, she can't spit out the fur trapped in those barbs so she swallows it. In small quantities, the hair moves through the digestive system with no problems. However, when she sheds and ingests too much, the hair can't pass out of the stomach, so the kitten hacks it up, and you find some squishy land mines.

Most of the time, hairballs are just a nuisance, but sometimes an oversized hairball can pass out of the stomach and cause an intestinal blockage. Read the section "Plumbing through intestinal blockage" in this chapter for more on that subject.

You can disqualify your kitten from the Olympic class projectile vomiting team by simply brushing her. To get things moving, you can rub a hairball remedy or petroleum jelly on her paws so she can't sling it everywhere when she shakes her feet.

I use Laxatone and Petromalt (both petroleum based) hairball medicines, as well as plain old Vaseline (petroleum jelly).

You can also buy special food designed to help control the hairball problem. The additional fiber in these diets acts like a plunger, pushing hair through the stomach. Hair doesn't accumulate because the fiber keeps it moving.

If your kitten continues to be constipated or begins to vomit, see your vet. The problem may not be hairballs at all.

Plumbing through intestinal blockage

If your kitten hasn't pooped in a day or so, she may have something stuck. An object that gets stuck in the intestines backs everything up like a stalled car during rush hour. A single stalled car can turn into a tragic pile-up and a first-class emergency.

You may see some string, yarn, tinsel, or even audiotape hanging out of your kitten's mouth or bottom. Don't try to pull it out! The stuff could be wrapped around his intestines. Even if it isn't, pulling the string could actually saw a hole in the intestines. Instead, grab your kitten carrier and your keys and rush your kitten to the vet, *now!*

Symptoms of an object lodged in his throat or intestines include

- Difficulty breathing
- Bleeding from mouth or bottom
- Convulsing
- Vomiting
- Coughing
- Drooling
- Swollen tongue

Without immediate medical attention, your kitten may not make it.

Getting Ticked Off at Parasites and Organisms

Your kitten may have a whole host of hitchhikers and freeloaders living at his expense. They can cause diarrhea and constipation and even anemia. Fortunately, most are easy to conquer providing you don't let your kitten get too sick.

Worms, worms, and more worms

In this section, I tell you all you ever wanted to know about worms. We have big worms, we have fat worms, we have mean worms, we have ugly worms. Read on for the squirmy facts about kitten worms.

Measuring tapeworms

Fleas tend to bring more than just themselves to the party on your kitten's skin. Even if you get rid of the fleas, they leave behind other little gatecrashers to make it an event your kitten will be reminded of long after the flea is dead: tapeworms. When a kitten with fleas grooms herself, she swallows tapeworm eggs. The eggs hatch, producing adult tapeworms that settle happily into the kitten's intestines, stealing nutrients intended for the kitty.

Tapeworms can grow up to 6 inches long and make lots of little segments. Unfortunately, each segment contains maturing tapeworm eggs. Later, the new egg segment breaks off of the worm and exits once again through the poop.

Most of the time, you don't need to give your vet a poop sample. You can see the evidence of tapeworms underneath the kitten's tail. It looks like dried white or yellow rice. You can treat for tapeworms, but you'll never get rid of them until you get rid of the fleas.

Symptoms of a severe infestation include weight loss, diarrhea, abdominal pain, and increased appetite. I had one 4-week-old foster kitty with such a big tapeworm infestation that he suffered a hypoglycemic episode that resembled a stroke. My vet wormed him for tapeworms and gave him glucose. He was fine, but don't let anyone tell you tapeworms aren't a problem in tiny kittens!

Over-the-counter tapeworm treatments don't work very well. Save yourself time and get something like Droncit from your vet. Clean up your litter boxes, and if you use clumping litter, toss all the old litter.

Going round about roundworms

I'd always heard that kittens come into this world already infected with worms, and dismissed it as an old wives' tale. But if the mother, or *queen,* has roundworms, the kittens do too. A worm-free queen has worm-free kittens (unless they're exposed at some point).

The roundworm larvae set up housekeeping in the kitten's intestinal tract where they can grow up to 5 inches long and where they lay eggs of their own. The kitten poops out the eggs, which can lay in the grass for years. He or another animal steps on the eggs and swallows them when he licks his paws. More roundworm.

Like other parasites, roundworms give the kitten a bulging tummy. Occasionally, the worms can actually be seen in kitten poop or puke. Sometimes a kitten has so many roundworms, he dies from an intestinal blockage. So take your kitten to the vet and get him wormed. Read more about parasite prevention in Chapter 10.

You need to follow up with a second worming two weeks later, because wormers don't kill eggs, and larvae aren't affected.

Discovering those pesky hookworms

Tapeworms steal your kitten's food from the inside. But hookworms steal his blood. Young kittens can easily die from the internal bleeding caused by hookworms.

Hookworms can grow up to 1 inch long and have hook-like mouths. These nasty little bloodsuckers attach themselves to the intestinal walls and open a blood bar. All they can drink — no limit. When one area of the intestine dries up, the hookworm moves, leaving behind a couple of tiny holes that bleed.

Kittens become infected by nursing from an infected queen, walking on infected soil, or using an infected litter box. They swallow the eggs through normal grooming and the larvae grow in the stomach and small intestines. Later, they poop out the eggs to start the cycle again. After the kitten ingests the cyst containing the eggs, the cyst can hang around in the intestine for some time before coming out for dinner.

Kittens with hookworms may puke and poop blood. They're prone to anemia and constipation and tend to lose weight.

Hookworms can infect *you* if you're careless in handling poop or walk barefooted in an infected area, so take your kitten to the vet and keep him parasite-free. And wear your shoes if you're walking in an area where neighborhood cats poop.

Finding out about cold-hearted heartworms

Heartworms have long been considered a dog owner's problem, but now vets realize that cats and kittens can be infected with these parasites. Outdoor kittens living in an area with mosquitoes find themselves most at-risk. But mosquitoes can sneak inside as well.

Kittens aren't infected as often as puppies, thank goodness. However, kittens with heartworms are in more trouble than puppies. Most puppies are larger than kittens, so they can survive longer with more worms. A grown cat can drop over dead from as few as ten heartworms. Even one worm can present a serious reaction because your kitten's heart and blood vessels are so small.

Some kittens show no symptoms, and other times they cough, have breathing difficulty, collapse, and experience seizures, vomiting, and diarrhea. Until recently, diagnosis required a chest X-ray, but now your vet can perform a blood test in the office. The test isn't terribly accurate, however, because the test needs several worms to detect the presence. Only one or two heartworms can cause serious damage in a kitty.

Unlike a dog, your vet won't kill heartworms in a cat because the medicine is toxic to cats, and if several worms die at once, they can leave the heart and block those tiny blood vessels. Most vets give steroids to make breathing easier, and then let the worms die on their own. As the worms die and dislodge, they can cause strokes and blockages in the arteries or veins where they lodge. Sometimes, the adult worms can be removed from the heart surgically.

If your kitten lands in the high-risk category — an outdoor kitten in an area with lots of mosquitoes — you may want to have her tested and start her on heartworm preventive. Talk to your vet.

Itching to find out about fleas, ear mites, and ticks?

If you want to see a miserable kitten, look at one who's got fleas, ear mites, and a token tick or two. Watch him scratch, scratch, scratch. All that scratching and itching are enough to drive a kitten crazy.

No fleas, if you please

Fleas have been bugging kittens since kittens first showed up. Several species of the little bloodsuckers even annoyed the dinosaurs.

You can tell whether your kitten has fleas by putting him on a white towel and dragging an extra fine flea comb through his fur. If he does have any bugs, you either trap a flea between the teeth of the comb, or tiny little black flecks land on the towel. Most vets call that black stuff *flea dirt,* which is a nice way of saying flea poop.

In the short two to four weeks that fleas live on this earth, those little vampires can certainly cause a lot of grief. Unlike Dracula, one flea can't suck your kitten dry. But if forty or so of his closest friends join him for dinner, your little kitten could have problems.

With your kitten providing the one-course meal to a bunch of insect freeloaders, he could begin to act lethargic with anemia. (One of my early fosters, a kitten named Diana, came to me with

over 100 fleas on her. Her gums had very little color to them.)
Check out the insides of his ears and his gums. If they're whitish
or grayish, you need to take the kitten and his flea circus to the
vet right away to show his guests the magical disappearing act.
A fleabite can infect a kitten with more life-sucking parasites: tapeworms. Read the section "Measuring tapeworms" in this chapter
for more info.

Fleabites can cause an allergic reaction called miliary dermatitis.
The kitten reacts to the flea's saliva and develops itchy bumps.
Your vet usually treats this with a shot of steroids.

Today you have lots of flea control meds you can use on kittens:

- **Capstar:** If your vet gives your kitten a dose of Capstar, the
  fleas drop like flies. Capstar, a quick fix for serious infestations, interferes with nerve transmission in the flea, but
  doesn't affect the kitten. The manufacturer doesn't recommend it for use on kittens lighter than 2 pounds or younger
  than 8 weeks. In a few minutes, the fleas drop off of the kitten
  stone cold dead. It's a beautiful sight. Talk to your vet; you
  have to get the Capstar from her. It doesn't kill larvae or eggs
  and only works for 24 hours.

- **Spot ons:** You can buy these from your vet or over-the-counter.
  Spot ons are applied only once a month to one convenient spot
  on the skin; they distribute over the skin surface to sit in the
  hair follicle or sebaceous glands to provide protection. Some
  of the prescriptions treat ear mites and prevent heartworms.
  I am not comfortable with many of the over-the-counter products, especially for kittens. I only recommend the spot ons
  you can get from your vet. Always read the label and make
  sure a product is designated for use on kittens.

- **Sprays:** I don't like sprays because they stay on the fur. When
  you hold the kitten, the residue rubs off on your skin and
  clothes. However, if you have a young kitten with a serious
  flea problem, you can spray a towel with a kitten-safe flea
  spray. Hold the kitten in the towel for a few minutes, and then
  bathe the kitten in a baby shampoo to get rid of the fleas and
  eggs. Make sure that flea sprays are kitten-safe.

- **Flea combs:** Combs are never a poison problem, but they're
  hard to use on a bony kitten. If you decide to go this route,
  you must comb daily. I use an extra fine-toothed flea comb.
  The flea gets caught in front or between the tines. Then I drop
  the fleas in a bowl of soapy water to drown them. I carry one
  around in my purse and flea comb my friends' pets. Really.

- ✔ **Garlic supplements:** I love natural supplements, and I know that many people use garlic as a natural form of flea control. But garlic can damage a kitten's red blood cells. It has the potential to cause hemolytic anemia, in which the body's immune system can begin attacking its own blood cells. I think garlic supplements are risky, especially because the kitten's already losing red blood cells to the bloodsucking fleas.

- ✔ **Collars:** Cut them up and put them in vacuum cleaner bag. They're not terribly effective on the kitten. Also a friend's kitten managed to get the collar caught over her mouth like a horse's bit. She almost didn't make it.

Especially for little guys, check with your cat clinic and follow the manufacturer's directions unless the vet indicates otherwise. My vet has given me both Frontline and Advantage spot ons and scaled the dose way down for 4 week olds. Your vet may do the same. If you don't feel comfortable going outside of manufacturer's recommendations, you can always get out the trusty flea comb.

All flea fighters are not created equal. Never use any flea or tick control products labeled for dogs on your kitten. Dog flea control products are so lethal to felines that a kitten who rubs up against or sleeps with a dog treated with *permethrin* (a synthetic pyrethrum) can suffer a lethal reaction. If your dog and kitten come in contact, then treat the dog with a cat-friendly product.

You need to try to get rid of fleas and their eggs around your house and yard. Otherwise, those eggs just keep providing you with new little fleas.

- ✔ **Wash bedding:** Wash all linens where your kitten likes to sleep including her bed and your bedspread.

- ✔ **Vacuum your house frequently:** Be sure to vacuum areas where kitty hangs out like cushions, couches, and carpeted areas. Toss out the vacuum bag to keep flea eggs from hatching back inside the house or put a piece of flea collar in the bag.

- ✔ **Treat the yard:** Especially if you let the kitten play outside.

Getting an ear full about ear mites?

You may notice your kitten shaking his head or scratching at it. Inside his ears, he has a mother lode of black goop that looks like coffee grounds. Your unlucky kitten's been cursed with ear mites. These pinpoint-sized parasites live and breed in your kitten's ear canals. Your veterinarian can verify the diagnosis by taking a look at the goo under a microscope, but the black discharge is usually a dead give away. A healthy ear should be clean and dry.

Giving your kitten pills

If you've ever tried to give a pill to a kitten, you know that you need the arms of an octopus to hold him. But giving medicine doesn't need to be that hard. Ask your vet if you can put the medicine in baby food or get it from a compounding pharmacist. Otherwise, read my advice on how to get that pill down a kitten's hatch:

1. **Hold the top of your kitten's head and grasp his cheekbone with the thumb and index finger of your free hand.**

2. **Tilt his head back until his eyes are facing upward.**

   His jaw should open a little, naturally.

3. **With the hand that's holding the pill (between the thumb and forefinger), use your middle finger to pry his mouth open.**

4. **Quickly place the pill as far back on his tongue as you can.**

5. **Close his mouth and keep it closed.**

6. **Stroke his throat, gently blow on his nose, and touch your finger to his nose. He'll reflexively lick his nose and swallow.**

If you're afraid of being bitten, you can use a pill popper. Get one from your vet or pet store. Follow steps 1 through 3. Place the tip of the pill popper in his mouth from the side and press the plunger (as shown here).

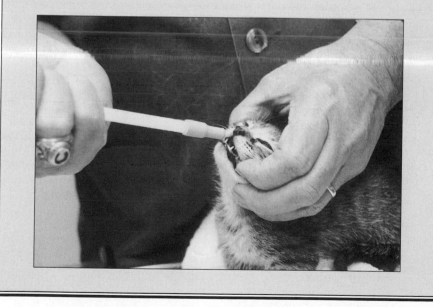

Not only do ear mites cause the inside of your kitten's head to itch around the clock, but they can eventually cause ear infections and, if left untreated, even deafness. Ear mites are a social disease. Outdoor kittens can get them from other cats or even mice and squirrels. If you have other pets, you need to treat everyone.

New advances in ear mite treatments cut down on the amount of work and stress that you and your kitten must endure, but the good ones come from a vet.

- ✔ Acarexx is a water-based suspension that you pour directly into the ear. The manufacturer states that you only need a single dose directly in the ear. Injections given a few weeks apart are available. Ask your vet which would be best for your kitten.

- ✔ A monthly spot-on application of Revolution permits the product to be absorbed into the body where it kills numerous parasites, including ear mites.

- ✔ An old standard in the war of the ears is a topical ear product called Tresaderm, which helps to reduce inflammation and to kill yeast, mites, and mite eggs. The ears have to be cleaned out for the medicine to work, and you should treat for 21 to 30 days.

Most older and over-the-counter products containing insecticides don't kill incubating mite eggs. Because of this, you have to continue to apply these products for the mite's life cycle or longer — at least 30 days.

The best time to use ear medications for mites is late in the evening when feeding activity is most intense. Next time your veterinarian cleans your kitten's ears, ask her to show you how to do it.

When you're treating ear mites with drops, they avoid the poison by taking a short holiday. They simply crawl out of the ear and enjoy new scenery on the kitten's face or body until the coast is clear. So before you treat, use a kitty-safe flea product on your entire kitten to keep the mites corralled in the ears where they belong.

Tickling your fancy for blood-sucking ticks

Like fleas, ticks suck blood from your kitten. As you would expect, kittens who hang out in wooded areas are more likely to have the little bloodsuckers. Ticks are usually found on a kitten's head and ears where he can't clean, but you can find them anywhere. I once rescued a 6-month-old kitten who had numerous big gray ticks deep inside his ears.

Understanding ear mites from the earside out

Have you ever wondered how it feels to have ear mites? Although we can't tell what a kitten's thinking, one vet knows exactly what a kitten with ear mites experiences.

In 1994, Dr. Robert Lopez won an Ig Nobel Prize (awarded annually by the science humor magazine *Annals of Improbably* to celebrate the unusual, honor the imaginative, and spur people's interest in science, medicine, and technology) for offering himself as a lab cat to see if ear mites could survive in a human ear. He took ear mites from an infested cat and transferred them to his own ear. Immediately, he heard scratching and moving sounds as the mites explored his ear canal. The itching started. With all those critters itching, scratching, and moving around within his ear, the sensations were almost overwhelming. Lopez felt helpless as the sounds grew louder and closer to his eardrum. The activity and noise increased at night when he should have been sleeping. After the ear mites ate, he could sleep. But the little parasites were up bright and early at 7 a.m. repeating the patter. At the end of a month, he couldn't hear out of the infected ear because it was clogged from debris. When he flushed out his ears, his hearing returned to normal.

If you notice that ear mites have started partying in your kitten's ears, get him to the vet right away to save him from all those sleepless nights.

Look for ticks by parting the fur and also by feeling with your fingers. If you find a tick, use tweezers to pick up the body. Pull straight out slowly, and the mouth should release. Don't twist the tick. When the whole tick has been removed, you should see a bloody little crater and maybe a drop of blood on the skin. Skin with no bloody spot, but a couple black spots where the tick was means the mouth's still imbedded in your kitten's skin; you may need to take her to the vet because the head can cause an infection. Don't use matches, cigarettes, or gasoline to remove the tick. He may just dig deeper.

Ticks carry a lot of diseases that people can catch, including Lyme disease and Rocky Mountain spotted fever; so wash your hands after handling ticks.

Other tiny, icky, problematic thingies

In this section, I tell you about other little microscopic varmints that can cause all sorts of problems for your kitten.

Catching on about coccidia

Coccidia are protozoa that are usually seen in kittens 4 to 12 weeks old, but even adult cats can get them. They live and breed in the intestinal tract. Kittens with coccidia get the runs. You can see traces of blood and mucous in runny poop. Kittens with really bad cases lose their appetites and may barf. With all that fluid escaping, dehydration is a big risk.

Kittens frequently get coccidia from their mother, and when one kitten in a litter gets it, they all get it. Even if your kitten hasn't been exposed to other cats, she could be exposed to coccidia from mouse poop or a roach. This is yet another reason to wait until kittens are 3 months old before bringing them home. They've already gone through that period when they're most vulnerable to the organism, and you don't have to deal with it. Look in Chapter 2 to read about the proper age to bring your new kitten home.

Your vet will want to look at a sample of poop to confirm that coccidia are causing the trouble; however, those single cells often evade microscope detection. When I have kittens with the runs and we can't see what's causing it, I have them treated for coccidia, and it usually goes away. However, it can take four or five days before you see a slowing of the going.

Kittens and cats with coccidia should be kept away from uninfected kitties for about three weeks.

Giardia isn't fancy chocolate

Like coccidia, giardia live in the kitten's intestines and pass through the poop. Giardia move from kitten to kitten through bowls or drinking water or by contact with another cat's poop. Hanging out inside protective cysts, giardia can live for several months outside of a body, waiting to hitch a ride.

Kittens with giardia get the runs, and sometimes gas. And you haven't lived until your sinuses have been cleared by kitten gas. I don't know how such intensity of odor can come from that little bitty body.

Giardia can be cleared up fairly easily by a couple of drugs: metronidazole and quinacrine. Take some poop to your vet and make sure to treat all infected kitties. Just because you don't see symptoms, doesn't mean they're giardia free. Although you can get giardia from an infected stool, you're more likely to get it from water. Don't forget to wash your hands.

Getting to know toxoplasmosis

Toxoplasmosis is the most feared of all kitten parasites because of what it can do to a developing human fetus. Although kittens do pass the organism in their poop, a few common sense sanitary habits can protect you. Be sure to do the following if you're pregnant:

- ✔ Keep your kitten indoors.

- ✔ Feed dry or canned food, or if you feed a raw diet, use only freeze-dried raw food. (Find out about the best kitten diet in Chapter 7.)

- ✔ Immediately dispose of any prey your kitten may catch or kill.

- ✔ Wear gloves when gardening, in case you come in contact with infected cat poop.

- ✔ Have the boxes cleaned daily. Toxoplasmosis takes 24 hours to become infectious.

- ✔ After cleaning the litter box, wash your hands for at least 20 seconds with soap and water. I sing "Happy Birthday" because it takes about that long.

- ✔ Avoid handling stray kittens.

Giving a dose of liquid medicine

To dose with liquid, use either a syringe or a dropper. I like a syringe because you can be sure your kitten got all the medicine, and it's faster.

1. **Check the label and your vet's directions for the proper dosage. Shake the bottle if necessary.**

2. **Fill the syringe or dropper with the proper dose.**

3. **Hold your kitten's jaws closed but tilt his head back slightly.**

4. **From the side, insert the tip into his mouth just behind the canines.**

    The medicine should go to the pouch between his teeth and cheek. If you're injecting a sizeable amount of liquid, give him a chance to swallow it. Don't choke him.

5. **Treat him to something he likes.**

For years, physicians have insisted that pregnant women get rid of their cats for fear that the woman would become infected with toxoplasmosis. Recently, the Centers for Disease Control (CDC) released the finding that relatively few cases of toxoplasmosis in pregnant women are caused by cats or kittens. In fact, most women were infected by eating meat that wasn't thoroughly cooked. (For more information, check out the CDC Web site at www.cdc.gov/ncidod/dpd/parasites/toxoplasmosis/factsht_toxoplasmosis.htm#8.) Bottom line: To get the disease, you have to ingest the toxoplasmosis by, for instance, biting your nails after handling raw meat or cleaning the cat box. Still, if you're pregnant and your kitten has toxoplasmosis, get to your doctor right away.

Diabolically Deadly Diseases

Your kitten faces four diseases that, if caught, could have him meowing with the choir invisible. It doesn't have to be that way. The four most deadly feline diseases are almost completely preventable by keeping your kitten inside and vaccinated.

Kittens are fragile, and these awful diseases can start a physical cascade that your kitten can't recover from. Proper precautions will keep your kitten safe from these devastating viruses.

Feline distemper

Feline distemper is the feline panleukopenia virus (FPV.) By any other name, it's still a kitten killer.

This severe FPV attacks the bowels, the immune system, and the nervous system and destroys the kitten's white and red blood cells. FPV kills up to 90 percent of infected kittens under 6 months of age. The good news is you can prevent it. So make sure your kitten gets his vaccinations as soon as possible. You can find out more about this lifesaving shot in Chapter 10.

A kitten with FPV usually gets fever, quits eating, and acts depressed for about 24 hours. He could twitch his head, make exaggerated movements and fall over on his side. Or he could die before he shows any symptoms. If you discover your kitten is infected, isolate him from other cats immediately.

Your kitten can contract FPV from direct contact with a sick cat, when he uses a litter box, or from your clothes if you've been handling a sick cat. Even fleas can spread it from cat to kitten.

Most veterinarians diagnose FPV based on the symptoms they see, whether a kitten's had vaccinations, and a blood sample. A vet can't do much for a kitten with feline distemper. Supportive treatment like fluids and blood transfusions can be given and medications to try to control diarrhea and vomiting, but chances for survival are bleak.

FPV is an extremely hardy virus and survives most temperatures and disinfectants (long after its victims are gone). If you lose your kitten to distemper, wash all bedding in bleach and toss any bowls and toys to keep from infecting any other kitties you adopt later.

Feline leukemia virus — ugly name, ugly virus

The feline leukemia virus (FeLV) is one of the most devastating diseases a kitten can face. It's passed from cat to kitten (and vice versa) through bodily fluids, mom's milk, and through the umbilical cord. Vets believe that it takes prolonged or repeated exposure to pass the virus around, because the virus dies quickly outside of the body.

About a third of the kittens exposed to FeLV come down with it and die. A kitten infected with FeLV and showing symptoms can live from several weeks to several months, depending on how far the virus has advanced before diagnosis. Another third of kittens exposed seem not to be affected, but then months or even years later, the disease breaks out — triggered by stresses to the immune system. And the final third of kittens can actually fight off the disease.

FeLV doesn't have to be a death sentence. Although a cure has not been found, interferon or lysine can help build up your kitten's immune system. Vitamin C may also help boost the immune system, but there's no proof that it helps fight the disease.

FeLV is a retrovirus that implants its own DNA into the host's cell. When the cells reproduce, the virus also reproduces. The human equivalents, AIDS and HIV, are also retroviruses.

The symptoms of FeLV are varied and often confusing because individually they could be symptoms of so many illnesses. Symptoms can include

- Anemia
- Colds

- ✔ Jaundice

- ✔ Decreased appetite and weight loss

- ✔ Diarrhea or constipation

- ✔ Blood in the stool

- ✔ Enlarged lymph nodes

- ✔ Decreased stamina

- ✔ Drinking more than normal, then peeing more than normal

Some FeLV kittens even develop cancer as a direct result of the disease.

FeLV hampers the kitten's natural immune system and prevents him from being able to fight off disease. My first encounter with FeLV involved D.B., an 8-month-old I rescued from the side of the road. A month later, he started suffering from chronic bladder infections. As soon as he finished his antibiotics, the infection returned. Unfortunately, he just kept getting worse and worse so I had to put him to sleep. For more on making such a difficult decision, see the sidebar "When the prognosis isn't good" later in the chapter.

No human or dog has ever had a case of FeLV, so if your kitten tests positive and he isn't with other cats, you don't need to rush into any decision.

If you have other cats, you need to take precautions to protect them. FeLV vaccinations can give you a high degree of comfort, but they aren't 100 percent effective. So you're still running a risk, even if it is a small one. For more on FeLV shots, flip to Chapter 10.

If your kitten tests positive for FeLV and you have other cats, you can try to find a sanctuary to take your kitten. Some organizations handle the difficult placement of an FeLV-positive kitten. And some people with a positive cat will adopt another positive kitten or cat for a companion. Be patient, and you may be able to find a home for your kitten.

Have your other cats tested for FeLV before bringing a new kitten into the house. If you lost a cat to FeLV recently, you only have to wait 30 days so that the virus lingering around your house dies. Fortunately, FeLV can't survive in the environment. To protect other cats against FeLV, scrub everything down with a cup of bleach to a gallon of water. Wash beds with bleach, wash bowls in a dishwasher, and toss litter pans.

Feline immunodeficiency virus — say what?

Like feline leukemia, feline immunodeficiency virus (FIV) is a retro-virus. However, FIV is classified as a slow virus. FIV works much like HIV (human immunodeficiency virus) and causes a disease in cats similar to AIDS in humans. Don't worry, you can't get it. FIV only affects felines.

Unneutered males who go outside looking for a good time most frequently get the disease. Inside kittens who aren't exposed to infected cats have little to worry about. The virus moves from cat to cat through bites; seldom through casual contact. Occasionally an infected queen can infect her kittens with infected milk. Kitty sex doesn't seem to be a common way to get the disease unless the male's bite breaks the skin.

It could take years for symptoms to appear. Eventually your grown kitten's immune system will wane, and he will begin to develop sec-ondary infections, including

- ✔ A persistent fever and chronically infected gums and mouth
- ✔ Chronic skin, urinary tract, and upper respiratory infections
- ✔ Eye inflammation
- ✔ Cancer
- ✔ Seizures and various neurological disorders

Vets usually diagnose FIV based on symptoms *and* a blood test they can perform at the clinic.

Nothing can kill the virus in a cat, so vets often treat FIV-infected kittens with steroids to steady inflammation and antibiotics to treat other ailments that arise from a suppressed immune system. Appetite enhancers and anabolic steroids may help to maintain the appetite. Some vets use lysine and interferon to help slow the repli-cation of the virus.

FIV can't survive outside the kitten's body more than a few hours, so if you recently lost a cat to this disease, you don't need to wait before adopting a kitten unless other infections or viruses were present. Some FIV cats also have either FeLV or feline infectious peritonitis, in which case you should wait before getting a new friend, to protect the health of your future kitten. Scrub everything down with one cup of bleach to a gallon of water. Wash all beds, food dishes, and toys.

An FIV vaccine has recently become available. You can read up on it and the problems it presents to FIV testing in Chapter 10.

Feline infectious peritonitis — this one's no fun

Most cats have been exposed to feline infectious peritonitis (FIP) at some time in their lives. FIP, a disastrous disease, is mainly seen in kittens and very old cats because their immune systems can't fight it. Kittens become infected by inhaling or ingesting the virus from saliva or poop from a cat or contaminated surfaces like beds, clothing, food dishes, and toys.

FIP is sometimes called the great imitator. Initially, maybe only one symptom, something vague like diarrhea or sneezing, may appear. You may think that your kitten only has a cold, when in fact he's in the early stages of FIP. Later, more symptoms appear.

The disease comes in a wet form and a dry form. Kittens with the wet form, or *effusive form,* have fluids that collect in their abdomen or chest that make breathing very difficult. After symptoms appear, these kittens die soon — in one to four weeks.

Kittens infected with the dry form usually suffer from weight loss, depression, anemia, and fever as well, but also drink more water and pee more because their kidneys are failing. Their skin and eyes look yellow because of liver failure, and they may vomit and have diarrhea. These poor things last longer than kittens with the wet form — they can hang on for four or five months — before kidney failure gets them.

Your vet can't actually test for FIP even though some vets may call it an FIP test. FIP is in the coronavirus family, and the test looks for the presence of a coronavirus antibody. Most cats coming from shelters or catteries have been exposed to *a* coronavirus. A perfectly healthy cat can test positive even if he's never been exposed to FIP. The Cornell Feline Health Center suggests that the test should be used only as an aid to help diagnose a symptomatic kitten. An FIP diagnosis must be made by combining the symptoms like lack of appetite, fever, collected fluids in the chest or abdomen, weakness in the hind quarters, and inflammation of the eye lining, along with a positive coronavirus test. If your vet believes an apparently healthy kitten has FIP because of the test, get a second opinion. One breeder told me that her vet wanted to put her kitten to sleep because she tested positive for coronavirus. A second opinion revealed that she had a treatable infection.

When the prognosis isn't good

Sometimes, despite your best efforts, your kitten is too sick or too injured to make it. You've done everything your vet suggested, and nothing is working. Or your kitten has been horribly wounded and will only live a short time in great pain anyway. You can offer your kitten a dignified and painless passing. The vet gives your kitten an injection. Within seconds, the kitten slips into unconsciousness. Death follows in less than a minute.

If you find yourself considering putting your kitten to sleep, it may help to ask yourself the following questions:

- **Can my kitten's pain or discomfort ever be relieved?** Does your kitten have a quality of life or is he in constant pain. Can he do anything he used to enjoy?

- **What are the chances that he will recover?** Some diseases are progressive and only grow worse and more painful over time.

- **How much more can I afford to spend with or without a guarantee?** Unless you're very wealthy, this nasty subject may rear its ugly head. Can you afford to spend $5000 on surgery that may or may not work when you have problems paying your own medical co-payments?

- **Does he want to live?** When a kitten stops eating (and I'm not talking about an upper respiratory infection where he doesn't eat for a couple days or so because he can't smell) that's often a signal that the kitten has given up.

After you make this difficult decision, you need to make an appointment with your vet and decide whether you want to be present when your kitten is put to sleep. Some things that you see may disturb you. If you can't emotionally handle that, your vet will probably have a technician who can hold and comfort your kitten. I prefer to be with my pets when they must be euthanized. I want them to know they're loved as they go to sleep. Ask if you can be present. If the answer is "No," you may want to speak to the vet directly. In an emergency situation, you'll have to comply with their rules: It's doubtful the vet is trying to rob you of the last few meaningful moments of your kitten's life. About 10 percent of euthanasia procedures simply don't go well, and the vet doesn't want you to experience this. You can even find vets who will come to your house for the procedure. You also need to think about what to do with your kitten's body. You can

- Take him home for burial

- Have him buried at a pet cemetery

- Have a private cremation and keep or bury the ashes

- Let the vet dispose of the body

After everything's over, ask your vet to give you a few minutes alone with your kitten to grieve and collect your thoughts.

TIP

Calling someone who cares

Losing a kitten can be very difficult to cope with because many people don't understand mourning a pet. After the unexpected death of my kitten, Sebastian, I became depressed and inconsolable. I don't want you to go through it alone. Here are the phone numbers of some free pet loss counseling hotlines.

✔ U.C. Davis College of Veterinary Medicine Pet Loss Hotline: 530-752-4200 or 800-565-1526. Call 6:30 to 9:30 p.m. PT, Monday through Friday.

✔ Iams Pet Loss Support Center and Hotline: 888-332-7738. Call 8 a.m. to 5 p.m.

✔ Iowa State University Pet Loss Support Hotline: 888-478-7574. Toll-free. Call 6 a.m. to 9 p.m. CST.

✔ Or try the Web site `www.petloss.com`.

The symptoms are so varied that diagnosis is difficult. The disease advances suddenly and aggressively. After symptoms start appearing, the full-blown disease arrives quickly. Common symptoms include

✔ Swollen stomach

✔ Labored breathing

✔ Lack of appetite

✔ Depression

✔ Unkempt coat

✔ Weight loss

✔ Fever

There's no cure for FIP. Some vets offer an FIP intranasal vaccine, but the effectiveness is questionable. Take a look at the pros and cons of the FIP vaccine in Chapter 10.

Knowing When to Take a Kitten to the Vet Immediately

Your kitten can't tell you he's sick, which can be very frustrating. In nature, hiding disease keeps him alive, so your kitten may hide illness and mask symptoms. Sometimes you have to be a detective and a psychic to figure out something is wrong.

To find out how to perform a monthly exam on your kitten that can help you find illnesses early, read Chapter 10. You need to get to know your kitten so well that you can tell when he's not quite right. Take a look at the following list to see some of the symptoms your kitten exhibits when he's trying to tell you, "Take me to the vet, now." If your kitten's feeling puny and you don't see the symptoms under illnesses, check the symptoms of poisoning or injury in Chapters 8 and 20.

- ✔ Blood in urine or poop

- ✔ Diarrhea, pooping more than twice an hour

- ✔ Straining in the litter box with no results

- ✔ Puking more than three times in an hour

- ✔ Fever over 102.5 degrees or a temperature of under 100 degrees if the kitten's depressed

- ✔ Lethargy

- ✔ Weight loss in a short time

- ✔ Labored breathing

- ✔ Flinches or cries when you touch him

- ✔ Something hanging out of her mouth (like string or tinsel, which could wrap around her intestines)

- ✔ Change in behavior; an outgoing kitten hides, or a shy kitten wants to be around you all the time

Chapter 10

An Ounce of Prevention

*I*n this chapter, I go over some inexpensive ways to prevent a cat-tastrophe before it happens. Included is information on vaccinations, the importance of keeping the kitten inside, microchipping, step-by-step instructions on giving him a monthly exam, worming, and regular visits to the vet.

Understanding Vaccinations: What You Don't Know Can Hurt Him

In Chapter 9, I go over all of the horrible, life-threatening diseases kittens can catch. The good news is that you can prevent many of these diseases by vaccinating your kitten. But remember, shots only protect him before he's been infected. If he catches a disease, a vaccination won't do him any good.

Although vaccines are vital to protect your kitten from infectious disease, most of them don't completely protect him. The amount of protection they provide varies from kitten to kitten. To further protect your kitten, you should reduce his exposure to infected cats or contaminated areas. Keeping him inside reduces his risk of exposure considerably.

Timing is everything: What shots your kitten needs when

Early on, a kitten receives some immunity to disease from his mother's milk. The first milk a kitten receives after birth is rich in antibodies that protect the kitten for his first 7 or 8 weeks of life.

The American Association of Feline Practitioners (AAFP) recommends that when your kitten reaches 8 weeks (6 weeks for a hand-raised orphan because she doesn't have mom's antibodies to protect her), she should receive her first shot. The shot will include protection for

- ✔ Feline herpesvirus (FHV), the disease formerly known as rhinotracheitis
- ✔ Feline calicivirus (FCV)
- ✔ Feline panleukopenia virus (FPV)

I discuss these diseases in Chapter 9. Vaccinated kittens can still catch a less serious case of these viruses, but they should be protected against the lifelong problems associated with the full-blown virus. After your kitten gets her first shot, she should get a booster in three or four weeks. After she's fully immunized, she needs an annual booster and after that, boosters every three years.

From there, AAFP and the Academy of Feline Medicine Advisory Panel on Feline Vaccinations suggest that a kitten's vaccination needs should be evaluated by your vet on an individual basis depending on the kitten's age, health, and how likely she is to come in contact with cats who may spread certain diseases. The vet should also take into account the likelihood that the kitten will get parasites that harbor an illness, or whether you live in an area where a specific disease is widespread.

When you pick up your kitten from the breeder or adopt-a-pet, be sure to ask for a copy of her medical history. That way you know for sure which shots she's received and what shots you need your vet to give her right away. Often the breeder or rescue organization where you get your kitten has given her most of these shots before sending her home.

If your kitten will live outdoors, or even if he stays outdoors only part of the time, he should also receive vaccination against the following diseases:

✔ **Feline leukemia virus (FeLV):** Your kitten can be protected from feline leukemia virus through immunization. She can get her first shot at 8 to 10 weeks of age (depending on your vet) and should get a booster in three or four weeks. Unfortunately, a small percentage of cats never gain immunity against the disease, even with an annual booster.

✔ **Feline immunodeficiency virus (FIV):** Recently, the first vaccine against FIV became available in the United States. Kittens should be tested for the disease before being vaccinated — as early as 8 weeks old. One problem with the new vaccine is that it taints current FIV tests because once inoculated, a kitten tests positive for the disease for the rest of her life. If your kitten should ever become lost, and rescued or adopted, she will show positive for FIV. The fear is that shelters will euthanize lost or stray kittens who have been vaccinated because they test positive for the dangerous virus. You can prevent this by having your kitten tattooed or microchipped when you have him vaccinated, because the chip can reveal a code that tells rescuers who he is, who he belongs to, and that he's been vaccinated for FIV. I tell you about tattoos and microchips later in this chapter.

✔ **Rabies:** Rabies is a virus found in the saliva of infected animals, which is transmitted most often to other mammals through bites. Most states and municipalities require rabies vaccines (either annually or every three years depending on the vaccine) for *all* kittens over 4 months (whether they live inside or out). For more about rabies, see the "Rabies" sidebar later in this chapter.

Feline Infectious Peritonitis (FIP)

Recently the American Association of Feline Practitioners and the Academy of Feline Medicine Advisory Panel on Feline Vaccinations issued a report that included recommendations concerning the FIP nasal vaccine. Because the vaccine has not yet been proven beneficial, neither of these two prestigious groups recommends it.

If you still want to have your kitten inoculated with the current FIP intranasal vaccine, she can get her first dose when she reaches 16 weeks. You'll need to get a booster in three or four weeks and then annually. The vaccine appears to be safe, but studies disagree on how effectively it protects. If you have a multicat household, the vaccine may be helpful when used together with good kitty hygiene: Clean boxes and bowls regularly. Discuss whether your kitten needs the FIP vaccine with your vet. Chapter 9 tells you all about the disease and the rather dubious test for FIP.

After your kitten is fully immunized, speak to your vet about when she'll need her next booster shot. Until recently, vets traditionally recommended annual booster shots for the life of the kitten. Now, depending on the vaccine, she may be protected for up to three years after her first annual booster shot. Be sure to follow the regulations in your city and state, which your vet should be aware of.

Keeping an eye out for reactions

Sometimes kittens suffer a reaction to vaccination. Most reactions are minor, including fever, diminished appetite, and sneezing. The calicivirus vaccine can cause aching in joints. However, in rare cases, your kitten could develop side effects, including a life-threatening allergic reaction or even a *sarcoma* (cancer) that develops at the injection point weeks, even years later (see the "Shots that bite back" sidebar in this chapter for more information about sarcomas).

To be safe, keep a close eye on your kitten for a couple of hours after he gets his shots. If you notice anything more serious than just feeling a little under the weather or if he feels bad for more than 36 hours, take him back to the vet.

Shots that bite back

When your kitten gets her shots, a little swelling often occurs at the injection point. But if the swelling persists for months or continues to grow, be concerned. The veterinary community has discovered an association between some shots (mainly FeLV and rabies) and *sarcomas* (a type of cancer) in cats. The sarcomas seem to appear three months to three years after vaccination, so you'll want to keep an eye on the injection site. Take your kitten to the vet if the swelling doesn't go away within a month.

While it's frightening to think that your kitten could get cancer from something that's supposed to protect her, she's more likely to die from the disease itself if you don't get basic vaccinations. These sarcomas affect between 1 and 4 cats out of about 10,000 vaccinated. But death among kittens who have contracted rabies is 100 percent and you would be at risk as well. Don't forego necessary shots because of the danger of the sarcoma. Instead when getting rabies or FeLV shots, ask your vet for the safer vaccine that doesn't contain adjuvant.

Rabies

In the United States, cats now surpass dogs in the number of rabies cases reported each year. Fortunately, these numbers are still low: The disease is always fatal for both animals and humans after symptoms begin to show. In medical history, only three people have survived rabies.

It can take between a week and a year for an unvaccinated cat bitten by a rabid animal to start showing symptoms. Infected cats become highly aggressive or weak and paralytic. They're extremely dangerous and very quick. They frequently snap at imaginary objects and attack anything that comes near them. They also have difficulty swallowing.

Always keep your kitten current on his rabies shots. If a rabid animal bites your kitten and he's not current on his shots, he'll most likely be euthanized and his head sent to a lab for testing. Unfortunately, the only way to determine if an animal is rabid is by laboratory examination of the brain tissue.

Forget Shots, Give 'Em Tabs or Dots: Preventing Heartworms

Like dogs, kittens can get heartworms from mosquito bites. But unlike dogs, kittens can't be treated after heartworms have infected them, and only one worm can kill a cat. However, a couple of monthly heartworm preventives have been approved for cats and kittens. Ivermectin has been shown to be a safe and effective kitty heartworm preventive given in a yummy chewable tablet. Heartguard, containing Ivermectin, is recommended for kittens at least 6 weeks old.

Your kitten can also get heartworm protection from an oral or *spot on* (a liquid applied to one spot between the shoulder blades once a month) as well. Revolution from Pfizer not only prevents heartworm, but also gets rid of fleas, ticks, and most internal parasites. Revolution is available only from your vet. The label recommends Revolution for kittens at least 6 weeks old, but I know vets who say it's so safe they use it on both newborn kittens and pregnant queens.

Although it's not absolutely necessary as it is with dogs, you may want to test your kitten for heartworms before you put her on a preventive. Find out more about for heartworms in Chapter 9.

"Spay"ing (Or Neutering) on the Safe Side: Altering Your Kitten

Altering your kitten may not seem like preventive medicine, but it can be a lifesaver. Spaying your female kitten can help prevent feline breast cancers, the most common cancer found among female cats. It can also help prevent most ovarian and uterine tumors and ten other cancers and tumors related to reproduction. In boys, neutering helps prevent prostate enlargement cancers, as well as reducing the occurrences of anal and rectal tumors. For more information about how spaying and neutering makes your kitten a happier and better-adjusted pet while not contributing to the problem of cat overpopulation, check out Chapter 14.

Giving Your Kitten a Monthly Exam

Just as you look for changes in your own body, you should give your kitten a monthly physical to keep an eye out for tumors and other potentially serious problems before they become a threat to his health.

Make the exam a pleasant experience for your kitten. Give him lots of soft, reassuring words throughout the process. Include throat scratches and a gentle body massage. Don't forget to give him a treat when you complete the more unpleasant parts, like taking his temperature. That way, he sees something in it for him and he doesn't mind so much when "that time of month" rolls around.

Perform his exam in a place where your kitten feels comfortable — like his bed or on your lap while you're brushing his coat or petting him. If he doesn't like a particular aspect of the exam, do it at the end of the session followed by an immediate reward. You may want to perform the examination in stages so he doesn't get antsy.

A wonderful book, *Cat Massage* by Maryjean Ballner (St. Martin's Press), gives you the lowdown on massaging your kitten. Borrow a couple of tips from there, and he'll be begging for an exam.

Keep a kitten-health notebook. It helps you to watch for patterns of weight loss or gain and figure out when certain minor changes occurred. If you don't want to keep a journal, make a note on the calendar whenever your kitten vomits or when you first notice a sneeze. If your kitten has health problems, your notes will help your vet pin down exactly when symptoms started appearing.

Step 1: Weigh in

Take your kitten's weight and record it. A baby scale works perfectly for this. If you don't have one, you can weigh yourself holding your kitten and then subtract your own weight. This method isn't extremely precise, but it still provides good information.

Step 2: Check the body for symmetry

Look at the whole kitten to see if his body is symmetrical. Does the left paw look like the right paw? Is the right shoulder shaped the same as the left shoulder? If something looks odd to you, be safe and ask your vet. He can tell you what's normal for your kitten. After several examinations, you'll know when something looks or feels different.

Step 3: Examine the nose and mouth

Start with the nose; make sure you don't see any gooey discharge. A normal kitten nose can be either moist or dry. If your kitten has light colored skin, the nose pad should look pink, not white.

Next, examine the mouth. Gum diseases and mouth cancer are more common among older cats, but you need to get your kitten in the habit of opening her mouth when she's still little.

Start the oral examination by pulling the lips back and looking at the teeth and gums. As you pet your kitten, just pull her lips back with your thumb. Start slow. Look at one side of her mouth, then the other. Treat her with a lick of baby food. When she's comfortable with you opening her mouth, put thumb and forefinger behind the fangs, tip her head back, and then she will drop her jaw. Take a look inside.

- ✔ The tongue and gums should be pale pink, not white or red. If they are white, she's probably anemic. Red gums mean she has an infection going on in her mouth. Both conditions mean there's a trip to the vet in her future.

- ✔ The teeth should be clean and white like your own teeth. If any of the teeth look a little pink, your kitten may have an infected tooth.

- ✔ Take a sniff. Kitty breath shouldn't be unpleasant or nasty. If her mouth smells rotten or like dog breath, you're looking at some sort of dental disease.

✔ Look for spots or changes in her mouth. Some kittens have dark spots in their mouths that are part of their own unique coloration. But some spots are abnormal. Your vet should check out any new spots immediately. Get familiar with your kitten's mouth so you can detect changes.

✔ Note excessive drooling. It could mean that a foreign object is stuck in the mouth or between the gums.

If your kitten objects to you messing with her mouth, then do a quick peek inside her mouth and give her a treat. Work on this daily until she cooperates. Don't force her. You don't want to risk a bite. If you can't or don't want to open your kitten's mouth, simply pull the gums apart and check out what you can see.

Step 4: Scan the eyes and ears

Check to see if your kitten is squinting or her eyes are watering. Look at the eye by gently pulling the lid down with your thumb. As with the mouth, the tissue should be pink, not white or red. The eyes should be clear and bright. The pupils should be the same size. She may have just a little sleep in the corners of her eyes, but you shouldn't see lots of goo.

Kittens' eyes each have three eyelids: the top, bottom, and a third on the inside corner. The third eyelid only becomes obvious when your kitten feels sickly. The problem could be something minor like intestinal parasites or serious like an infection. Get her to the vet to check it out.

Look inside the ears. They should be pink and clean. A healthy cat ear shouldn't have any dark gunk or discharge that you may see in dog ears. You shouldn't smell any odor. A foul smell indicates an infection. If you see goo or something that looks like coffee grounds, your kitten probably has ear mites or an ear infection. Both are uncomfortable. Get your vet to check him out and give you some medicine. Read all about these microscopic annoyances in Chapter 9.

Step 5: Examine the jaw, neck, back, and legs

Feel the angle of your kitten's jaw for lymph nodes. They feel like soft jellybeans. Play around the folds of the neck and eventually you'll feel them. Lymph nodes (seen in Figure 10-1) are the body's filters. Swelling or tender lymph nodes could be the first indication of an infection, cancer, or feline leukemia virus. Your vet can show you what a normal gland feels like.

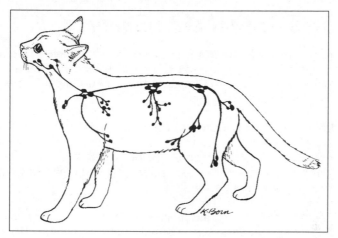

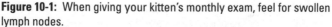

Figure 10-1: When giving your kitten's monthly exam, feel for swollen lymph nodes.

Run your hands firmly down the spine as if you were giving a massage. If the kitten winces repeatedly when you touch a certain spot, she may have a wrenched muscle or other injury. If you find a touchy place and she limps, she could have a fracture or broken bone. Give the leg bones a gentle squeeze. Look for bumps, lumps, and scabs, which can be warning signs of abscesses, injuries, or skin conditions.

If you find a boo-boo or your kitten's sensitive to touch, either give your vet a call to ask her about the problem or make an appointment. It may be nothing, but then again, you may have uncovered a serious condition in the early stages.

For the best results (and the least amount of scratches), be gentle. Your kitten should think he's getting a firm massage.

Step 6: Inspect the skin

The skin is the kitten's largest organ. It should be clean with no scabs, sores, pimples (yes, kittens get acne), or missing patches of fur, which could be the result of ringworm (discussed in Chapter 9) or fleabite dermatitis. Feel all over with your hands. Without getting rough, check for sensitive spots. Also examine the coat. Run a flea comb through the fur. Look for matting and flea dirt.

A dull or clumpy-looking coat could be a symptom of a more serious health concern.

Step 7: Feel the tummy

As you feel your kitten's tummy, you may not have a clue what each bulge and cranny does, but after you've examined her a few times, you should be able to recognize that a new lump has appeared or when an organ feels bigger.

When you palpate your kitten's tummy, be very gentle. The stomach is a cat's most vulnerable place. Under different circumstances, exposing her soft belly could get her killed. Your kitten may be alarmed. She needs to trust you to let you do this. So give her a treat when you're finished.

Stand your kitten up and place your hand under her belly. Put your fingers on one side and the thumb on the other side. Bring them together. See how close you can get without hurting her. In a kitten, sensitivity in the abdomen usually means she has a bladder infection, an intestinal blockage, or an intestinal infection. Gently knead the abdomen. Part of feeling the flanks is looking for excess weight. Also, feel the nipples for swelling. Sensitivity or anything out of the ordinary should be referred to a vet.

Step 8: Check heart rate and respiration

You can cup the chest with your hand and feel the heartbeat. Your kitten's heart rate should fall somewhere between 160 to 240 beats per minute: It depends on size, age, and breed and whether the kitten's just laying there or anxious and jumping around.

Check her respiration when she's at rest. She should breathe 20 to 30 times per minute.

Step 9: Peruse the paws and pads

Don't forget the paws. Make sure nothing is caught in your kitten's pads. You may want to take this opportunity to trim his nails. I tell you how to do that in Chapter 11. Don't forget the reward.

Feel between the toes and pads for cuts or sores.

Step 10: Don't forget the back end

Now, it's time to check out the back door. Run your fingers down his tail to check for lumps or scabs. Feel the tail all the way down.

Lift her tail and take a look. Make sure you don't see anything that looks like rice clinging to his fur — telltale signs of tapeworms. To find out more about tapeworms, look in Chapter 9.

Finish up the process by taking your kitten's temperature using a digital thermometer. I prefer to use a digital thermometer, because the tip flexes if the kitten struggles or moves, and because it beeps when you're ready to read it. It works faster than a standard rectal thermometer. For more information, take a look at the "Taking the temperature" sidebar in this chapter.

I recommend the Vicks Comfort-Flex, BD Flexible Digital Thermometer, or an Eckerd Flexible Thermometer. Both retail for around $10.

Taking the temperature

Ask your vet to show you how to take a temperature, but after you've been instructed, this explanation will give you a little reminder on how to do it. You need:

✔ A slick flat place like a counter

✔ Rubbing alcohol

✔ Digital thermometer (never try to take your kitten's temperature by mouth or using an oral thermometer)

✔ Lubricant like Vaseline or KY Jelly

✔ A towel to wrap him in if he's not cooperative

✔ A watch with a second hand

✔ Another person to assist you

1. **If you're using an old fashioned rectal thermometer, shake it down before using it.**

2. **Sterilize the thermometer in the alcohol.**

3. **Once dry, lubricate it with the Vaseline or KY Jelly.**

(continued)

(continued)

4. **Have the other person hold the kitten while you hold up the tail and insert the thermometer no more than one-half inch.**

   Inserting it further could cause her serious injury.

5. **Hold the thermometer and tail together. Never let go of the thermometer. If the kitten breaks away, don't let her run off with the thermometer still in her bottom.**

6. **Keep the thermometer in place for one to two minutes. The digital thermometer beeps when it's done.**

The temperature should read between 101 to 102 degrees on a healthy kitten. Anything below 100 or above 102.5 degrees justifies a trip to the vet.

Other things to watch for

Always keep an eye on your kitten for signs that he's under the weather. Watch your kitten as he uses the litter box. Check his poop; it should resemble a firm little log, not a bunch of little balls, and have no mucus or worms. Pooping should be effortless. The kitten should go for every meal he eats.

Is the kitten straining to pee so hard that the urine lands outside the box? This usually indicates it hurts him to pee. Is he sitting on the box, but never goes? Is he using the carpet instead of his box?

These could all be signs that he has a lower urinary tract infection, another one of those darn "can't wait" problems. Visit your vet.

Also, look for changes in habits like

- ✔ **Straining when he uses the litter box with nothing coming out:** If he's trying to poop and nothing comes out, he may have a blockage. Run, don't walk, to the vet. Constipation is often caused by dehydration, parasites, or another illness. You can give him some hairball remedy to grease the wheel, so to speak. If this doesn't move things along, take him to the vet. Don't give him an enema. Human enemas are toxic to felines.

- ✔ **Stops eating, drops food, or changes food preference from dry to canned:** Loss of appetite can mean your kitten has a cold and can't smell. He may go off his food because of parasites or if something has lodged in his intestines, like a furball. Dropping his food or a sudden preference for canned could mean that he has a dental problem. Or he may have swallowed poison or have something caught in his throat or stuck in his mouth. More serious diseases like anemia, diabetes, and cancer can cause lack of appetite. If your kitten quits eating, take him to the vet immediately.

- ✔ **Sudden weight loss or gain:** As with increases and decreases in appetite, this could be related to parasites, kidney disease, diabetes, or even cancer. Any sudden change in weight needs to be checked out by a vet.

- ✔ **Eats everything in sight:** If he seems to be hungry all the time and tends to drink and pee more, it could be a warning sign of diabetes. A kitten who's constantly hungry, but loses weight could also have worms (see Chapter 9).

- ✔ **Drinking more:** This could be a sign of diabetes or dehydration.

- ✔ **Sudden change in personality:** A kitten who uncharacteristically begins to hide under beds or in closets may be experiencing some pain. I had a shy kitten who liked to hide, but when she became ill she also became disoriented and couldn't find her way back to her hiding place. Personality changes warrant a trip to the vet.

- ✔ **Starts biting:** A non-biter who for no reason starts feeding on human flesh definitely needs to go to the vet. She could be suffering from pain or tenderness.

✔ **Shaking his head or scratching his ears:** This is a give-away that he's got an ear problem. Look in his ears for black stuff that looks like coffee grounds and sniff to detect a foul odor. The coffee grounds are a result of ear mites. The odor means your kitten probably has an ear infection. Off to the vet for him!

✔ **Tenderness:** Take your kitten to the vet. You need to find out what's causing that sensitivity.

The Latest in Identification and Loss Prevention

The kids have left the door open, and your kitten darts out the door. You put up signs and call all the shelters and wait. Even if someone finds him, your kitten can't tell her where he lives. He may never return home. Hopefully, you'll never have to worry about living through a scene like that, but just in case, I go over some things you can do now, such as microchipping or tattooing your kitten and outfitting him with a collar and tags, that can improve his chances of returning home with nothing more than the memory of a big adventure.

Collars and tags

The easiest and cheapest way to ensure your kitten's safe return is to outfit her with the proper collar and identification tags. I give you pointers on choosing a collar in Chapter 5. Now for some tips on tags:

✔ Buy a durable tag. If you have tags engraved, try to get unbreakable plastic.

✔ Unless you subscribe to a pet registration service (which I discuss later in this chapter), include your phone number on the tag. Make it large enough to read from a few feet away, in case your kitten doesn't let anyone near her. Security experts say that you shouldn't put your kitten's name on the tag, because knowing his name would make it easier for a stranger to bond with your kitten should she decide to keep her. Also, don't put your address on the tag because an unscrupulous person can use that information to case your home for a break-in.

✔ Choose a tag that has easy-to-read type.

✔ Law probably requires your kitten's registration tag and rabies tag, but don't depend on those tags to bring him home. You need the ID I mentioned above because most cities don't handle pet information on a 24-hour basis. If your kitten disappears after hours or on a weekend, it could be a couple of days before you're contacted. Some rescuers may not be that patient.

✔ Consider specialty tags that provide your cat's rescuer with a toll-free number and a code. You don't receive calls from strange people. The service contacts you directly. In the event you are not available, some services even approve medical care and boarding for your kitty.

If the dangling tags annoy your kitten, order a collar with a brass ID plate attached to the nylon web or buy a collar with your information woven into it.

Collars can work beautifully in tandem with a microchip (discussed in the following section). When your kitten receives his microchip, he's given a tag with the microchip identification number and a 24-hour toll-free phone number of the retrieval service. The rescuer can contact the service and get the kitten back to you. If the kitten winds up at the animal shelter without a collar, he should be scanned.

Microchips

A microchip is a tiny computer chip, not much larger in diameter than a grain of rice, preprogrammed with a unique identification code (see Figure 10-2). The microchip provides permanent, positive identification of your kitten.

The whole thing fits inside a hypodermic needle (granted, a large one). Your vet injects the chip under the kitten's skin and muscles between the shoulder blades. It can't be lost, altered, or even intentionally removed. You don't have to worry about it accidentally getting into his bloodstream, digestive tract, or lungs. Implanting a chip takes just a few seconds. And inserting the chip is only slightly more uncomfortable than a shot.

Most vets charge between $25 and $50 for the chip and registration. Vets and shelters handle two main brands of microchips: Home Again and AVID chips.

Figure 10-2: A microchip provides rescuers with information.

The manufacturers recommend that you get the chip implanted when you get the first set of shots (8 weeks) because the kitten is large enough.

If your lost kitten is brought to a vet or the pound, the vet, rescue organization, or animal control officer scans your kitten for the microchip and then calls in your code so he can get your contact information, information about any medical conditions the kitten has that may require immediate care, and whether he has received a vaccination for FIV.

Fortunately, more and more shelters are scanning animals for microchips these days (the microchip companies even donate scanners to city shelters at no charge), but you may want to call your city animal shelter and make sure that it scans all animals that it picks up before you have one implanted in your kitten.

One problem many animal shelters have with the chips is that when people move they forget to update their contact information. So make certain to keep your contact information updated.

Another way to identify your kitten is to tattoo a significant number on his ear, stomach, or the inside of the leg as I describe in the following section. But one advantage of microchips over tattooing is that if a car hits your kitten, the chip still provides the animal shelter with information that can help it contact you. A tattoo may not be readable if the body has been too badly damaged in the accident.

Tattooing

Although I prefer microchips, a tattoo is still better than no permanent ID. And in areas where the shelter refuses to scan for chips, a tattoo could be a lifesaver. A tattoo is commonly placed on the animal's right hind leg

If you're considering tattooing your kitten, keep these points in mind:

- Many animal shelters scan for microchips but don't look for tattoos. Perhaps because kittens are so furry, a rescuer may not think to look for a tattoo. Or the kitten may not appreciate being examined by a stranger.

- Several of the tattoo services I checked charged close to the same price a vet would charge to implant a microchip.

- Most people use a significant number like a driver's license or social security number. Others use coded numbers supplied by one of several tattoo registries. People rescuing the animal or animal control officers may not understand the significance of the number.

When a kitten goes in for her spay, you can have the vet tattoo her abdomen around the spay site with the word, "Spay." You can't usually tell from the outside that a female kitten has been altered. If your kitten is ever lost, stolen, or given up, a tattoo will save her from having to go through an unnecessary spay surgery.

Pet recovery services (owner notification services)

Hopefully your kitten will remain safely in the house for his entire long life, but in case he gets lost and found, he needs a way to communicate with his rescuer. Because the people holding him may not have read Chapter 13 on Felinese, you need to implement Plan B. Plan B is a pet recovery service; some use microchips implanted under the kitten's skin, others use tattoos and still others have a tag with a unique ID number so some strange person can't show up at your home.

Make certain the service you choose provides around-the-clock service, and that its phones are answered 24 hours a day. Some services use voice mail on nights and weekends. Kittens don't recognize the down time concept, and some people who rescue them can't hang on to them until the next working day.

I tested a number of pet recovery services and was most impressed with 1-800-HELP-4-PETS. The service is available 24/7. Regardless of what time I call, I always talk to a real person. When my cat was found, they kept the rescuer on the phone until they reached me. Not only that, the tag is light for the kitten and can be read from several feet away. When I first called about my fictitious loss, they made valuable suggestions about putting up signs, how and where to look for the lost kitten, and even what foods to use for bait.

Chapter 11

Cleanliness Is Next to Catliness

*W*hen you groom your kitten, you not only help her maintain good hygiene, but you address her overall well-being (and that of your furniture). Grooming your kitten is important, because in doing so, you're

- ✔ **Creating rapport:** Gentle brushing reminds her of her mom's tongue. This gives her a sense of security and trust in you.

- ✔ **Monitoring for illnesses:** Regular combing or brushing helps you get to know your kitten's body. With regular grooming, you find new lumps and scabs soon after they appear (but hopefully they don't appear, of course). It's also good training for the kitten's monthly health exam that I explain in Chapter 10.

- ✔ **Reducing hairball landmines:** Removing dead hair from both longhaired and shorthaired kittens minimizes hairballs and painful mats. (Imagine what your hair would feel like if you never combed it!)

- ✔ **Preventing furniture damage:** Trimming your kitten's nails cuts down on damage to carpet and furniture.

- ✔ **Warding off future dental problems:** Regular tooth brushing reduces cavities just like with people.

- ✔ **Cleaning up ear mites:** Ear cleaning can prevent ear mites and ear infections.

Get in the habit of grooming your kitten regularly early on, because he'll need regular grooming as he gets older and his fur gets thicker; start now to make tomorrow's grooming sessions easier.

Lucky for you, this chapter gives you the basics on establishing your kitten's grooming ritual. I show you how to trim your kitten's toenails, care for her coat, give her a bath, clean out that junk in her ears and eyes, and brush her teeth.

Perfecting the Pedicure

The first step in any grooming regimen is to clip his nails to disarm your kitten in case you have a disagreement. Clipping his nails also prevents him from tearing up carpet and furniture and from puncturing your guests' legs if he cuddles up on their laps. Before you start, you need

- **Nail clippers:** Use clippers for cats, not people. Human nail cutters will splinter his claws.

- **Styptic:** This stops bleeding in case you accidentally cut him. It comes in a pencil or powder. Get it at any pet store.

Begin touching your kitten's feet and trimming his nails regularly right after you bring him home, so that from the get-go you train him to expect it. After he's accustomed to you touching his feet, try cutting a few nails. You can even give him a treat every time you finish, so he associates the reward with having his paws handled. This will, in turn, make him less likely to freak out and run up the wall when he finds out it's that time again.

Getting started

Before you get started, take note of a few important recommendations that make clipping your kitten's nails easier for you and safer for both of you:

- **Be sure to handle nippers correctly.** When handling scissors-style nippers, you have more control (and don't contribute to your carpal tunnel syndrome or tendonitis) if you hold them correctly. Put just the tip of your thumb inside the top hole and place your ring finger through the bottom hole. Rest the blade on your front two fingers to steady the nippers. Move only your thumb when clipping.

✔ **Stand your kitten on a flat, slick surface like a kitchen countertop.** Restrain your kitten in the crook of your arm (see Figure 11-1). On a slick surface, the kitten can't get traction to dart away.

✔ **If your kitten is extremely uncooperative, you may want to try giving him something to calm his nerves.** Such soothing agents include Bach Flower Remedies, such as mimulus, rose rock, and Rescue Remedy. A few drops of these safe flower potions down her gullet should take the edge of any anxiousness. Buy them at any health food store.

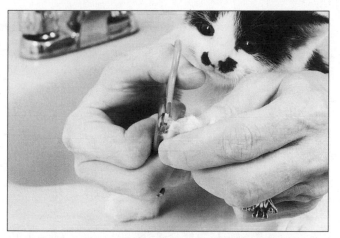

Figure 11-1: Working quickly is the key to successfully trimming her nails.

Trimming the tips

To trim your kitten's claws, perform the following steps:

1. **Expose the nail by gently pressing on the top and bottom of the toe pad with your thumb and index finger.**

2. **Locate the *quick* — the vein that carries blood to the nail as shown in Figure 11-2. It looks pink against a semi-translucent white nail. If kitty has dark claws, you can see the quick from the side.**

   Place a drop of baby oil or mineral oil on the nail, and the quick is easier to see.

3. **Snip off only the small hook or about ⅛ inch of the claw (see Figure 11-2).**

   Take care — cutting into the quick is very painful. If you do so, your kitten probably won't cooperate in the future (and you may have to peel him from the ceiling).

If you accidentally cut into the quick, don't panic. Touch a styptic pencil to the claw end or pat on styptic powder to help staunch the bleeding. The claw may bleed for a moment, but it should stop very quickly. Soothe him by speaking softly and stroking him head.

Give your kitten a pedicure every couple of weeks, or at least once a month.

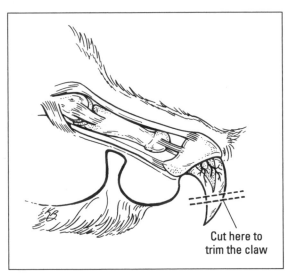

Cut here to
trim the claw

Figure 11-2: Find the veins or pink quick before trying to trim your kitten's nails. Just nip off the very tip of the claw.

Don't forget to talk to your kitten throughout the procedure and praise him after you cut each claw, much like you may talk to a child who's getting a vaccination — this helps your kitten feel safe and reassured. If one paw is all your kitten allows you to do at a time, don't fret. Finish up tomorrow.

Brushing Up on Coat Care

Even though your kitten is her own professional groomer, she still needs a helping paw from you regularly. How often she needs it and what tools you use depend on the length of her fur, how dense her undercoat is, the amount she sheds, and whether shedding season has arrived.

No matter how often you have to do it, make grooming a pleasant experience for your kitten. You want her to look forward to grooming, not avoid you like a plague of fleas. Give her treats and praise her. Remember, the key to grooming success is being gentle: comb her gently, never pressing harder than you would on your own arm. If your kitten's nervous, give her a tiny stuffed animal to bite, speak to her in a reassuring voice, and start with a short grooming session.

Deciding how often to brush your kitten

To pick up the dead hair, you ought to run a brush or comb through your shorthaired kitten's coat every week and your medium to long-haired kitty's every few days (although it varies from breed to breed and even kitten to kitten). Your Persian needs a comb-through daily. During those times of the year when your kitten leaves enough fur around to knit another whole cat, brush or comb daily. Always comb out the tangles before you give her a bath. Check out the "Bathing for Beauty" section later in this chapter.

Don't put off grooming your kitten, especially if he's furry (unless you're going for the dreadlock look); otherwise, you may wind up having to change his name from Fluffy to Matty. Tangles left untended for a week or two can turn into bona fide mats. Neglecting kitty's coat only saves you a couple of minutes a few days a week, and can end up costing you a pretty penny when your cat groomer has to shave the mats out of his coat.

Using the right tool for the tangle

You have many grooming tools to choose from; pet store shelves are full of combs, brushes, and mane-taming tools (avoid the ones that look like medieval torture devices). Unless you're planning on showing your kitten, you only need to worry about the same basic tools that you use on your own hair: the slicker brush and metal comb. As a rule, brushing gets rid of dead hair, and combing finds tangles. Take a look at some of the most common grooming tools below:

✔ **Soft slicker brush:** This is the only tool you need if you have a kitten with a close-lying or very short coat. When you buy a slicker, check the label to make sure the brush has soft fine wire bristles or that it's made for a cat's coat. Some dog slickers are hard and can scratch or irritate your kitten's tender skin. Look for one with a curved, not flat, surface. I especially like the ones with coat tips.

✔ **Comb:** For kittens with a dense, short coat or long hair, pick out a metal comb with both coarse and fine teeth. Comb all over with the coarse tines then with the fine side. The comb helps you find any stubborn tangles that are hiding in your kitten's fur. When you find a knot, use the slicker brush to remove it and then use the comb again. If you can't get a comb through the coat, you haven't brushed enough.

I use the Classic Products Comfy Care Combs because they're easy to hold on to, comfortable, and well made (order by calling 800-228-0105).

Professional groomers cut through the thick of it

From time to time, your longhaired kitten's fur gets out of hand and you find yourself in the thick of a matted fur epidemic. Often mats form next to the skin, and the only safe way to remove them is to shave them out. If you try cutting them out of your kitten's fur, you could wind up at the cat clinic getting stitches. A professional groomer should always remove mats.

You may just want to simplify your life by getting seasonal grooming — a lion cut summer hairdo shaves everything but the ruff (hair around the neck), legs, and tail — or a monthly shampoo and set.

Whoever you use, make sure they are used to grooming cats. Ask your vet if she has a groomer on site or can recommend one in your area. Ask whom your friends trust or get a recommendation from an animal shelter or a kennel. Some areas even have mobile groomers who travel to your house with a fully equipped cat beauty shop in a van.

Visit the shop to make sure it's clean and if they let you, watch how they treat the animals. Before you take your kitten there, get references and call the Better Business Bureau to check the groomer's record.

Other specialty grooming items you may want to invest in include

- ✔ **Flea combs:** These tiny combs have fine teeth to trap fleas in. They're also good face combs.

- ✔ **Zoom Groom:** This is the best tool for removing dead hair from a short coat. It's a rubbery plastic tool that loosens up the hair. Kittens love it because it massages them as it grooms. Check it out at www.kongcompany.com.

- ✔ **Grooming gloves:** These gloves loosen dead undercoat of shorthaired kitties. If you don't have one on hand, you can dampen your palm and groom as you pet. This is called hand grooming.

Working from head to tail

When you brush or comb your kitten, start at her head, because that's her favorite place. Never brush against the growth; she finds that uncomfortable and irritating. Brush around her head and down her back and sides. Then very gently brush her legs and tail. Finish up by getting the tummy and the inside of the hind legs (your kitten's least favorite place). End the session with a yummy reward.

When you're grooming a shorthaired kitten, brush her fur from the head toward the tail. If your kitten has long hair, brush from her body out to the ends of her hair. If you find a knot or tangle, brush it out with the slicker brush. The comb also will help locate those shy knots hiding in her undercoat. After you detangle her, comb through the longhaired kitten's entire coat. Pay close attention to her underside. That's where most people miss, particularly the chest between the front legs and the britches in the rear.

Put some white paper underneath your kitten while you comb her so you can see if flea dirt falls off her. Flea dirt looks like black specs that fall off the coat of an infested kitten. To find out how to treat fleas, flip to Chapter 9.

Dealing with mats

Unfortunately, mats happen. Knotted fur starts out as a small tangle nourished by dead hair that winds around the original snarl of fur. Before you know it, your kitten has a wad of fur right next to the skin. This can happen almost overnight during shedding season.

Don't cut out mats, especially if you can't see the roots. Mats often grow so close to the skin that you can seriously cut your kitten without realizing it. Gently work them out with a comb or take your kitten to a vet or groomer. Never bathe her if she's matted — you'll only make mat(ter)s worse.

If you have a 1/4" clearance between the mat and the skin you can slide a Solo Groom Pet Groomer underneath the tangled wad and squeeze the handle. A blade slides across the top of the comb (opposite the skin.) Get it from the manufacturer at 888-730-8115.

When working out a small or loose mat:

1. **Hold the mat down and against the skin and pick at the tip with the teeth of the comb.**

   Work slowly and patiently.

2. **As you loosen the ends of the hair, comb them out and then work gently on the next layer.**

   Don't rush. If you pull her hair, she won't sit still next time you get the comb out.

3. **Go slowly and break up the mats a little at a time.**

If you can't train your longhaired kitten to tolerate having her tummy touched, go for a *tunnel cut* — where the groomer shaves the kitten's underside and the fluffy fur on the back of the hind legs. After she's shaved, your kitten can get used to having her belly groomed when it's not tangled and matted.

Bathing for Beauty

I once saw a bumper sticker that read, "The only thing self-cleaning at my house is the cat." Thank goodness for cats' natural grooming tendency — it makes your job easier. Nonetheless, your kitten needs your helping hand once in a while.

Deciding how often to bathe your kitten

Because cats do such a good job of bathing themselves, you only need to bathe them when they get into something that you don't want them to ingest or if you suffer from allergies and you want to rinse off cat dander on a regular basis.

If you kitten gets into something caustic, like liquid potpourri or household cleaning products, bathe him immediately. If you think he's already licked some of the chemical call the ASPCA Animal Poison Control Hotline (800-548-2423 or 888-426-4435) to find out if there are additional steps you should take to flush the product out of your kitten's system. (You will be charged a fee of $45 for the call.)

If you need to bathe your kitten regularly, start a bathing routine when your kitten first comes home. Teaching an old cat new sinks can be traumatic for both of you, but if you start early, a kitten accepts bathing as a normal part of life. If your kitten isn't accustomed to being bathed, you may find yourself competing in the kitten wrestling Olympics. Be patient; comfort your kitten with gentle talk and work quickly. Hopefully, with time, he'll tolerate bath time better.

Using the right supplies and suds for the situation

Before you break the news to your kitten that it's time for a bath, get all your bathing tools together:

- **Shampoo and conditioner (or detangler):** I recommend using shampoo on shorthaired kittens and shampoo plus conditioner and a detangler on kittens with long hair or thick undercoats. Use products formulated for cats such as BioGroom Protein Lanolin Shampoo, because it's tearless and leaves the coat soft and clean. Human shampoo, even baby shampoo, is the wrong pH for your cat and can dry out his skin, but it can do in a pinch. Only use shampoo labeled safe for kittens. I like Mycodex Pet Shampoo with Carbaryl for fleas and tick problems. Get it from your vet. Avoid dog shampoo altogether, especially flea and tick products formulated for dogs, which may contain permethrins that can poison your cat.

- **Homemade rinsing agent:** Made of ½ cup vinegar in two quarts of water, this rinse helps remove soap and conditioner residue from the coat.

- **Towel and/or blow dryer:** Just towel her dry and/or blow-dry on low. Never use a hot dryer on a cat, but don't let her get chilled either.

- **Treats:** Speak to her in a soft, comforting voice and praise her with treats as you bathe.

If your kitten struggles or tries to scratch you, consider giving her Bach Flower Remedies to keep her calm (described in the "Getting started" section earlier in this chapter).

Lathering up!

You need to comb your kitten's fur before you get him wet, especially if he has long hair. If he has any mats or tangles, remove them (see the "Dealing with mats" section earlier in this chapter). Otherwise, the mats will only get worse when they dry.

Make the bath as untraumatic as possible. Avoid getting water in his face (kitties hate that). Wet him down with warm water using a sprayer on a hose. Keep the room warm so he doesn't get chilled.

Dilute the shampoo with water before you pour it on your kitten's coat, to make lathering easier. How much shampoo you use depends on the length of his fur; a shorthaired kitten may take just a quarter-size dollop. Longer hair requires more. If you don't use a tearless shampoo, put a drop of either mineral or castor oil in his eyes to protect them from irritation. While you're at it, stick a couple of small wads of cotton in kitty's ears to keep from getting water in them.

1. **Place your kitten in the sink or tub.**

   Hang on to her by the scruff of the neck.

2. **Wet the kitten with lukewarm water.**

   Use a faucet sprayer to spray her, start at her tail and move slowly to her shoulders. Avoid getting water in her eyes and ears. Keep water pressure light, not hard.

3. **Put shampoo on your hands, dilute, and then lather the kitten.**

   If you're using a kitten flea shampoo, lather around the ears and face first so fleas don't escape into the kitten's ears. Move from the head, then go down the back to the shoulders. Skip down to the tail and lather the tail, hips, and legs, then move toward the shoulder. This corrals the fleas and eventually overwhelms them with flea killer. If you shampoo your kitten regularly, the order doesn't matter.

4. **Rinse her well.**

   Rinse her neck first so it's easier to hang on to her. Then rinse the rest of her. Try not to splash water in her face. After you think you've removed all the soap, rinse her again — there's always a little shampoo evading the spray.

5. **If your kitten has long hair, apply a conditioner, then rinse the fur until the water is clear.**

   Conditioner helps detangle the hair so you can comb her out without hurting her. Shorthaired kittens don't usually need conditioner or detangler.

6. **Rinse her in the homemade rinsing agent (see "Using the right supplies and suds for the situation") to remove the last traces of soap and conditioner.**

7. **Pat her dry with a towel.**

   Don't rub; that just causes hair to tangle and mat.

8. **Blow dry.**

   If you're feeling adventurous, try blowing dry her hair on low heat. You can place her in a carrier and blow-dry her on low or no heat. Don't over dry her. A kitten's skin is very sensitive, and you can badly burn her with a hot blow dryer.

   Comb her long hair as you blow it; otherwise, the hair may mat. And watch her body language for signs that she may be losing her temper.

If your kitten fights you tooth and nail and you swear you're never going to bathe her again, read the "Professional groomers cut through the thick of it" sidebar in this chapter.

Checking eyes and ears

Kittens keep their ears relatively clean on their own. But after the bath is a good time to take a small cotton ball and wipe out the ears. A little wax is okay, but if your kitten has something that looks like coffee grounds in his ears, he probably has ear mites and needs to see a vet. Read more about ear mites in Chapter 9. Wiping out his ears also helps dry them out and avoid trapping water inside the ear canal that could cause a painful yeast infection.

Don't clean his ears with a cotton swab. You may drive it too far down and injure his ear. Use a damp cotton ball. Real cotton won't scratch that sensitive ear tissue like synthetic cotton will.

If you have a kitten who tears, wipe the lower eyelid with a warm, damp cotton ball. Don't apply any pressure to his eye. Let the warm water soften and loosen the crusty crud until you can gently wipe it away. Each time you go over the gunk, use a clean piece of cotton.

Cleaning Kitty's Canines

When it comes to your kitten, don't grab a tube of your toothpaste and an old toothbrush and expect to get the job done. Human toothpastes can be harmful to your cat, because fluoride is toxic to kittens. After all, you can't teach your kitten to spit, so he's bound to swallow the stuff. Instead, invest in some poultry-flavored cat dental paste and ask your vet for a kitty-friendly toothbrush. He can sell you a tiny little toothbrush from C.E.T. (www.cetdental.com) that's perfect for a little kitten mouth. You can get poultry-flavored toothpaste at any pet store.

Warm your kitten up to the idea of having his teeth brushed by letting him lick some of the yummy toothpaste off the toothbrush. Then quickly move the brush to the back teeth on one side, then the other. Remember, you only need to brush the outside of the teeth next to his cheeks. Your kitten "brushes" the inside of his teeth with his tongue. The whole process takes 40 seconds, daily is best, but weekly at the least. Take a look at Figure 11-3 to see a kitten getting his teeth brushed.

If you don't remove plaque, it mineralizes and turns to tartar. Tartar cannot be removed with brushing. When tartar forms, periodontal disease and gingivitis follow, leaving infection, pain, and missing teeth in its wake. Worse still, oral infection can spread to other organs, including the lungs, heart, liver, and kidneys. When tartar forms, it takes a veterinarian and usually putting the cat under anesthesia to remove it. Schedule a dental appointment for your kitten annually to maintain proper dental health — treating dental disease costs much more than prevention.

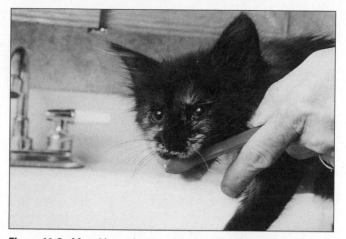

Figure 11-3: Most kittens love poultry-flavored cat toothpaste. Get him used to it by letting him lick the paste off the toothbrush.

Chapter 12

I'm Leaving on a Jet Plane: What Should I Do?

*E*ventually you'll have to leave town. When you have a kitten, traveling becomes infinitely more complicated than it used to be. You can't just pick up and leave a kitten anymore than you could leave a toddler home alone without supervision. Fortunately, you've got a number of care options to choose from. You could get a pet sitter to check on your kitten at your home, board your kitten at a facility, or take her with you on your trip.

This chapter discusses guidelines for screening pet sitters and boarding facilities and suggests information to get from and give to your kitten's caretaker. If you have a friend or family member to take care of things for you, skip ahead to "Preparing for your departure" later in this chapter. This chapter also gives suggestions that will make traveling with your kitten less stressful. Read on to find out all about this stuff.

Leaving Kitty with a Qualified Pet Sitter

You may reject the idea of disrupting your kitten's routine or, if you have a multi-pet household, boarding may not be economically feasible. In this case, using a pet sitter may be your best choice. If you don't know a trustworthy sitter, get recommendations from your friends or your vet. Frequently, vet assistants or techs moonlight as pet sitters. Failing that, request recommendations from your local humane society.

Making that initial contact

Unless you already know the person, when you first contact potential pet sitters, give out only vague information; use approximate dates (early March) and locations (near Fox Avenue and Regency Street). Save specific addresses, dates, and destinations until after you have agreed to hire someone.

Conducting the interview

Before you hire a pet sitter, ask her some questions. Remember, you're entrusting her with the safety and wellbeing of your kitten as well as your home.

Here are some questions to ask a potential pet sitter:

- ✔ What's the contact info for your last three pet-sitting clients?
- ✔ May I have three other references, including a veterinarian?
- ✔ Do you have cats?
- ✔ How are you going to charge me (by the animal, by the trip, or by the hour)?
- ✔ Who will actually care for my kitten? (I once had a sitter give my key to her friend because she was too busy to come herself.)
- ✔ What's your backup plan if you become incapacitated?
- ✔ What services do you provide? How do you charge for them?
- ✔ Do you take time to play with the pets you sit for?

Nosing around

If you think checking the background of a potential pet sitter is overkill, think again. The pet sitter will have access to your entire home, including your valuables, papers, credit cards, mementos, and of course your kitten. An unscrupulous person could wreak havoc that could last for years.

When a sitter has provided the phone numbers for her references, call them. Talking to the pets would be the best way to find out about a pet sitter. Since that isn't an option, you'll have to talk to the pet owner. Try to carry on a casual and friendly conversation. If you run across some questions the client hesitates to answer, consider it a red flag. Ask them

- ✔ When did you last hire this pet sitter?
- ✔ How often have you used this person?
- ✔ How do you feel about the job they did?
- ✔ What problems or misunderstandings did you have?
- ✔ Will you use this pet sitter again?
- ✔ Do you recommend this person to your friends?

Closing the deal

After you're comfortable with the pet sitter and her references, make an appointment to meet in your home. Introduce her to your kitten and show her everything you require. Take note of how your kitten responds to her and she responds to your kitten.

Before you commit, ask yourself how you feel about her. If she checks out and you feel good about her, find out if she's free when you need her. If she's not the right person, thank her and send her on her way.

Preparing for your departure

You're going to be busy. You've got to make contact lists, call vets, shop for pet supplies, and set things up in the house so the sitter can find what he needs. Without detailed preparation on your part, your sitter won't be able to do his job.

Right before you walk out the door, look for your kitten to make sure that you haven't accidentally locked her in a closet.

Doing the little things

You need to do a million little tasks to get ready for a trip. Your pet sitter will thank you for remembering to

- ✔ Check that you have enough kitten food and litter to last until you return.
- ✔ Set out all medications and clearly label dosage and when to cease medicating.
- ✔ Put ID tags on your kitten in case he accidentally gets out.

✔ Make a note of his favorite hiding places.

✔ Let your vet know you're leaving.

✔ Make a list of emergency info.

Compiling emergency info

Be sure to gather vital information for your pet sitter. He needs to know

✔ Your itinerary

- Departure and return dates

- Contact info

✔ Home security stuff

- Temporary codes

- How to arm and disarm

✔ All local emergency contacts

- Neighbors who can help in case of emergency

- Police and fire departments

✔ Your vet info

- Phone number and directions to your vet clinic

- Phone number and directions to the closest emergency clinic

✔ Your wishes in an emergency

- Decision maker if you can't be reached

- Whether you want the pet sitter or a friend to make a decision to euthanize, if necessary

✔ The names and descriptions of your cats

- If you have more than one cat, leave a photo and point out differences

- Or give them different-colored collars

✔ Your expectations

- How often to visit

- When to visit (daily, morning and night, and so on)

- What else to do, like answer phone, get the paper and mail, water the plants

- Medication requirements

- How often to scoop or change the litter boxes

✔ Important locations

- Feeding locations

- Location of kitten food, medications, litter boxes, fresh litter, liners, scoops, and so on

- Location of cleaning supplies (brooms, vacuum, trash bags)

Letting the pros know

Contact your vet ahead of time and give approval for treatments in your absence and set monetary limits if you feel you need to. Give written consent for treatment in case your pet sitter has to take the kitten to the emergency clinic. As unpleasant as it seems, contact the person who you've designated as the euthanasia decision-maker in case you can't be reached. Give him instructions.

I never thought this would happen, but while I was visiting relatives across the country, my best friend had to take my 6-month-old hydrocephalic kitten, Maynard, to be put to sleep when pressure on his brain started building again. Although it was heartbreaking for all of us, I'm glad that I had a plan in place and that my friend could spare Maynard unnecessary pain.

Notify local police that you'll be out of town. Give them your sitter's name and automobile description. Unless you know the pet sitter extremely well you may want to put your valuables in a safety deposit box. Don't tempt fate or your sitter.

Making a surprise visit

The first time I hire a sitter, I tell her I'm coming back a day later than I actually plan to. I want to see the condition of the house and kitten's facilities when I'm not expected. If the place is satisfactory, I pay her for the promised number of days. If not, I take the key and pay her for the actual days I was away.

Although fibbing about your return is duplicitous, I've found that it pays. I started doing this when I returned early, out of necessity, and found maggots in my kitten's food bowl and their boxes stinking with old poop. My trusted sitter, whom I'd used for eight months, had simply dumped new canned food on top of the old stuff, instead of tossing out the old food and using a clean bowl. Prior to this event, the house was always clean and tidy on the day the sitter expected me to arrive home. Needless to say, I got a new pet sitter.

Boarding Kitty

If you have a special needs kitten or feel uncomfortable about an unsupervised person having access to your home, you can board kitty at your vet's office or another facility.

It doesn't hurt to find a boarding facility right after you bring the kitten home. You never know when an emergency will suddenly crop up requiring you to leave town at a moment's notice. For this reason, it's also a good idea to keep your kitten current on his shot. You don't want to be scrambling to get vaccinations right before you go on vacation.

Locating potential candidates

As with so many things about kitten ownership, the best way to find a good boarding facility is to ask your friends and your vet for recommendations. Your vet may even be able to board your kitten for you.

Before you call the facility or drop by for a visit, call the Better Business Bureau and check on the kennel's record. The bureau can tell you if the boarding facility has any outstanding complaints against it.

Interrogating the management

If it checks out at the BBB, give the boarding facility a call and ask to speak to the manager. Ask him

- ✔ Do you require current vaccinations for upper respiratory diseases and distemper? (If they don't require shots, keep dialing.)

- ✔ Do you board cats on a regular basis? Do you board cats only? If not, do you have a separate room for cats or do you place dogs and cats in the same area? (Kittens hate being stuck in a room with barking dogs.)

- ✔ How do you prevent the spread of fleas, ticks, and ear mites?

- ✔ How do you monitor cats for illness, and what do you do if they get sick? Which vet do you use? Do you give medication? Do you charge extra for medication?

- ✔ What kind of supervision do you provide?

✔ What kind of food do you provide and how often do you feed? What will you do if my pet won't eat? (Boarded cats have a tendency to stop eating.)

✔ How often do you scoop and change the litter box? (Verify this during your surprise inspection.)

✔ What form of entertainment or human interaction do you give cats (exercise room, TV, employees play with cats)?

✔ How much do you charge? What other services, such as grooming, do you provide? Are there additional charges?

✔ Do you allow cats from the same household to share the same pen? Do you ever put unassociated pets together?

Dropping by unannounced

If the questions are answered to your satisfaction, then conduct a surprise inspection of the facility. With the exception of a vet clinic involved in a life and death emergency, any facility should let you look at its boarding area. If they ask you to come back later, don't bother. When you visit the kennel, the place should look tidy and smell clean with no odors except for brand new poop. Watch how the people and the cats interact.

Reserving a spot for your kitten

Make your reservations as far in advance as possible. Reputable facilities book up; some places book up years in advance around holidays.

Making it feel like home

Your kitten is going to be a stranger in a strange cage. She'll be frightened and alone. To help your kitten adjust to the kennel, bring her favorite toys and a blanket or her favorite bed from home. Leaving an unwashed T-shirt with your scent on it will help her feel close to you.

Don't forget to provide facility workers with phone numbers where you can be reached, your vet's information, and info about any medical conditions or special needs your kitten may have. You must also have your inoculation records.

Traveling with Kitty

Traveling with a kitten is much like traveling with a baby. Whether you plan an overnight visit across town or a two-month tour, you need to bring an entire war chest of necessities. Everything your kitten needs at home, he will need abroad. See the complete list in the "Packing kitten's suitcase" section. Most importantly, he'll need to wear a harness with ID.

Packing kitten's suitcase

Just like you need toiletries, medicines, and a change of clothes when you travel, your kitten has necessities, too. I keep a kitty suitcase packed to make sure I don't forget anything important when it's vacation time.

Among your kitten's travel supplies be sure to include

- **Dry food in zip-up bags, small cans of food, and a bottle of water** from home or commercial bottled water because unfamiliar water could cause diarrhea. Don't forget treats!

- **Calming remedies and medications** such as prescription motion sickness meds from your vet or Bach Flower Essence Rock Water or Rescue Remedy, which helps calm a frantic kitten. Get Bach at your health food store.

- **Litter box and litter** are a must. Disposable boxes work well under the circumstances. Flushable litter usually weighs less than clay, and it simplifies disposal.

- **Scoop and plastic bag** for kitty poop and other nasty throwaways. You may also want to bring along some larger plastic bags for trash.

- **Alcohol-free antibacterial baby wipes** for kitten bottom cleanup and wiping your hands.

- **A roll of paper towels** for general cleanup and to line the kitten's carrier.

- **Health certificates and proof of rabies vaccinations** are required for air travel.

- **Little whiskbroom and dustpan** to clean up litter tracking at hotels.

- **Unbreakable food and water bowls, grooming supplies, and toys** round out your kitty's suitcase and help make your vacation fun for you and your kitten.

Driving little Miss Daisy

Whether you take the entire trip in your car or hop a cab for the airport, any kitten travel begins with a ride in an automobile. Both you and your kitten will enjoy the excursion if you prepare her ahead of time.

Getting accustomed to the carrier

The trip begins long before you load up the car. It actually starts when you acquaint her with her carrier. Some people only bring out the carrier to take the kitten to the vet. When kitty sees the carrier, she hides. But when the carrier represents pleasant things, she's not going be as upset when you whisk her off to the car.

Let her sleep in it. Turn it into a game; give her treats when she goes to it. Next, take short trips; first travel around the block, then to the closest city. Put her toys inside and reward her when she gets inside and plays with them. Wow, what an adventure! When it's time to take a big trip, she'll just think she's going for another ride around town.

If you plan long distance motoring, get your kitten a large carrier, big enough to hold a litter box and a bed. See Chapter 5 for more advice on finding the right carrier for your kitten.

Cruising in the carrier

While traveling in a car, always keep your kitten in a carrier. I've known people involved in traffic accidents to lose their cats through broken windows. Some of the most innovative carriers have seat-belt safety straps to keep the carrier from bouncing around in the event of a wreck. Just as you would strap in your kid, secure your kitten's carrier in the backseat with the seatbelt. If it doesn't have special seatbelt loops, run the seatbelt through the handle.

Wad up a lot of paper towels and put a thick layer in the carrier floor. Nervous kittens often have runny diarrhea when they travel. Just pull out the soiled paper wads so she doesn't step in them, throw them in a plastic bag, and replace with fresh paper. The crumpled towels will keep the kitty waste confined to one area provided you clean it up right away. Don't feed or give your kitten water just before leaving. All the excitement could make her break-fast seek escape through one of several body openings. When you're underway, feed her some treats; chicken or turkey baby food always accompanies my trips. When you get to your hotel or final destination, feed kitten a real meal.

If your kitty's really scared . . .

If you haven't had time to acclimate your kitten to the carrier and traveling, she may cry and show other signs of anxiousness. I don't recommend giving tranquilizers — especially to kittens. But if kitty acts apprehensive, you can safely give even the smallest one Bach Flower Remedies to calm her down. For apprehension, I like Aspen, Rock Rose, Walnut, or the old standard: Rescue Remedy. Bach Remedies help with numerous fear-based behavior problems. For more about behavior issues, read Chapter 14. A friendly feline pheromone product called Feliway, sprayed inside the carrier, also has a calming effect on kittens. Find out about these remedies at www.bachcentre.com.

On a warm day, never leave your alone kitten in a car. Even with the windows cracked, the temperature can soar to 120 degrees in a matter of a few minutes. I take my foster kittens into just about any business provided they stay in the carrier.

Flying with your little feline

Some people would rather have a root canal than get on a plane with their kittens. Granted, you have to lug extra weight around the airport, and then you have to pass through security, but I can give you some tips to simplify the process and take some of the mystery out of it. Flying with kitty is still quite a bit of work, and your kitten may not appreciate it, but you can do a few things to make the process easier on both of you. Remember, you can't take your kitten out of his carrier after you board the plane.

Feeling out the airlines

Call the airlines and ask about their requirements and restrictions. At the airport, you'll be asked to provide a *health certificate* — a document signed by your vet certifying that your kitten is free of contagious diseases and is healthy to fly. When you make your reservations ask your airline how long the health certificate is good for; some airlines accept them for 30 days, others for only 10 days after the vet has issued the certificate. You'll also need to show proof of rabies vaccination if your kitten is over 6 months.

Also, establish what they charge for in-cabin pets. They often charge an additional fee despite the fact that they consider your kitten carrier (like the one in Figure 12-1) one of your carryon items. Make your reservation early because they limit the number of pets that can be taken in-cabin.

Figure 12-1: Soft-sided carriers, like this SturdiBag, allow you to position your kitten comfortably in the plane's cabin.

When discussing seating, ask that you not be seated in front of a bulkhead or in a row with an emergency exit. The carrier must fit under the seat in front of you, and if you have a wall in front of you, you don't have a spot to stow the carrier.

Harnessing your kitten

Put a harness on your kitten with ID. Your home information should be engraved on one side and a travel number or nationwide cell phone or pager taped on the other side. If your kitten accidentally breaks free while you're traveling, this may be his only ticket back home. You can find out about identification and information registries in Chapter 10.

Minding your hotel manners

Not all hotels welcome pets, so when you make your room reservations ask about your kitten. Some places may tell you to find another place to stay, or they may book you in a special section, charge you a small service fee, or require an additional deposit. Some travel guides list pet-friendly lodging, or you can check out either www.petswelcome.com or www.travelpets.com.

Deciding whether to sneak or not to sneak

I know folks who sneak their kittens in hotels, but I believe your kitten is safer if you travel with full disclosure. Traveling aboveboard will give you the opportunity to make special arrangements with housekeeping for the cleaning of your room.

Going unsecured through security

The most frightening moment of any trip for most kitten owners traveling by air is walking through the security X-ray checkpoint. Officers will instruct you to remove the kitten from the carrier, place the carrier on the conveyor belt, and carry your kitten through the human X-ray scanner. Never place your kitten in the carrier to send through the X-ray conveyer.

While you try to walk through those X-ray arches and return your kitten to his carrier, alarms are blaring, people are dropping change and keys into metal bowls, and any number of other unfamiliar noises, sights, and motions are scaring the fur off of your kitty. He *will* struggle. Make sure you have a harness on him. Security may not be too helpful. They may even watch nonchalantly as your kitten scratches three layers of flesh from your chest while you try to fit a spread-eagle four-legged acrobat into a carrier opening. (In all the years I have been traveling with my cats, I have only had one person offer to help me get the cat back in the carrier.) If you're traveling with a companion, have him go through the checkpoint first so he can hold the carrier door open for you.

Thinking about safety

When you arrive at your room, check for things that could be hazardous to your kitten. (To read more about dangerous items, check out Chapter 8.) I know a lady who found roach pellets underneath her bed at the designated cat show hotel. Thankfully she spotted them before her kitten did.

Both for my kitten's safety and my peace of mind, I travel with a *kitten cage*. I especially like SturdiProducts Show Shelter because it weighs just a couple of pounds and springs into a usable cage in seconds (www.sturdiproducts.com). A cage or enclosure provides a safe haven for my kittens when I can't be in the room. When my Siamese-mix, Sam, got sick right before I left for a trip, the exclusive no-pets bed and breakfast allowed me to bring him along because of the cage. He was also invited to visit again — anytime. They liked that he was confined in the cage and not contaminating their room with kitten dander. Keeping your kitten in a sealed tent or carrier while you're out of the room also assures that someone checking on the room won't accidentally let him out into the hall. It also keeps him out of mischief.

I always arrange with the housekeeping department to have the maid clean up while I'm in the room. I give her a good tip because kittens guarantee she's going to have to do more work, even if it's just vacuuming up tracked litter in the bathroom or dealing with more and smellier trash.

Part IV

Kitten Psychology: Understanding Your Furry Friend

The 5th Wave By Rich Tennant

@RICHTENNANT

"It's called a 'Dork Doll'. I'm hoping it will socialize my kitten for when your boyfriend comes over."

In this part . . .

Your kitten has a complex personality: He looks at things very differently than you do. This part helps you translate cat language into English. I tell you what kitten body language means to help you better understand your kitten's likes and dislikes and how little things can really bother him. And I give you advice on how to handle behavior problems and when to call a kitty shrink.

Chapter 13

What Did You Meow? Understanding Felinese

In This Chapter

▶ Listening to "kitten talk"

▶ Paying attention to feline body language

Kittens have a way of letting you know what they want. Mine do it all the time. Watch your kitten's body language and, when she's insistent, where she takes you. The tone of her voice can give you a clue. Does it sound like a polite request or is she frantically trying to get you to do something *now?*

A friend of mine has sibling kittens. One day, one of the boys weaved in and out of her legs, urgently meowing and running back to the refrigerator. She ignored him for a while, thinking he just wanted her to feed him, but when he kept after her, she opened the fridge door to find his shivering brother inside. In her case, it paid to realize her kitten had something important to tell her.

Not all communications between you and your kitten are likely to be this urgent, but understanding what your kitten is trying to tell you can help you bond and prevent future behavior problems.

In this chapter, I introduce you to what I like to call *Felinese,* the language of cats. Your kitten may not be able to speak to you with human words, but if you pay attention and know how to interpret his actions and vocalizations, the meanings become fairly clear. Try to focus on all the different ways your kitten communicates with people, other cats, and even the dog.

Felinese 101: Kitten Vocalizations

The vocal part of Felinese is much more than just "meow." It includes purring, chirping, and even growling.

A Cornell study has documented hundreds of different cat vocalizations — ranging from soft purrs to the battle yowls of a tomcat. No human knows what every one means, although some of the vocalizations do appear to mean the same thing to most kittens. Other kitty words and sounds may vary from kitten to kitten.

The more you talk to your kitten, the more he will respond and begin to understand. Speak to your kitten, and the two of you will develop your own language together, verbally, through body language, or both.

Among the most common and universal vocalizations in Felinese are:

- ✔ **Meow:** "Meow" is the first word you probably think of when you think about kitten language; it's primarily spoken by a mother to her kittens and from a kitten to his owner. Meow isn't usually used in mature cat-to-cat communications. Your kitten uses this word almost exclusively with you or other humans.

  Meow has a variety of meanings; the pitch helps you with all the different definitions. Experts say that the more disturbed the kitten is, the lower the pitch of the meow. A higher pitched meow says, "I'm glad you're home." Your cat can also convey urgency; "Feed me, now!" Slightly different sounds and emphasis convey a request or a complaint.

- ✔ **Silent meow:** The silent meow is a polite request. Your kitten waits until you're looking in her direction and mouths meow. You almost have to have kitten ears to hear the subtle sound she makes, if she makes any at all. My Siamese-mix kitten, Sam, has mastered the silent meow. He uses it when he wants a treat or snack. I find the silent meow almost impossible to resist.

- ✔ **Purr:** Purring is usually the first thing that endears a kitten to a person. Kittens begin to purr when they're just a few days old. For a long time, people thought that kittens only purred when they were happy. And a kitten does purr strongly and loudly when she feels content. But she also purrs when she's anxious, hurt, in labor, or even dying. A kitten purring with a relaxed body and partially closed eyes feels very contented. Purring with a tense body is a sign that she's fearful or nervous about something and is reassuring herself. For more about purring, see the "How kittens purr" sidebar in this chapter.

How kittens purr

Until recently, no one really understood the mechanics of purring. Now some scientists believe that kittens purr by forcing inhaled and exhaled air down into the larynx and diaphragm, producing intermittent signals at frequencies between 25 and 150 hertz. Researchers believe that sound produced at those frequencies improves bone density and promotes healing. That could explain why severely ill or anxious kittens purr — and why humans find a kitten's purr so comforting.

✔ **Chatter and chirps:** You hear these sounds when your kitten has her eye on prey. They have an "ack ack ack" sound. She may be stalking a fly at rest, a fat little bird outside the window, or a really convincing interactive toy. Sometimes you can hear her clicking her teeth, too. I've also had kittens make this sound when they've done something they know is naughty.

✔ **Hiss, spit, growl:** When your kitten growls, he's telling you that he means business. If the growl fails, he escalates to the hiss. You can't misunderstand this: He feels threatened, angry, or both. If you hear your kitten hiss, back off and let him calm down. He's showing his teeth, and his claws stand ready; he may bite if you force him. A spit may follow the hiss, which certainly inspires me to retreat.

✔ **Yowl:** This sound means it's time to get your little girl fixed; she's in heat. She's calling out to find herself a man, or rather, a tomcat. Get used to it. She's going to keep this up until she either gets pregnant or you have her spayed. (See Chapter 14 for more info about altering your kitten.)

Felinese 201: Reading Kitten Body Language

Not only does your kitten use her mouth to talk to you, she also speaks through her eyes, ears, tail, body posture, and even her scent. Felinese is like any other foreign language: If you talk to a person from a foreign culture and listen to the words only, you may be confused. But if you look at how someone stands, whether he's smiling or frowning, and whether his hands are loose or clinched, you start to understand more of what he's saying.

Understanding body talk

Your kitten uses different parts of her body in combination to get her message across. If you're going to be a good kitten communicator, you can't just listen to what the kitten says. You have to think feline and look at her big picture, at the whole kitten.

Like a line of kitty greeting cards, kittens have facial expressions and body positions to handle all situations.

Tail

Your kitten's tail is one of his most effective communications tools. How he holds his tail can clue you in to how your kitten feels at any particular moment:

- When the tail is held up high like a flagpole, he's confident and contented.

- A kitten wiggles his tail at either the base or the tip as a friendly greeting.

- With a tail safely curled under his body, he feels threatened. This is a submissive posture that says, "Curses! Caught red-pawed."

- The tail can fluff to more than twice its normal size when he's terrified. Be careful, he can switch from retreat to charge in the blink of an eye.

- A flick of the tail tells you that your cat's disappointed in some way.

- A wagging tail means you're bothering her (the exact opposite of a wagging dog tail).

As a cat grows more frustrated with the situation, she'll use her tail more forcefully. When motion escalates to thumping against the floor, look out and stop whatever you're doing to annoy her. She's getting ready to nail you (or the other cat).

- If you see your kitten staring at something and slowly twitching her tail tip while crouched, she's curious or excited. My kittens will assume this position when they sit on the window perch and spy a bird.

Ears

Your kitten's ears not only hear, they speak volumes: The position of his ears reflects his mood (see Figure 13-1). Because 30 muscles control each ear, your kitten can move his ears 180 degrees and change their shape. Although it may vary from kitten to kitten

✔ When he's feeling friendly, content, or relaxed, your kitten's ears face forward and are slightly tilted back.

✔ Erect ears mean he's alert even if he's lounging.

✔ Ears pointed forward indicate he's curious about something.

✔ A fearful or defensive kitten will usually have his ears back and down — lying flat against his head. He does this to protect his ears from being scratched or bitten in case the ruckus escalates into a full contact brawl. He also avoids eye contact. A submissive kitten holds his ears like airplane wings

✔ The aggressive cat on the offensive rotates his ears so the inside of his ears are folded up, but facing behind him. Beware! You don't want to bother a kitten with flattened or rotated ears.

Relaxed | Frightened | Ready to Attack

-Contented
-Relaxed whiskers
-Irises contracted
-Eyes half closed

-Ears flattened
-Whiskers forward
-Big, round irises

-Ears flattened and
 pointed back
-Irises between
 round and contracted
 Whiskers forward

Figure 13-1: Kitten facial expressions. The ears, pupils, and whiskers say it all.

Eyes

Your kitten's eyes provide a window into what's going on inside her mind (refer to Figure 13-1). Take a close look at her eyes. Every part of her eye sends its own message. Especially pay attention to her *pupils* (the black dot at the center of her iris). Not only do the pupils contract and dilate to control the light, they react to emotional responses:

✔ **Contracted pupils:** A relaxed or contented kitten will hold her eyes half-open with her pupils contracted.

✔ **Dilated pupils:** When your kitten's bug-eyed with fully dilated pupils, look out; she's either fearful, defensive, surprised, aggressive, or maybe even preparing to attack.

✔ **Staring:** An unblinking stare from her means she's challenging you. For more on the ins and outs of cat staring, see the sidebar "A cat can look at a king, but a king shouldn't look at a cat" in this chapter.

I use dominance staring as a discipline tool on occasions when the kittens play with me too roughly or attack bare skin. Silly as it sounds, I get down on the kitten's level, make direct eye contact, and hiss. Most of the time they stop what they're doing and start to groom their paws or butt as if to change the subject.

✔ **Blinking:** The opposite of the stare is when your kitten deliberately blinks at you. He's telling you he likes you and feels safe and comfortable with you. You can return the favor by blinking slowly back. Some people call it a kitty kiss. You will know that your kitten has developed real affection for you and feels comfortable with you if he slowly closes his eyes.

A cat can look at a king, but a king shouldn't look at a cat

When someone speaks to you, you tend to look at him. If you avoid eye contact, you may be considered rude or untrustworthy. Your kitten, however, translates staring as a threat or a sign of your dominance. In the kitten world, staring isn't considered friendly. Which explains why, in a room full of cat lovers, the kitten always homes in on the one person who doesn't like cats. Everyone else stares at the kitten, trying to get his attention or to grab him — aggressive signals and signs of dominance. So the kitten's drawn to the one person who's avoiding him, because in Felinese, the poor guy who doesn't like cats has the best cat manners and is making the friendliest kitty gestures.

Under normal circumstances, cats don't make eye contact with each other or even humans. Your kitten doesn't like it when you stare directly at her, either. You may look at your kitten because you love her and admire her beauty, but she won't understand your reason. Eventually, she may become accustomed to you looking at her, but because of her psychological hardwiring, she'll never be comfortable with it.

On occasions, one of my Turkish Vans (a very assertive breed) plants himself a few feet away from one of the more mellow cats and simply stares with his pupils fully dilated. The other cat avoids eye contact, and after a while yowls for my help. A submissive kitten avoids making eye contact to prevent getting pounded in a fight. If you ever see kittens vying for dominance in this way, you'll notice that the dominant kitten holds her head up, and the submissive kitten lowers his head. I wouldn't want to be on the receiving end of that stare. Even I find the angry, challenging stare of a dominant cat uncomfortable.

A kitten's eye view

Kittens can see almost as well as humans with 20/20 vision can. In some ways, kittens can see even better. Kitty vision is designed to aid in hunting. Consider these interesting tidbits:

✔ Kittens are slightly nearsighted so that they can focus in on a nearby mouse or lizard rather than distant prey.

✔ Kittens' retinas have more rods than cones. (*Rods* are the cells used for night-time vision; *cones* are the cells used for daytime sight and seeing colors.) Having more rods helps a cat see at night, enabling him to pinpoint sudden motion with his peripheral vision. (Of course, having fewer cones means that your kitten can't see colors as vividly as you do.)

✔ Your kitten has large, elliptical pupils that contract and dilate much faster than your round pupil can. Because of its size, the kitten's pupil lets more light in. His eyes have a *tapetum membrane* that reflects light through a second time in the opposite direction creating a visual double exposure of light (this is why your kitten can hunt in near darkness). The yellow glow seen when light shines onto your kitten's eyes is the light reflecting off of the tapetum membrane.

If you don't mean to discipline your kitten, but he catches you looking at him, try slowly blinking at him to break up the stare. That should put him more at ease. Also try this during stressful times to calm your kitten down.

Whiskers

Although your kitten uses his whiskers like a probe to determine whether a hole is big enough for him to go through, he also uses them to communicate (refer to Figure 13-1).

✔ When your kitten feels relaxed, he holds his whiskers to the side, allowing them to droop down.

✔ A curious kitten perks his whiskers up and forward slightly.

✔ A hunting kitten moves his whiskers forward — a great help for locating prey in the dark.

Making sense of scents

Your kitten marks his territory using pheromones from glands located in his chin, temples, the corner of his lips, and at the base of his tail. If a male kitten is unneutered and becomes sexually mature (between 6 and 9 months of age), he may start marking territory with pee pee graffiti. If he becomes the dominant tomcat, he'll mark his territory by leaving his poop uncovered for all the other cats to find, as if to say, "I'm the king of my world." The other cats and kittens cover their poop, leaving themselves in protective anonymity. Early spaying and neutering helps prevent the need to do this kind of marking. However, older neutered kittens sometimes spray to express anxiety about changes in life. Chapter 14 tells you all about marking with pee.

Head butts mean "I love you"

Kittens not only speak to you through vocalizations and posture, but their physical contact with you also speaks volumes.

Following are some of the ways your kitten's going to communicate to you (see Figure 13-2):

Trusting   Friendly

Frightened   Ready to attack

Figure 13-2: Kitten body language.

✔ **Head butt:** The head butt is a friendly cat-to-cat greeting that your kitten may extend to the favorite people in her life — the equivalent of a kitty hug. She's greeting you like you would greet another cat at a family reunion. She's also marking you with scent from the glands around her mouth and ears.

✔ **Kneading:** Whether you call it kneading, milk treading, or making biscuits, kneading is a sign that your kitten is a very happy camper. When she's resting on your lap and massages your legs with her paws, she may feel as if she's gone back to her mother's nest. After all, you feed and protect her like her mother did. When she was a baby kitten, she massaged her mother while she suckled to make the milk flow faster. An older kitten kneads because she feels safe and content. For more on you as kitten mother, take a look at the "But M-o-o-om!" sidebar in this chapter.

This kind of affection can be a bit rough on your legs when those needle-sharp claws dig into your thighs. Like several other kitten responses, this one is a compliment, so don't get mad or brush your kitten away; you'll confuse him. A real queen would never push her kittens away like that. Instead, trim his claws regularly. You can find out just how to do that in Chapter 11. Another way to protect your legs is to lay a thick towel or blanket across your knees as you sit down, before your kitten climbs into your lap.

✔ **Drooling:** You may notice as you pet or stroke you kitten that he's not only purring, but he's also drooling, too. The petting has sent your kitten into such a state of euphoria that he's actually forgotten to swallow. Take this as a wonderful compliment. Still, if you object to a little kitten spit landing on your clothes, occasionally press your finger against your kitten's nose or the side of his mouth. He'll swallow instinctively without shattering his mood.

This kind of drooling isn't a problem, providing it only happens when you're petting your kitten. If he dribbles all the time, he may have a problem with his gums or teeth, which would justify a trip to the vet's office. More on kitten medical problems in Chapter 9.

✔ **Licking:** When your kitten licks you, it doesn't mean that she's kissing you. She's probably grooming you. But don't be insulted. Kitties only groom other kitties they feel are in their own family. When she licks you, she's telling you that you're one of the clan.

✔ **Wanna smell my butt?** Your kitten may approach you, turn around, and present his bottom to you as if to say, "Ya wanna sniff me?" This is something he only invites his friends to do, whether the friend is human, feline, or even canine. Some experts say the kitten is offering an invitation to take a sniff of his anal glands so you'll know who he is — sort of a kitty handshake. Others say you remind him of his mother, and he's asking you to groom his bottom. I don't recommend you go to that extreme to bond with your kitten, but thanking him and scratching the base of his tail when he presents his butt is an acceptable response. Regardless of whether he's asking for grooming or greeting, take the presentation of his bottom as a compliment — an intimate and meaningful moment, at least for a kitten.

✔ **Leg weaving:** As with most of your kitten's affectionate actions, leg weaving originated with mom. A kitten greets his mom with his tail upright, and then wraps his tail around her rear end to get her to lie down so he can eat. As he gets older, he continues to rub against friendly cats to place his scent on them. His tail has scent from his anal gland on it. As he rubs his tail against another cat or you, he's marking you — another display of affection and a good way for him to get attention or food. It works on me.

✔ **The classic Halloween cat posture:** When something frightens your kitten, she may assume the classic Halloween cat posture. (Sometimes playing kittens assume this position out of excitement rather than fear.) She fluffs up her tail as big as it can look, puffs up her fur by making it stand up on end, and arches her back. She assumes this posture when she wants to look bigger and meaner in the hopes of bluffing a potential attacker into believing she's invincible. This terrified kitten won't approach you head on. She stands with her profile to you and, instead of turning and running away, hops off to the side so that her opponent (you in this case) continues to see a big scary cat even as she's madly retreating. When you see this posture, back off. Even though she's a cute, adorable kitten, she may bite you. If you do get bitten, speak to her in a gentle voice and leave her alone until she calms down.

✔ **See my tummy:** If you've ever watched littermates play, you may have seen one roll over with all four paws in the air. With her claws sheathed, she's inviting contact. The other kitten jumps right in, and the growling and tumbling mock battle begins. Your kitten may also greet you with this position. When she shows you her belly, it could mean that she's so relaxed and so totally trusts you that she's showing you her most vulnerable position. She's not saying, "Scratch my belly," like a dog would. It's a show of trust, not an invitation.

But M-o-o-om!

Because you assume many of the duties of the mother cat, or *queen,* your kitten will begin to look at you as Mom. Before long, you may notice that many of the things your kitten does around you and for you go back to things she did with her furry mom. You should feel flattered. You can return the compliment and bond with your kitten by mimicking some of her mom's behavior. A kitten likes being stroked and petted because it reminds her of her mother's tongue grooming her. To find out about other ways you can bond with your kitten, read Chapter 21.

If your kitten offers you her belly when she gets older, you may want to reconsider before you reach down to rub that feline Venus' flytrap. Look a little closer. When lying on her back, your kitten is in a heavily armed defensive position. On her back, she can attack an adversary with claws from all four feet plus her teeth.

Chapter 14

Managing Behavior Problems

· ·

In This Chapter

▶ Understanding your kitten's nature

▶ Putting him back in the litter box

▶ Keeping kitty from spraying

▶ Stopping the scratching

▶ Preventing kitty from climbing on counters

▶ Halting aggression

▶ When all else fails, seeking a kitty shrink

· ·

*H*ave you ever noticed that the first syllable in catastrophe is
"cat?" Trouble comes as naturally to cats as breathing does.
They have a knack for getting into whatever causes the most havoc,
like chewing toxic plants and electric cords or scratching furniture.
Some high jinks are par for the course, but what if kitty is acting
out of control? You don't have to put up with that! Products and
procedures exist to help you tame your little tabby.

In this chapter, I explain *why* your kitten does those things that
annoy you so much. Then I go over some of the most common
problems and give you tips on how to best overcome each of them.
I tell you why preventing an unacceptable behavior is better than
changing an entrenched habit. And I let you in on why training or
behavior modification can sometimes be as simple as making inappropriate behavior unpleasant and appropriate behavior fun.

The first step to dealing with any new behavior is taking a trip to the
vet. Peeing outside the box can sometimes be caused by something
as simple as a bladder infection that can be easily treated with a
round of antibiotics. Your kitten may be biting people because of a

painful abscess or other injury that gets jostled when you pet her. And hiding or other sudden behavior changes could also be caused by an illness.

Understanding His Antics

Before I describe specific misbehaviors, or what most people perceive as misbehaviors, I want to point out that often your kitten believes he's acting perfectly fine when you think he's tearing the house apart. What your kitten does makes sense to him. Scratching furniture, jumping on the counter, and climbing curtains are normal, healthy kitten behaviors. They're the same actions he'd be enjoying if he lived outside as a natural cat. They just don't translate well to living in the house, so you need to take the time to understand his kitten desires and give him a way that he can still express them (see Chapter 15).

When your kitten does something naughty, don't spank him or put him in "time-out" like you do with kids. He just isn't able to understand these punishments. Instead, redirect his attention to an agreeable activity (such as scratching a post instead of the couch) and reward his good behavior. After your kitten figures out that he gets a treat whenever he uses the litter box, scratches on the cat tree or the cardboard scratcher, or sits on the window perch instead of the counter, he continues to be good because he sees something in it for him.

Overcoming Litter Box Avoidance

An odor is coming from the living room. Your kitten has missed the box — again. The house smells like a kennel, and you're getting tired of it. I don't blame you. You may be surprised to find out that your kitten is tired of something as well, or that he's feeling under the weather. Because he can't tell you that something's wrong in words, he's leaving you a message next to the litter box. Try to listen to him.

Pinpointing the problem

Kitty could be avoiding the litter box for a number of reasons. Perhaps she doesn't like the type of litter you bought or maybe she's trying to tell you to keep her toilet cleaner. Whatever the reason, you need to pinpoint and correct the problem right away.

If your kitten has had fastidious litter box habits until recently, take an immediate trip to the veterinarian's office. Your little friend's problem may not be a bad attitude at all, but a urinary tract infection. Bladder infections make the kitten feel like he's got to gooooo all the time, and when he does pee, it hurts. Kittens with bladder infections begin to believe that the box is hurting him, so if he doesn't pee into the box, it won't hurt when he goes to the bathroom. Peeing outside the box is a distress signal that requires immediate medical attention.

If your kitten receives a clean bill of health from his vet, you've got some detective work ahead of you. The most likely culprits for your kitten being on the outs with his box follow:

- **He doesn't like the litter.** Maybe he doesn't like the way the litter feels. If you're using litter made from pellets or large crystals, or even regular clay litter, stop. Studies show that kittens prefer soft sandy litter, which feels good against their feet. For more on the textures that kittens like, read about litter in Chapter 5.

  Maybe he doesn't like the way the litter smells. Kittens don't want their cat litter to smell like anything but kitten. You may like rose-scented litter, but it turns your kitten's stomach. According to kittens, many scented litters aren't fit to pee in. Find out more about how his sense of smell affects his litter preference in Chapter 5. Switching to unscented litter may solve his problem.

- **She doesn't like the size or shape of the litter box.** Companies make litter boxes to appeal to humans, not cats. If your box isn't large enough to accommodate a big kitty, she may hang her bottom out the opening or not even bother to get into it in the first place.

  I converted a 35-gallon covered storage tub into a litter box for my larger kittens and cats. The box is even large enough for my 22-pound bruiser. Talk about a master bathroom!

- **The litter box is filthy.** I hate using bathrooms at gas stations along the highway. Some of them are just nasty. Your kitten likes his litter box to be clean, too. He shouldn't have to perform bathroom gymnastics to avoid stepping in all the poop collected in his box. You have to scoop everyday.

  Also, think about the chemicals you use to clean it. Despite the advice of columnists and cleaning experts who suggest that you're supposed to sanitize and deodorize the litter box, your kitty isn't Captain Kirk; he wants to go where other kitties *have* gone before. He wants to go where *he's* gone before.

If you scrub his box down with bleach and remove all of his scent, he may not recognize it. He likes the way his pee smells, providing you don't let the box stink like an ammonia factory. Never clean his box with pine cleaner or citrus cleaner. Instead, clean his box with hot water only. If cocciddia or other viruses worry you, use very hot water to clean the box. If you must clean or disinfect it, sprinkle some previously used litter in the sparkling clean box to make it seem more familiar.

✔ **Litter is scattered outside the box.** Maybe your kitten is just confused. After all, in her mind she's not doing anything wrong; she's still going in cat litter. Clean up litter tracked outside the box. Also consider using a litter that doesn't track or purchasing a litter mat that you can regularly empty back into the litter pan.

✔ **Someone's bothering him.** Watch your kitten. One of the kids or other cats may be picking on him by blocking the box or harassing him while he's using it. Have more than one litter box in a room (a bully can't block more than one box at a time) and keep the boxes in a room with more than one door, so the bully can't block the only escape from the room either.

✔ **He hates the location.** You may be inclined to keep the litter box in an out-of-the-way spot where you don't have to look at it or smell it. Unfortunately, if the box is out of the way for you, it's out of the way for your kitten, too. Instead, make sure you have at least one litter box for each cat plus at least one additional box on every floor of your house. Convenient places to position the boxes include in a bathroom or utility room. But remember washers, dryers, or furnaces make scary noises, so don't put the box next to a gadget that makes a lot of racket.

✔ **Something's changed; she's stressed out.** Your kitten gets worried very easily. Think back to when the transgressions first began. Did you move the litter box? Is there a new mat in front of the box to catch the tracked litter? Did you bring home a new baby or pet? Did a companion kitty die? Something as insignificant as placing a new chair a few feet away from her litter box may annoy her. If stress is causing the problem, be sure to read the following section about how to get her back in the box.

Getting him back in the box

To get your kitten back in the box, you may simply have to switch to the fine (sand-like) unscented clumping litter.

Ordinarily I would never recommend clumping litter for kittens, but providing your kitten is at least 5 or 6 months old, you can try out a new cat litter called Dr. Elsey's Cat Attract that just begs to be peed on. They use some herbal additive that cats just love and that seems to make using the cat box downright fun. After he's using the box again consistently, you can gradually switch back to your other litter.

If Dr. Elsey's doesn't work, then it's back to litter box 101 for your kitten. He needs to return to his safe room (see Chapter 6). Confine him to a small room, like a bathroom, with his litter box and food. Give him a chance to get used to using his proper facilities again. Then let him out for short, supervised periods until you feel comfortable giving him total freedom. If that doesn't work, then you may need to consider getting professional help. See the "Seeking Professional Help" section later in this chapter for more information about finding a shrink for your kitten.

Calling in the cleaning crew

While you're pinpointing and correcting the problem, be sure to thoroughly clean the spot or spots outside the box where the kitten relieved himself. As long as it smells great (that means great as in just like kitten pee), he will always want to go back there.

When cleaning up a recent mistake

1. **Place a towel over the spot.**

2. **Blot it up by pressing down until you get no more moisture from the carpet.**

   Don't rub the carpet. Rubbing just pushes the pee deeper into the carpet pad.

Locate older pee spots, which are often hard for the human nose to smell, with a black light or ultraviolet light. You can purchase a black light from a pet supply or janitorial supply store. (Don't bother with a cheap black light from a novelty boutique; they work fine for psychedelic posters, but they don't show cat pee.) Turn out the lights except for your ultraviolet lamp, and your kitten's indiscretions show up in florescent yellow. Mark them with a piece of masking tape, turn on the lights, and start to reclaim your home.

1. **Apply an effective pee neutralizer, such as Enzyme D or Tuff Oxy, to the spot on the carpet, pad, and sub floor.**

   If possible, pull up the carpet and pad and scrub the sub floor (it doesn't matter if it's concrete or wood). If the sub floor has been hosed with cat pee and you don't treat it, that spot is a likely target for future hosings. If you can't pull up the edge of the carpet to treat the pad or sub floor, use a large syringe (needle is not necessary) to inject sufficient quantities of the cleaning chemicals through the carpet and into the carpet pad.

2. **Keep the area wet with solution according to the product directions.**

   The type of solution that uses enzymes and/or friendly bacteria to break down and eat odor-causing bacteria needs to be wet to work. Some solutions need to stay damp for 24 hours.

3. **Remove excess moisture from the carpet with a wet vacuum, shop vacuum, or carpet cleaner to prevent mildewing.**

4. **You may need to treat the carpet a second or even a third time.**

   If you can still smell urine, so can your kitten. And if he can smell the pee, he sees it as an invitation to come back and party.

If your kitten gets in the habit of peeing in a particular spot, make it unappealing to him. I cover the spot with Sticky Paws XL (www.stickypaws.com). I also spray a deterrent like Boundary Indoor/Outdoor Cat Repellent on the area. You can purchase both products at most pet supply stores. It takes two or three weeks to break a habit, so keep the tape and the repellent working for the full time.

Nixing the Spraying: Spaying and Neutering

Older kittens claim their territory by marking with pee. They also spray and mark instinctively when they're in new and stressful situations. A kitten who's marking stands on all fours, holds his or her tail straight, and wiggles it at the base. Instead of squirting down, he sprays out against a tree, wall, or other vertical surface. In your house, the couch is often the closest thing to a tree.

Boy kittens start spraying when they reach sexual maturity, at about 7 months old. Girls can do it, too. Although the unspayed girl sometimes sprays to mark territory, she usually does it to announce to all eligible bachelors that she's in heat starting at about 5 months of age. You can prevent spraying in most kittens simply by having your kitten spayed or neutered.

The cost of altering your kitten varies from region to region and vet to vet. Neutering runs between $50 and $90, and spays cost somewhere between $85 and $150. (Spaying costs more because it's major surgery requiring more anesthesia and cutting incisions in the abdominal wall, whereas a neuter takes a tiny incision in the testicle.)

If that seems like more than you can afford, have no fear. Some organizations can help you find low-cost spay and neuter services. You can contact

- **Your local animal control or local rescue society:** It may know who offers a low-cost spay/neuter program in your community. It may even sponsor one.

- **Spay/USA:** This national spay/neuter referral network can connect you with a low-cost spay/neuter clinic in your area. You can reach Spay/USA toll-free at 800-248-7729 (800-248-SPAY) or check out its Web site at www.spayusa.org.

- **Pets911:** Call this referral network at 1-888-738-7911 (1-888-PETS-911) or check out the Web site at www.1888pets911.org.

- **Friends of Animals:** Yet another referral network. You can reach it toll-free at 800-321-7387 (800-321-PETS).

If putting an end to stinky kitten sprays isn't a big enough selling point for altering your kitten, consider the following added benefits:

- **Altering your kitten increases his chances of living a long, healthy life.** Spaying prevents certain diseases, like uterine and ovarian cancer. It also reduces the possibility of developing breast cancer. Neutering the male kitten reduces the chances of testicular and prostate cancers, as well as prostate enlargement and hernias.

- **Altering your kitten reduces aggression (see the "Dealing with Aggression" section later in this chapter).** He's less likely to scratch or bite you, your children, or other animals, and he's also less likely to engage in aggressive play.

✔ **Spaying your kitten keeps her (and you) from suffering through a heat cycle.** A female in heat can be really maddening. The poor little thing cries out until she gets what she wants — a little tomcat action. While she cries and carries on, she may be peeing all over the place hoping to attract Mr. Right.

✔ **Altering your kitten ensures she doesn't contribute to the population explosion.** Every year millions of cute, healthy kittens are euthanized because they don't have homes. The Humane Society of the United States statistics show that between 4 and 6 million cats and kittens are killed annually in shelters.

✔ **Altering your kitten keeps him closer to home.** If you permit your neutered kitten to go outside, he's less likely to roam far from home.

If you decide to alter your kitten, schedule the operation right after his 7-week birthday or as soon as he weighs 2 pounds. Now this may seem early to some, but both the American Veterinary Medical Association and the American Humane Association endorse early spay and neuter, because research shows that early sterilization doesn't appear to affect the health of kittens in a negative way. Actually, early-neutered kittens consistently recover quicker from the anesthesia and bounce back from surgery sooner than their 6-month-old counterparts. For example, my newly neutered boys climbed the 7-foot cat tree as if nothing special was going on. And even though I try to stop it, the girls also get into a little rough and tumble play the day of surgery, too.

If you adopt an older, unneutered kitten who sprays your walls or furniture before you have a chance to have him neutered, don't scream at him or punish him. Hitting or rubbing his nose in the mess doesn't work either. He thinks you've flipped and that just adds to his stress. Instead, thoroughly clean the carpet (see "Calling in the cleaning crew" earlier in this chapter), walls, and baseboards.

After cleaning off all of the pee, try a little spraying of your own. Spray Feliway at your kitten's nose level. Feliway is a synthetic facial pheromone that marks the wall with a friendly, soothing smell. This soothing scent should calm him so he doesn't feel the need to mark.

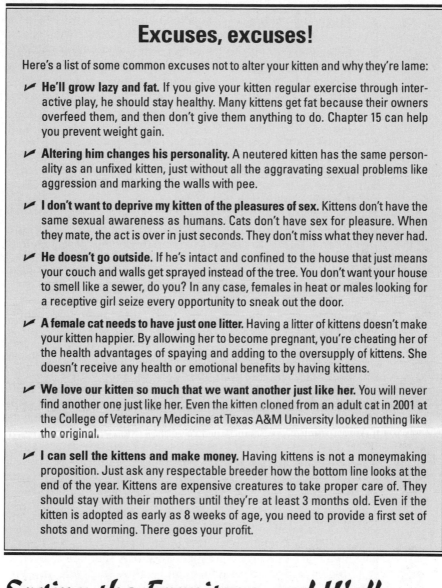

Excuses, excuses!

Here's a list of some common excuses not to alter your kitten and why they're lame:

✔ **He'll grow lazy and fat.** If you give your kitten regular exercise through inter-active play, he should stay healthy. Many kittens get fat because their owners overfeed them, and then don't give them anything to do. Chapter 15 can help you prevent weight gain.

✔ **Altering him changes his personality.** A neutered kitten has the same person-ality as an unfixed kitten, just without all the aggravating sexual problems like aggression and marking the walls with pee.

✔ **I don't want to deprive my kitten of the pleasures of sex.** Kittens don't have the same sexual awareness as humans. Cats don't have sex for pleasure. When they mate, the act is over in just seconds. They don't miss what they never had.

✔ **He doesn't go outside.** If he's intact and confined to the house that just means your couch and walls get sprayed instead of the tree. You don't want your house to smell like a sewer, do you? In any case, females in heat or males looking for a receptive girl seize every opportunity to sneak out the door.

✔ **A female cat needs to have just one litter.** Having a litter of kittens doesn't make your kitten happier. By allowing her to become pregnant, you're cheating her of the health advantages of spaying and adding to the oversupply of kittens. She doesn't receive any health or emotional benefits by having kittens.

✔ **We love our kitten so much that we want another just like her.** You will never find another one just like her. Even the kitten cloned from an adult cat in 2001 at the College of Veterinary Medicine at Texas A&M University looked nothing like the original.

✔ **I can sell the kittens and make money.** Having kittens is not a moneymaking proposition. Just ask any respectable breeder how the bottom line looks at the end of the year. Kittens are expensive creatures to take proper care of. They should stay with their mothers until they're at least 3 months old. Even if the kitten is adopted as early as 8 weeks of age, you need to provide a first set of shots and worming. There goes your profit.

Saving the Furniture and Walls from Kitty Claws

Furniture scratching is a natural feline behavior. Some kittens scratch due to stress or boredom. Some kittens scratch to sharpen their claws or get a full-body workout. (Watch her. She's stretching every muscle.) Still others scratch to mark the furniture as theirs or because, darn it, it just feels good!

Your kitten has scent glands in the pads of her feet. When she gives a piece of furniture a good working over, she's depositing scent to tell everyone that this is hers in a friendly, non-threatening way. She does the same thing when she rubs her head against your legs or gives you head butts (see Chapter 13).

If you don't want a sofa that looks like a deranged haystack, start deterring the damage early, and your kitten, his claws, and your grandmother's antique settee can live intact and in harmony. If nothing seems to work, consider declawing your kitten as a last resort, which I talk about later in this section.

You should start trimming your kitten's nails shortly after bringing him home. This way he gets used to having his paws handled. Trimming your kitten's nails every few weeks establishes the good habit and helps keep your furniture and skin intact. You can find out how to cut your kitten's claws in Chapter 11.

Scratching off bad behavior

Most people try to change a kitten's behavior by punishing or yelling at her. That approach doesn't work. Rather than wasting your energy by trying to stop an unwanted behavior, you're better off rechanneling the kitten's energy toward something acceptable. A two-tiered approach is the most successful: Make scratching the furniture unpleasant and offer her something she *can* scratch.

Providing distractions

Providing your kitten with something substantial that she can scratch is the first step to protect your furniture. Your kitten uses the couch or recliner because it's big and doesn't move when she gives it a good tug. Entice her away from the recliner with a heavyweight scratching post, preferably a tall cat tree. (Kittens love high places, so give her a place to satisfy that need.) Even a stout log or cardboard scratcher can be more satisfying than your heirloom Queen Anne couch if it's presented right. By being presented correctly, I mean by making the Queen Anne unattractive (see "Removing the appeal of your appointments" later in this chapter) and, at the same time, making the alternative enticing.

Make sure the scratching post of choice is heavy enough to support climbing and stretching. If the post tips when the kitten puts her weight into a full-body stretch, she's going to find something better to scratch (for instance your recliner). For more about buying a great scratcher, check out Chapter 5.

Placement is very important. Place the new scratching post right next to your kitten's favorite place of destruction. Don't force her paws onto the post. She'll figure it out on her own. You may not need to do anything to get her to attack it. If she doesn't warm up to the post right away, you can entice her with catnip or a favorite string toy. Praise her and give her a food reward whenever you see her use or interact with her post. After she begins using the scratcher on a regular basis, move it closer to where you would like to keep it, preferably in a high-profile location. Otherwise she may not remember the scratching post when the urge to scratch hits her.

Removing the appeal of your appointments

Make your furniture less inviting by

- ✔ **Applying double-sided tape.** The most effective anticlawing product is a double-sided tape called Sticky Paws for Furniture (www.stickypaws.com). I've used it, and it's nothing short of amazing. Kittens absolutely hate it. The adhesive is water-soluble and works safely on most upholstery fabrics. The stuff is almost completely invisible, and you don't have to remove it even when you expect company (see Figure 14-1).

- ✔ **Spraying a deterrent around the area where the kitten scratches.** These sprays often contain citrus oils that kittens can't stand. Most of these products are not detectable to the human nose. Unfortunately, the spray deterrents don't create a force field the kitten cannot enter. Use them with other deterrents and positive reinforcement. Ask for spray deterrents at your pet store.

- ✔ **Changing the feel of the furniture.** Safety pin bubble wrap to upholstered furniture. When the kitten punctures it, bubble wrap makes a scary pop, sending him running for the hills. Also try fixing sheets of aluminum foil to the floor in the place the kitten likes to stand while she's shredding your couch. You can also apply it to the couch arm. Most cats don't like the way it feels.

- ✔ **Firing a water pistol at her rear end.** A good old-fashioned squirt gun permits you to administer correction from some distance away from the kitten. In order for the squirt gun to work, the kitten can't know that you're the one manning the trigger. Otherwise, you only stop the behavior right at that moment. But if you do things right, your kitten soon discovers that the water only shoots from nowhere while she's in the act of scratching the sofa. But remember, the previous solutions, which don't depend on your presence, are more effective.

Figure 14-1: Put Sticky Paws where your kitten's ripping up the furniture. If you place a scratching post or cardboard scratcher nearby, he should abandon the sofa for the scratcher because it feels better.

Declawing: The last resort

Perhaps the most controversial aspect of kitten ownership is declawing. Some people are passionately against it, so much so that some countries, including England and Brazil, have made declawing illegal or permissible only under extreme medical circumstances.

Those who oppose declawing argue that the practice is a painful, invasive operation that offers no health benefit to the kitten and that is performed solely for the convenience of the owner. People involved in humane work swear that other behavior problems, such as nervousness and aggression, crop up in kittens who have been declawed, but the American Veterinary Medical Association doesn't acknowledge any behavioral problems as a result of declawing because no documented studies have been done to confirm the change in personality of declawed cats.

Those who endorse declawing say that the procedure is no worse than any other operation. It solves behavior problems that could cause a kitten to lose her home.

In the United States, some states are looking into making declawing a cat a crime. While I don't agree that the state should outlaw declawing, I hope that you make every effort to retrain your kitten before you have her declawed. Please don't declaw her unless you have a destructive kitten who doesn't respond to training. Under no circumstances should you declaw your kitten as a preventive measure, or because you're afraid she *may* scratch the kids.

Like any other surgical procedure, the declaw operation involves risk, including the possibilities of infection, permanent sensitivity, hemorrhage, nail regrowth, and altered feeling in the toes for some time after surgery. Although it rarely happens, sometimes declawing can cause the kitten's toe tendons to contract, making it uncomfortable for the kitten to walk. Because the last joint in the toe is removed (see Figure 14-2), kittens must change the way they walk, shifting weight to the hindquarters. Occasionally, this can cause muscle atrophy in the kitten's front quarters.

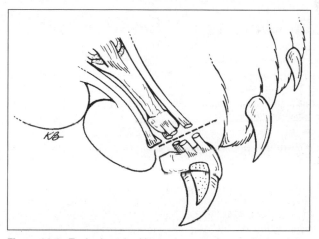

Figure 14-2: To declaw the kitten, the vet removes the last joint in each toe on the kitten's front feet.

If declawing is necessary, talk to your vet about what procedure he prefers. Most vets today perform either laser declaws or tendonectomies, which I describe in the "Lasers aren't just for alien invaders" sidebar in this chapter. The age that vets prefer to perform a declaw may vary from clinic to clinic, but vets should do it between 4 and 6 months. However, don't be surprised if your vet refuses to do a four-paw declaw unless you can provide a good reason. Most vets only remove the claws from the front two feet.

Also ask how you can prepare for your tender-footed kitten's homecoming. Remember, the kitten's feet will be sore for several days, so you may need to set up a safe room (see Chapter 6) to keep her confined and quiet. If she gets too active — jumping or climbing — her feet could start bleeding. You also need to put newspaper litter in her box, because dust from clay litter can become trapped in the incisions and get infected. Most kittens prefer Yesterday's News Softer Texture litter, which you can buy at your local pet store.

Under no circumstance should a declawed kitten be allowed outside unattended, *ever*. A kitten defends herself with her claws and uses them as her primary escape from danger. Without claws, she can't climb a tree fast enough to get away from dogs. She stands little chance of escaping an attacker and, if cornered, is forced to rely on her teeth to defend herself.

Lasers aren't just for alien invaders

If you must declaw your kitten, laser declawing is a more humane option than conventional surgery. Vets perform traditional declaws with a guillotine-type instrument. The laser method seals the nerve endings and cauterizes the blood vessels, significantly reducing the pain the kitten experiences compared to traditional scalpel surgery. Kittens declawed with lasers heal faster and walk sooner. Laser surgery also reduces the amount of time the operation takes, so it requires less anesthesia and speeds up the recovery time. But the equipment is expensive, so the laser operation usually costs more. Remember that even with the state-of-the-art laser procedure your kitten can experience complications. If the bone is overheated, it can lead to infection.

Another alternative to the traditional declaw operation is the flexor tendonectomy. Under general anesthesia, the vet cuts the tendon attached to the end of the toe. That tendon allows the claw to flex, but the severed tendon keeps the claw permanently sheathed. The kitten still has her claws, but she can't extend them to scratch or claw furniture. Even this procedure has drawbacks. You need to trim the nails frequently. If you don't, the nails grow into your kitten's pads. As your kitten rubs her paws on the furniture, she can still get her claws caught in fabric and carpet. And the American Veterinary Medical Association actually doesn't recommend tendonectomies for cats.

As with a declaw, a kitten with a tendonectomy has difficulty climbing trees and has a hard time protecting herself from other animals. So after a kitten has had this procedure, you need to keep her strictly inside.

Keeping Kitty off the Counters

Kittens want to be where the action is. They also want to hang out where the food can be found. I can guarantee that at some point your kitten will jump up on the counter and try to help you fix dinner. You don't want him up there because you don't want cat hair in your food and you don't want him around the sharp knives and the hot stove. You need to make the countertop experience unpleasant for him.

One of my favorite deterrents for counters is Sticky Paws XL; a large sheet of double-sided tape with removable tabs that sticks to the counter only by the edges. After the kitten jumps up on the counter and lands on the XL, he jumps right back down. When I need to use the counter, I pull the tape up and stick it to the refrigerator. When I'm finished, I return the XL to the counter. You need to make sure your countertop is covered for a week or two, until your kitten gets out of the habit of jumping on it. After your kitten lands on that sticky tape a couple of times, and decides he doesn't like the way it feels, he looks for a nicer spot.

Other ways to keep your kitten off the counter include

- ✔ **Motion sensors:** Motion sensors are essentially electronic tattletales. SSSCAT is a motion-activated spray product in a can that makes counters, furniture, and other off-limits areas unattractive. When the device senses the kitten's movement, it emits a beeping tone and a burst of pressurized air sprays in the kitten's direction. The motion sensor and direction of spray are adjustable, and the scentless spray is stainless, ozone friendly, and has no side effects. The device also has two levels of action: a sound/spray option that gives a warning sound just before the spray is released and a sound only option that can be used after the cat begins associating the sound with the spray. It's pricey — costs around $50. Get more information from Premier Pet Products by calling 800-933-5595 or checking out its Web site at www.Premier.com.

- ✔ **Snappy Trainer:** These look like mousetraps with a huge plastic paddle on them. When the kitten steps on the paddle, the trap goes off. The trap sometimes goes flying through the air with that nerve-racking mousetrap snap. That only has to happen a couple of times to convince a kitten to start avoiding the device and the counter altogether. Although not likely, if the kitten lands in the wrong place, he could hurt his paw. One behaviorist suggested putting a piece on newspaper over the trap to avoid injury. Check out this device at www.interplanetarypets.com/snappytrainer.html.

Teaching good table manners

Although begging at the table is more associated with dogs, kittens can be just as annoying. If you ignore a kitten, he may just jump up on the table and fight you for your plate. If you don't want your kitten eating dinner with you

✔ Don't feed him while you're eating.

✔ Don't feed him human foods or anything from the table.

✔ Don't feed him out of dishes from the table — not even a bowl.

✔ Don't allow him on the table for any reason.

✔ Don't eat before you feed him. When his stomach is full, he isn't interested in what you're eating.

✔ Don't leave food on the table even accidentally. One positive experience makes him want to come back.

✔ Don't pay attention to him while you're at the table. You shouldn't pet or talk to him around the table.

If your kitten insists on bothering you while you eat, lock him up during mealtime.

✔ **Water trap:** Try filling shallow aluminum trays with water and lining them up next to the edge of the counter. When the kitten jumps on the counter, he lands in a pan of water. After this experience, he thinks twice about jumping up there again. This training exercise may create a mess, but cleaning up water isn't difficult.

✔ **Water pistol:** The three previous methods work better than yelling or water pistols because your presence isn't necessary. However, when you're using the counter and the kitten decides to check out what you're doing, give him a little squirt with a plant mister or squirt gun. Aim at his rear end, not his face and say firmly, "No." Don't yell. Just place him on the floor and ignore him.

Dealing with Aggression

Kitten aggression comes in all forms. He could be hiding in the darkness of the hall and attacking your feet as you walk past (predatory aggression). He may bite or scratch you when you touch a certain spot on his body or he may be in the throes of ecstasy when he suddenly clamps down on your hand (stimulus biter). He may simply be afraid or take out his anger or frustration at another animal or situation (redirected aggression). Whatever the cause, the violence must stop.

Don't ever encourage aggression. Never let your kitten attack your hand or any other part of your body. For example, you may think it cute to wiggle your toes and let your kitten attack them, but the same game won't be fun when he's grown to 10 pounds and can hurt you. Prevention is better than having to change an unacceptable behavior. Teach your kitten the difference between acceptable and unacceptable play, and make sure your children follow the rules as well when playing with the kitten.

After the first attack, you need to correct him immediately. If your kitten likes to ambush your ankles in the hallway or from under your bed, ready a couple of correction devices such as

- ✔ Water pistol
- ✔ Balloon and needle
- ✔ Soft drink can filled with 10 pennies

When you see your kitten in ambush position and ready to pounce, sternly say, "No!" and either give him a squirt (not to the face), drop the penny can near him (don't hit him with it), or pop the balloon. If you don't have any of these on you, clap your hands.

If you have problems correcting him in the act, set him up, but don't let him think you're condoning his actions. Walk past his favorite ambush blind with balloon or water pistol in hand. When he takes the bait, discipline him.

Now that you've shown him he's either going to get wet or get the pewaddle scared out of him if he jumps you, you have to give him a way to use up that predatory energy. Give him a lot of playtime where he can pretend to be the great predator (see Chapter 15). He quickly discovers that ankles get him wet, and it's much more satisfying to bite into and kill Da Bird toy.

If things appear to be getting out of hand, and your kitten seems uncontrollable, you may need to seek professional help — read on.

Seeking Professional Help

If you've tried everything I've suggested and your kitten's still in hot water over soiled carpets, aggression, scratching or any inappropriate behavior, you need to call in a cat behaviorist or a cat shrink.

A cat behavior counselor treats your kitten holistically — treating the entire kitty, not just the symptoms. Your kitten's counselor will want to make sure you're kitten is getting

- ✔ Medical treatment for medical conditions that may be causing him pain or discomfort

- ✔ Sufficient exercise

- ✔ A good diet

- ✔ Communications training so the owner can begin to understand what the kitten is telling him

- ✔ Plenty of things for him to do around the house like scratching posts, hiding places, and even high up places to enrich the kitten's environment

- ✔ Desensitizing training to help the kitten understand that the object of his fear is less scary than he thinks it is by exposing him to it in a safe environment

- ✔ Tranquilizers — when necessary

If you decide you need to call in an expert to help your kitten, ask your vet to recommend someone. If she can't refer you, check with the Association of Companion Animal Behavior Counselors (www.animalbehaviorcounselors.org) or the American Veterinary Society of Animal Behavior (www.avma.org/avsab/default.htm). You can also ask any nearby veterinary colleges or universities whether they have a behavior clinic.

Failing that, you can contact Tufts University of Veterinary Medicine Behavior Clinic, which offers PETFAX for remote behavior consultations. The sessions are conducted together with your vet. Sometimes medication can help you and your kitten work through the problem together. The service costs less than $200. You can reach PETFAX at 508-887-4640.

Chapter 15

Keeping Your Kitten Entertained and Out of Trouble

In This Chapter

▶ Playing with kitty when you have the time

▶ Making sure he's busy when you are

I've heard many behaviorists say, "A tired cat is a good cat." If your kitten has used up all his energy, say, chasing a laser pointer or scratching his favorite post, he's too tired to attack your ankle.

You can't bully your kitten into behaving the way you want him to, but you can persuade him by giving him proper attention and rewarding him when he does what you like.

In this chapter, I tell you how to keep your kitten entertained and out of trouble both while you're home and while you're out.

Showering Him with Attention When You're Home

Many people have the wrong impression about kittens. They believe you can feed them, scoop their poop, and — ta da — you have a happy, well-adjusted pet. It's true kittens don't need constant attention, but they do need someone or something to properly channel their curiosity and drain their energy. Otherwise, your kitten will be in a mood for attack-the-toes-under-the-covers after you've gone to bed. Play some of the hunting and chasing games I discuss in this chapter, and you'll both be happier and well-rested.

Going for a walk

If he enjoys it, taking your kitten out for a morning or evening stroll provides him with a mental diversion and some much-needed exercise. Under the proper circumstance, leash training your kitten adds excitement to his housebound life.

Before taking your kitten outside, think about whether you can safely walk your cat in your neighborhood. If you live in an area that has heavy, loud traffic or dogs running free, then taking your kitten for a walk may not be a good idea. On the other paw, if you live in a quiet neighborhood with no unrestrained dogs, or if you have a peaceful park nearby, both you and your kitten may enjoy the exercise.

Right off the bat, buy your kitten a comfortable harness. The harness should fit snugly, allowing you to slip two fingers between it and the kitten, showing you that it's not too tight. The harness should fasten with plastic safety latches that click into place, not buckles. Test the snaps before buying the harness to make certain it can't inadvertently come loose while the kitty is scratching or struggling.

Although they're cheap and available everywhere, I don't like the thin little figure-eight harnesses. Kittens can turn into contortionists, and if this type of harness is a tad too loose, your kitten could wiggle out. And don't bother with harnesses that fasten underneath the kitten. They're too much trouble to put on. Make sure the one you buy fastens on the side.

Before taking kitty for a walk, give him a chance to get used to wearing the harness. After he's strapped in, don't be surprised if he just falls over like his bones have decalcified. Help him adjust to wearing his harness by rewarding him as soon as you fasten the snap.

Harness manufacturers say never make your kitten wear a harness unsupervised. Because it has no quick release, if the harness becomes caught on something and the kitty panics, he could hurt himself.

After he's okay with the harness, attach the leash and let him drag it around. Turn the leash into a toy by letting him bat at it. When he's used to dragging the lead, try walking him around your yard. Let him explore at his own pace. Go where your kitten wants to go. When you're walking, remember he's not a dog; don't expect him to heel. If he gets too distracted, you can say "come" and give a gentle tug. Don't drag him. If he starts to fidget, bring him back inside.

After each romp, take off his harness and praise him. Tell him how wonderful and brave he is. Take him out for a little longer each time. If your kitten simply doesn't enjoy going outside, abandon the idea. Don't force a reluctant cat to go on walks. The point is for him to enjoy himself. If it's not fun for him, find another way to entertain him.

Even if dogs don't usually run loose in your area, I recommend carrying a can of a pepper spray just in case a stray threatens your kitten.

Killing da wabbit so to speak

Kittens are tiny tigers that hunt with amazing proficiency. Bringing one into your home doesn't take the wild out of her. You need to channel her predatory instincts in a way that isn't harmful to either of you. Daily bouts of interactive play not only bond you and your kitten, but also release her tension, distract her boredom, and keep her fit and healthy.

Start your morning with a rousing "chase the prey" game. It takes only 15 minutes but uses up plenty of your kitten's excess energy that would otherwise be used to get into mischief while you're at work or the grocery. Here's how you play:

1. **Dangle a cat lure from a pole, a little like a cat fishing pole.**

   You can make your own toy by attaching a fake mouse to a string or you can buy one of my kittens' favorite toys, called Da Bird, which makes a fluttering sound like the beating of a bird's wings when you flip it through the air. Buy one at www.go-cat.com.

2. **Get your kitten's attention by dangling the toy in front of him.**

   Wiggle the toy just a little. That's the way prey behaves.

3. **When you have his attention, move the toy out of kitty's reach. Then let him chase and pounce on it.**

   Make the toy act like prey on the run. Make it zigzag, stop for a moment, then dash a little farther, just like a mouse, lizard, or insect would. With a little practice, you can get your kitten to leap and do back flips.

4. **Let your kitten catch the toy every so often.**

   No game is fun if you never win.

5. **After the prey "dies," give your kitten a treat and then put the toy away.**

   Remember, if he killed it in the wild, he would get to eat it. After he's had a treat, he may give himself a bath and then take a snooze. Don't be surprised if he sits by the closet or wherever you keep the toy, staring. My cats can't get enough of this game.

Another popular toy you can use to encourage active play is the Kitten Mitten (see Figure 15-1). Break this toy out when you get home and help your kitten burn off some steam. Dance the fingers around your kitten and watch her pounce and play, getting a full workout in the process.

Never allow your kitten to bite or swat a bare human hand. That sends the message that hands are fair prey. It may be cute to see a 2-pound Maine Coon pounce and swipe at your hand, but it becomes a serious matter when he's fully-grown and acts out those instinctive behaviors. If you don't have a Kitten Mitten "on hand," use an oven mitt instead.

Figure 15-1: The Kitten Mitten allows your kitten interactive play without hurting your hand.

My kittens love chasing the light from laser pointers and flashlights as much as they love chasing Da Bird. They play with the red dot until they drop, even though they never have the satisfaction of the kill. A flickering light certainly diffuses some of that hyper kitten energy.

Don't permit children to use a laser pointer without supervision. If the laser is shined in an eye (either human or kitten) it can cause permanent damage or blindness. Also, remember the kitten's going to be so focused on the light beam she's not going to see that wall or that rocking chair she's heading for. Make sure you steer her in an area that's safe and free of room mines.

Do fence me in: Installing a kitten fence or run

Look into a cat fence or run that allows your kitten to explore the great outdoors safe from cars and dogs. Under the right circumstances a cat fence can save both your sanity and your kitten's life.

No fence or run can protect your kitten from airborne viruses like feline calicivirus and feline herpes virus, so make certain that he's current on his vaccinations before you let him outside. And after you install your kitten fence or run, make sure it doesn't have holes or open spots where your kitten can escape. The most ingenious cat fence in the world can't hold a kitten if it's made with rotted wood that has holes big enough for him to squeeze through.

Supervise outdoor play for several days or until you're sure your kitten can't find a way out. Some kittens exploit any weakness they find to make a break for it. It took a couple of months to contain Basil, our foster kitten, with a kitten fence. He jumped to the small planters, then onto our storage shed, then over our brand new 8-foot cedar fence. We blocked one exit, and he figured out another one. We finally had to install 12-foot poles and hang plastic mesh from it to keep our nomad home.

When you're certain your kitten can't escape, let him play to his heart's content while you get ready for work or fix dinner.

Putting up a kitten fence

Installing a cat fence is a snap if you have a secure existing fence. Installation requires a drill, a screwdriver, and a ladder. Simply attach special plastic mesh to metal brackets mounted at the top of a secure chain link or wood fence. Cats can't get over it. For a closer look at a nice cat fence, take a look at Figure 15-2.

Figure 15-2: A cat fence gives your kitten all the joys of the great outdoors without having to worry about him wandering away or being hit by a car.

Several manufacturers offer these fences including Cat Fence-In and Affordable Cat Fences (see the "Where to look for cat fences" sidebar in this chapter for company Web addresses). I bought the Cat Fence-In system for my kittens. Now Sam and the rest of my kitten clan can enjoy some fresh air without the hazards of coming in direct contact with unvaccinated cats. And the inside of my house has been restored to a degree of sanity.

Where to look for cat fences

If you're in the market for a cat fence, check out the following Web sites. Some of them, including Cat Fence-In and Affordable Cat Fences, provide commercial options. Others provide free plans that may do the job.

www.catfencein.com

www.catfence.com

www.friendlyfence.com/ff/prod_fence_cat.asp

www.feralcat.com/fence.html

www.hsus.org/ace/13937

www.lisaviolet.com/cathouse/backyard.html

www.scvhumane.org/behavior/cat/cat_fence.htm

www.corporatevideo.com/klips/secret.htm

Don't expect a cat fence to be a cheap form of kitty entertainment; however, it does cost less than replacing a home full of carpeting torn to shreds by a bored kitten. Most cat fences cost somewhere in the $1.50 and $2 per square foot range for the materials.

In case you're wondering, invisible fences, or fences that shock your pet when he wears a special collar and crosses the invisible barrier buried around your yard, are not meant for kittens. Most of the receiver collars are designed for dogs and are quite large — way too big for a cat, much less a kitten. And the fence only protects him against wandering away from home. It doesn't protect him against dogs, predators, or malicious kids that may wander into *his* yard.

Building an outdoor run

Not everyone has a fence that can safely support a cat fence. Then again, not everyone has a yard. But you can still offer your kitten outdoor excitement in safety by building or buying an enclosure or kitten run. Install a strategically placed bird feeder to give your kitty hours of entertainment.

Outside enclosures and *window patios* (a mini sealed enclosure that fits inside your window like a window air conditioner) are a couple of options that can bring a little of the out of doors inside. They can also help your kitten with the transition from outside stray to inside kitty who has a room with a view. Kitty can get closer to where the action is — or more accurately, where the birds are — without being exposed to the risks.

Midnight Pass has an entire line of inexpensive cat enclosures, most of them under $100. It even offers a portable netted enclosure called a Kittywalk that connects to a window or cat door. A net supported by metal wickets extends 10 feet. This is a neat idea if your fence can't support a cat fence, but don't leave your kitten unattended if dogs and other animals can get into your yard. For more on this item, check out www.midnightpass.com/kittywalktm.html.

You can also make a run out of an existing structure. After I decided my kitties couldn't go outside anymore, I screened in our covered patio. It wasn't too expensive, and my kittens loved it. Reasonably priced enclosure kits can be purchased from www.cdpets.com/enclosure.html.

Teaching your kitten tricks

Another way you can bond with your kitten and also keep her mind leaping is to teach her to perform some tricks. Kitties love the one-on-one attention. Nixie, my Siamese-mix, has "shake" down so well, she'll try to give me her paw even when I don't ask for it just to get the treat.

Try your home schooling right before you feed her. That way she'll have incentive to perform.

The following tricks are easy to teach your kitten and very impressive. It may take a couple of weeks for your kitten to put two and two together and come up with "sit," but after she catches on, you can make up your own act. I like to use baby food (without onions) as a reward because she gets lots of flavor with a quick lick that doesn't fill her up.

- **Come:** Show your kitten the treat. In a pleasant voice call her name and add, "Come." When she does, say, "Good come," and give her a treat. Never use her name to scold.

- **Sit:** Show the treat. Put light pressure on his rump. Say, "Sit." When he does, say, "Good sit!" and reward him. Repeat the process four or five times or as long as he's interested.

- **Shake:** Tell her to "Sit." Reward her. Now, put your hand behind her front right leg and bump her paw. Say, "Shake." Instinctively, she lifts her foot up. Gently hold her paw. Say, "Good shake" and reward. Repeat.

- **Sit up:** Instruct him to "Sit." Then hold your baby food-dipped finger above his nose slightly out of reach. Say, "Up." He rises up on his haunches to reach your finger. When he sits up, say, "Good up!" and reward.

- **Wave:** Have her sit. Now, hold your finger with the baby food at her eye level just out of reach and say, "Wave." She reaches up with her paw to touch your finger. Praise with, "Good wave!" and reward.

- **Kissy:** Put a tiny dab of baby food on your nose or cheek. Point to it, tapping your finger and say, "Gimme kissy." Let him sniff the baby food and lick it off. As he's doing it, say, "Good kissy!" and immediately give him a bigger lick from your finger. Repeat as long as you can stand it. During the initial training, you may lose a few layers of skin, but just think of it as exfoliating the pores. The kitten soon understands that whether or not he finds anything on your nose or cheek, the reward for licking is on your finger.

Home Alone: Encouraging Safe Play While You're Away

When you're out of the house, give your kitten something to do. Try to keep his mind working instead of letting him cook up things he shouldn't be doing. The following sections describe things you can do to keep your kitten entertained and out of your potted plants all afternoon.

Buy toys that make kitty play hard and that simulate prey he'd hunt in the wild. Introduce your kitten to his new toy or special area before you leave him alone with it for the first time. If he's not interested, figure out a way to make it fun. Run the laser pointer up the new scratcher or into the new window perch. Then reward him when you see him using them. Rotate his toys so he doesn't get too used to them. Playing with the same toy over and over again is like watching a rerun on TV. He wants to play with something new and exciting. If it disappears and suddenly appears a week later — he may see it as a brand-new toy.

Getting your kitten a kitten

Arriving home from work, you find toilet paper unrolled all over the bathroom, the drapes torn up, and the furniture scratched. You definitely have a problem. But it may be a different problem than you think. Your kitten isn't bad, but like a kid home on summer break, she has too much time on her paws. If she doesn't have something to do, she finds her own activities. A surprising answer to this problem is to get the kitten a kitten. What? You read right.

Your kitten would probably enjoy a friend, especially if you work outside the home or if you travel frequently. An extremely active kitten would also benefit from a feline diversion to help use up some of that seemingly endless kitten energy.

Two kittens aren't that much more work than one. You need just a few seconds more to scoop the poop and only a little additional time to groom. But at 10 in the morning, when your kitten is normally asking herself, "Do I climb the lace curtains or pull everything out of the trash can?" the new kitten jumps right in, and the games commence. She doesn't make it to the curtains because she just can't fit it into her busy schedule. A kitty companion can fill those boring days with hours of mutual grooming and wrestling.

Although I almost always encourage people to adopt an older cat, if you're getting a companion to keep your kitten out of trouble, another kitten would most likely work out best. When you have two kittens you don't have to deal with territorial issues. Another kitten can match the boundless kitten energy.

It you decide to give your kitten a friend, be sure to read Chapter 6 on introducing the new kitten to the resident cat. You may see a little hissing and some whiskers out of joint in the beginning, but before long they should be best friends. When looking for a companion for your kitten, look for someone with a similar personality. Don't get an assertive kitten hoping he can help make your shy kitten more outgoing. Instead, an aggressive companion may have her cowering in the closet. For more on finding kitty companionship, read Chapter 2.

Simulating the wild

Being a strictly indoor kitten is not all sunshine and joy. As a matter of fact, it can be a drag, especially when he's home alone several hours each day. Like a teenage kid on a permanent summer break, many inside cats become couch potatoes with nothing to do. You're keeping him in the house to assure he has a long, happy life. Now, you need to supply the "happy" part. You need to give your kitten activities and exercise.

Look for ways to mimic your kitten's natural habitat. Consider the following ideas:

✔ Kittens love to hide. They like to feel that they are spying on the household completely unobserved. Provide a place for them to do this: Leave paper sacks unfolded on the floor for your kitten to crawl inside. Or turn a cardboard box on its side for the kitten to nest in. By hiding in a box or sack, the cat feels safe and enclosed on all sides. He's protected. And who knows, an unsuspecting mouse may scurry past. The cat can spring into action before the mouse even knows what's happening.

✔ Give your kitten a taste of the great outdoors, literally, by planting a cat grass garden full of grasses and herbs such as oat, wheat, rye, barley, and blue grass as well as catnip and catmint that your kitten can hide in and munch on (see the color insert). The beauty of a cat grass garden is that anyone can grow it. And it's quick; a week after you plant most grasses, your cat can start nibbling away. Simply purchase stylish planters and pots at garage sales or nurseries and give kitty his own corner of greenery without exposing him to airborne viruses. For a complete list of cat-safe plants compiled by National Animal Poison Control see `www.cfainc.org/articles/plants-non-toxic.html`.

✔ To add ambience to your kitten's garden, you could give him some running water via a kitty drinking fountain or a decorative fountain. Try the Drinkwell Pet Fountain, which holds 6 cups of water (you can also buy an optional 6-cup reservoir). The spout is 5 inches above the floor, about kitty mouth level, and pours down to a "receiving ramp" that almost eliminates splashing but aerates the water. The motor makes a very, very faint hum, but that is drowned out by the splashing sounds made by the water. My kittens enjoy watching and listening to the water, but they don't dare take a dip — the only time I found water on the floor was when I accidentally bumped the fountain with my foot. You can order the Drinkwell Pet Fountain for around $50 including shipping at 800-805-7532. Or find a retailer at www.vetventures.com.

Keeping kitty high on life

Kittens love to hang out in high places, so try to satisfy that need by buying or building a tall scratching post (see Figure 15-3).

My kitties love the Cat Loft, which comes with a penthouse and a spiral staircase. A kitten or cat is always sleeping on it, because it appeals to everyone from the 3-month-old to the 15-year-old. The kittens especially love to run up and down the staircase. It costs about $200 plus shipping from Iroquois Innovations. You can reach the company at 216-381-1369 or check out its Web site at www.iroquoisinnovations.com.

Figure 15-3: Kittens need things that mimic their life as it would be in the wild. They love high places and hidey-holes.

Watching Tweety from a window perch

What kitten doesn't love to sit by the window and watch the excitement going on outside? From his little window to the world, your kitten can see birds and watch the neighborhood kids play.

One of the easiest perches to install is the Deluxe Window Seat by Omega Paw, Inc. You can buy it at most pet retailers for under $25. To install, just bolt two screws into the windowsill. The window seat is a white elegant-looking molded plastic perch that fits in any room. You can phone Omega Paw to find a nearby store that carries its products at 800-222-8269.

After you've chosen the window and installed the perch, make the view a little more interesting: Install a birdbath, hummingbird feeder, or squirrel feeder right outside the window. With the flurry of animal activity that follows, the window perch soon will be the most popular sleeping place in the house.

I actually place birdseed on the brick right outside the window to entice the birds to fly in for a close up. At first they flew away when the kitties pressed their noses against the glass. But now the birds have figured out that the kittens can't get to them and they put on quite a show.

Treating kitty with a treat ball

When you're away, take up your kitten's dry food and give him a treat ball so he can spend his mental and physical energy working for his dinner, just like a natural cat (but without those pesky bird and mouse carcasses).

Treat balls are neat devices you can get at almost any pet store and are another way to keep your kitten's mind occupied and his body doing something that doesn't involve damaging the furniture. Small openings allow a treat or piece of kibble to drop out one at a time. Your kitten quickly figures out he can get something to eat by pushing the ball around with his nose or paw. I recommend that you buy some kitten food that moves through the hole easily, but not too easily. This way you're feeding him something healthy, not junk food.

You don't even need a treat ball. You can send him on a treasure hunt. Plant treats or even dinner kibble around the house in nooks and crannies. He can spend his free time hunting down the goodies.

Part V
Welcoming the Unplanned Kitten

The 5th Wave   By Rich Tennant

"We found an abandoned kitten about 2 weeks old. We think he's a little hungry, but seems perfectly content at the moment as long as my boyfriend doesn't sneeze."

In this part . . .

You ou may find a stray or abandoned kitten who really needs some help. Don't panic! This part tells you how to remove him from a dangerous situation without getting hurt yourself. I also give you a step-by-step guide on how to care for a nursing kitten who's lost his mom. Remember, you need to be careful with this little guy! I describe how to bottle-feed him and how to keep him healthy. And I give you some pointers on finding him a loving home.

Chapter 16

Rescuing an Older Kitten in Need

● ●

● ●

It happens every day. Someone pulls up beside a dumpster or into a roadside rest stop, drops a kitten off, and drives away. Confused, frightened, and hungry, the kitten cowers. She doesn't know it yet, but her life is now a struggle for food. She has everything to fear — people, predators, and roaming dogs. If someone doesn't rescue her, it's only a matter of time before she becomes pregnant and has a litter of wild kittens or is hit by a car. She needs help now.

Whether you end up reluctantly rescuing one kitten or decide to make rescuing a way of life, you need some help in figuring out what to do and when. In this chapter, I go over some different approaches to catching a stray kitten who's old enough to be on his own and tell you what you need to do to make such a kitten comfortable after you get him home. And I go over some tips for (hopefully!) finding his owners.

If you find a very young kitten who should still be nursing or doesn't know how to eat solid food yet, be sure to read Chapters 17 and 18.

Capturing the Kitten Safely

If you have the right kind of bait (and about any food is the right kind of bait), a hungry stray will allow herself to be caught.

When you come across a kitten dangerously close to a busy road, you must be especially careful. Although your first instinct may be to rush over like Superman and scoop her up, don't. She's scared to death. Seeing you rushing toward her may send her right into oncoming traffic. And regardless of the situation, you must always consider your own safety first. Approach her slowly; pretend you're moving in slow motion. Circle around and move toward her from the traffic side. That way, if she bolts, she's more likely to run away from the traffic.

Coaxing a kitten to come

The stray kitten is way more likely to trust you if you don't look like you're in a hurry (as a hungry predator would be). Be patient and call her gently. If, by luck, she walks up happy to see you, pick her up gently, wrap her in a towel, blanket, T-shirt, whatever fabric you have handy, and slide the kitten — towel and all — into a cardboard box or cat carrier. You don't go everywhere with a carrier in the trunk? Use the fabric to confine her until you're both out of harm's way. Then head to the nearest convenient or grocery store, where you can probably talk the clerk into giving you a cardboard box.

If the weaned kitten seems shy but doesn't run away, it's a good bet she's hungry. She believes you have food, so she won't go far. Kneel nearby, but not too close, and call to her. Get down as low as you can. A big person can be very frightening to a little kitty. Put your hand out with your open palm toward the kitten. That will give her the impression that you have food, even if you don't. If you do have something a hungry cat would eat, it couldn't hurt to dab a little on your finger so the kitten can smell it. Let her come to you. Offer her a small sample, but hold most of it back. Talk in a soft, soothing voice; be friendly and comforting. When she's close to you, gently pick her up and wrap her in a T-shirt or slip her into a box if you have one handy.

If after some time the kitten won't approach you, flip ahead to the "Rounding up a reluctant kitten" section or the "Rescuing a wild child" sidebar in this chapter for tips on catching this little bundle of fluff.

Rounding up a reluctant kitten

If the stray acts reluctant and terrified or you suspect he may actually be *feral* or wild, don't try to grab him with your bare hands. At this point, if you're committed to capturing this kitten on your own, you need to round up some supplies to help you capture him.

Rescuing a wild child

Before I ever had a kitten of my own, I tried to save a 5-week-old *feral* (or wild) kitten from a colony near my office. He didn't understand that I was his ticket to the land of plenty. I didn't understand that he thought I was picking up my evening snack. That adorable little orange kitten sent me to the emergency room with a bite through my knuckle down to the bone. A scared kitten can do a lot of damage. Fortunately, I didn't have to take rabies shots, but those antibiotic shots to my bottom hurt like the dickens!

If you decide to take on the responsibility of a feral kitten, be aware that she was born outside and hasn't had contact with humans. While she may look like the cute little kitten you had as a kid, she's a wild animal with a strong sense of self-preservation. Feral kittens require a great deal of care when you handle them so *you* don't get hurt. So before you decide on a feral kitten, read up on ferals and make sure you know what you're getting into.

Experts tell me it takes between two and six weeks to tame most feral kittens. Of course, the younger the kitten, the easier the job and the faster the process. However, some kittens trapped when they are 4 and 5 months old can become very affectionate pets. Alley Cat Rescue has a wealth of information on its Web site at www.saveacat.org or call the group at 301-699-3946.

Go get

- A towel or blanket
- Leather gloves
- A can of cat food with a pull-tab or a pouch of cat food
- A safe container for the kitten:
  - A cat carrier

    I carry a Kitty Kabby in my trunk (www.stickypaws.com), which is a corrugated plastic carrier that folds down to just a couple of inches. It's waterproof and works great for rescue.

  Or

  - A cardboard box

    Ideally the box should be about 18-x-10-x-24-inches with a lid and air holes.

Without a fence or barrier available, you'll need to use the food as a distraction. Put the opened can on the ground and wait until the food consumes the kitten's attention. Toss the towel over him like a net (see Figure 16-1). Quickly, scoop him up in the towel and put him in the carrier, which should be waiting nearby with the door or lid open. Quickly, close the carrier door or box lid; otherwise he'll fly out the opening.

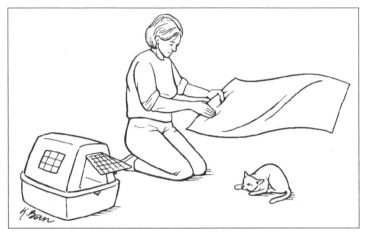

Figure 16-1: Never pick up a frightened kitten with your bare hands. Instead throw a towel over him like a net.

Don't give up if you don't catch him on the first trip. It may take several trips to win the kitten's confidence, or to trap him.

Of course there's always the unfortunate case of a kitten who's obviously sick or injured. Be very careful. You don't want to be bitten while moving a kitten in a lot of pain. Call animal control for help with a hurt kitten. If he's too badly hurt, they can put him to sleep. Although not the outcome you would have hoped for, it's much better than allowing him to suffer on the side of the road.

Treating a kitten bite

Hopefully you won't have to use this 35-minute wash-and-soak routine for cat bites, but just in case, here it is. Wash the bite with soap and running water for five minutes. Then soak it for another 30 minutes in warm water and Epsom salts. After that, seek medical advice. If you've caught the kitten, quarantine him for ten days, an adequate rabies quarantine.

Scratches don't usually become infected as badly as bites, but still need to be cleaned carefully and watched.

Making Your New Friend Comfy

You don't know anything about this kitty (except that he's cute), so get him to a vet right away, especially if he has gooey eyes, crusty junk around his nose, missing patches of fur, or fur that looks spiky. Your vet will look him over and test him for less obvious diseases such as feline immunodeficiency virus (FIV), feline leukemia virus (FeLV), and feline infectious peritonitis (FIP). He can also give you an evaluation of how tame or feral the kitten is.

If you have to bring the kitten home before he goes to the vet, keep him quarantined in the bathroom until you know he's disease and parasite free. Even when my fosters have tested negative for major diseases, I keep them sequestered for a couple of weeks to make sure they're free of upper respiratory infections, ringworm, or contagious illnesses that could spread to my other pets or family members. Don't forget to wash your hands before and after handling him.

If your kitten loves people and thinks a full tummy is heavenly, put him in a "safe room" (see Chapter 6) such as a bathroom with kitten food, water, and a litter box. He won't be much work; just get him healthy, altered, and find him a good home.

If you find a needy kitten when you're not in a position to help, contact local no-kill shelters and see if they can take him. Although most of these shelters stay full, you may be able to persuade them to take the kitten if you make a donation or offer to cover the initial veterinary expenses. Or you can ask a friend or relative if he or she can hang on to the kitten until you find his owners or a new home.

If the kitten has a collar and you think she simply ran away from home, take her to the vet to be scanned for a microchip. Read the following section on uniting the kitten with her family.

Finding the Stray's Family

He's friendly, and he's sweet; surely, he belongs to someone. You're convinced he escaped accidentally, and his family must be broken-hearted. You want to return him.

The quickest way to find the kitten's owner is to take him to the city shelter or your vet so he can be scanned for an identification microchip, which many smart pet owners have implanted in their animals these days. If she has a microchip, the shelter will call the registry and inform the owner that the kitten's been found. (Read more about microchips and how they work in Chapter 10.) If she doesn't have one, report her as a found kitten and either take her home with you or to a local no-kill shelter. If her owner calls the pound, the animal control officer will contact you.

When the kitten hasn't been microchipped, don't worry; I've got some suggestions for helping you return the stray to where he belongs. Follow the steps outlined in the next sections, and if someone is looking for him, they'll find him. However, don't be surprised if you get no response. Unfortunately, adorable and loving kittens get dumped every day.

Notifying the agencies

To try to get your kitten back to his home, report the kitten to all of the animal authorities (the city or county animal shelters) near where you found him. If your community is near several towns or you found the kitten near a city boundary, call them all. You should report the kitten to local authorities because the owner will call when he realizes the kitten's missing.

When filing a report with the different agencies, don't describe the kitten head to toe. Leave off the color of his collar or a distinctive mark. Make the person that claims him tell you that he has that white spot on his nose or that his tail kinks. You don't want to hand this kitten over to just anyone, and, sadly, there are unscrupulous people who will claim kittens (and puppies) to sell to labs, feed to a snake, or use as training bait for fighting dogs. It's more common than you think.

Don't just call animal control once; try back several times to see if the owner has contacted them. I once found a kitten and reported her to the city shelter. Somehow, clerks lost that report. When the owner called they told him that they hadn't heard anything. A week later, I reported her a second time. When the owner called again, we made a connection, and Katy returned to her home. Persistence pays.

Putting up signs

Next put up "Found Kitten" signs near where you found him. Don't forget to put one up in the exact spot you first saw the kitten. Put the signs up everywhere you can think of and everywhere they'll let you.

Contact the newspapers about taking out a free "Found Kitten" ad. As before, be vague about the details. It's the owner's responsibility to prove you have his kitten, not visa versa. Ask the caller to describe the kitten in detail before you give any information out. Otherwise an unscrupulous person will take info you've fed him and say, "Yes, that's my little Skippy." Remember the lab animal dealers!

Screening the "families"

It's so shocking, it's almost unbelievable, that someone would pretend to be a kitten's "family"; but they do. That's why you must screen each caller by asking the following questions:

✔ **What is your name and phone number?** Someone's who's not legit will be very hesitant to give this information. You may even want to make an excuse to call them right back just to make sure the number's real.

✔ **What does the kitten look like?** Ask her to provide details. What color are his eyes? Does he have any distinctive markings? Is he declawed? What color collar was he wearing when he escaped? Is his tail kinked?

✔ **Where was kitten when he escaped?** The house, the car, the vet. Is that near where you found him?

When you're convinced the owner is who she claims to be, you may suggest that you meet in a public place to return the kitten. Call me paranoid, but a kind hearted person may be an easy mark for a con artist or thief. Also, tell her if you've had to spend money on vet bills and politely ask if she'd be willing to reimburse you for the expenses. There's no guarantee you'll be able to recover your expenses, but you can always ask.

If all your efforts fail and you can't find the kitten's family, or he's been intentionally abandoned, you'll have to decide whether you want to adopt him yourself or if you should try to find him a new home. If you decide to adopt the kitten, read Chapter 18 on critical care for orphans. Take a look in Chapter 19 for helpful advice on placing him for adoption.

Chapter 17

Critical Care for Orphans

· ·

· ·

*Y*ou never expected to be a mother or father, especially not now with so many things on your to-do list! But somehow you find yourself caring for some helpless little kittens who depend on you for everything. Whether the mother cat, called a *queen,* abandoned them, is too ill to nurse, or died in an accident, you're in charge now.

An orphan kitten can do almost nothing for himself. This chapter discusses the importance of keeping these unweaned kittens warm, what and how to feed them, and how to help them potty. A young kitten can't even go to the bathroom without help! A trip to the veterinarian is in order to check your youngsters out for parasites and to get a little instruction about scary things like tube feeding and diarrhea.

The first time I cared for an orphan kitten, the mother had been hit by a car two days earlier. My neighbors and I quizzed each other about who should take the 2-week-old in. I mentioned that I had once read an article about how to care for an orphan puppy. Suddenly, I was a mom. With that thimbleful of knowledge I raised him to a healthy 6-week-old and found him a home. You can save a kitten life too!

Making the Rescue

When you happen upon a tiny kitten or a young litter, make sure they're real orphans before you leap to the rescue. Just because you don't see a mom cat doesn't mean she's not around. If you find a nest of fat, contented, sleeping kittens, then mom's most likely lurking nearby — unless you've actually found her body. However, if you find cold, dirty, hungry, crying kittens they're probably real orphans.

After you're sure a kitten has been abandoned, put him in a warm place. Immediate warmth will be your first order of business. Later in the chapter, I discuss setting up a toasty nest at home, but I'll wager that when you first come across an orphan, you don't have a heating pad on you. If you have a towel or an extra T-shirt, wrap him up in it and place him next to your skin. He's been away from mom for a while and he needs a little old-fashioned body heat.

Next take a good look at him and try to figure out how old he is. Table 17-1 should help you.

Table 17-1	Figuring Out an Orphan Kitten's Age
Days Old	*What Happens*
2 or 3	Umbilical cord falls off
5 to 14	Eyes open
6 to 14	Ears open
7	Holds up head and chest
14	Stands up, crawls around, plays, explores
17 to 21	Poops and pees on her own
21	Walks, swivels ears
21 to 28	Baby teeth break gums
28	Eats canned food, runs
42	Weaned from milk completely
49	Uses litter box

While you're making your examination, check for dehydration. Open the kitten's mouth. His gums should glisten and feel slightly moist to your touch. His mouth shouldn't feel gummy, tacky, or dry. If it does, he needs to be hydrated. Give him ½ to 1 teaspoon of water or unflavored Pedialyte every hour. As soon as possible, take him to a vet for an examination. (The section "Taking a trip to the vet" later in this chapter goes over what you should have the vet look for.)

After you've got the little guy settled in, call around to local vets, humane groups, and breeders to see if a surrogate mother with the proper number of legs and whiskers may be available. Queens love kittens and usually accept an orphan when he's around the same age as her own brood. A kitten raised by a queen usually gets along better with both people and other cats than one who is raised by people. The queen can keep the kitten clean and healthy — plus, she speaks kitten.

If the local humane or rescue societies can't take him and you feel up to the challenge, offer to foster the kitten yourself. Although not every group will accept your offer, others would be delighted. This would allow you to use their vets and their systems for adopting the kitten out. I volunteer to care for my foster kittens at home.

Roll up your sleeves and wash your hands. It's time to get started. You're going to raise a kitten!

First Things First: Setting Up Your Home and Seeing a Vet

A queen doesn't need a lot of accessories to set up a kitten nursery. Unfortunately, human foster moms are not nearly as well equipped to handle a tiny orphan. Keep reading to find out how to make him comfy.

Feathering his nest (so to speak)

Kittens need warmth more than anything else — even more than they need food. The younger the kitten, the more vital is his need for warmth. Because tiny kittens can't shiver, they can't control their body temperature like older cats do. Put bluntly, the cold will kill him. So the first thing you should do when you bring your orphaned kitten home is set up a warm, safe place for him.

The best way to regulate the heat is to use a heating pad designed just for pets. Simply place the kitten in a cardboard box on the heating pad covered with an old sheet or even a towel or light blanket. (I like using a sheet because those itty-bitty claws snag in the towel and blankets.) The kitten should have plenty of room in his box to crawl away from the pad should it become too warm. Monitor the heat closely. Even when using a pet-safe pad, make certain your kitten can't crawl under the protective sheet and be burned by the pad.

Heating pads intended for use on humans aren't recommended for pets and can rise to dangerous temperatures. Several years ago, I nearly lost a whole litter when a brand new heating pad set to the lowest setting shot up to 108 degrees Fahrenheit. In an emergency, use heating pads for human use with extreme caution.

If you worry about using a heating pad or don't have one, try filling a heavy sock with ½ cup uncooked rice and placing it in the microwave for 60 seconds. The sock should stay warm for three hours.

Table 17-2 shows you the approximate temperature your kitten needs.

Table 17-2	Warmth Table
Age	*Room Temperature*
Birth to 7 days	Around 90° F
8 to 30 days	80° F to 85° F
1 month	75° F

Taking a trip to the vet

The most life-threatening concerns to orphans are

- ✔ Chill
- ✔ Dehydration
- ✔ Starvation
- ✔ Diarrhea

As soon as possible, take your orphan to a vet for an examination. Have the vet check him for dehydration and internal and external parasites and evaluate his overall health. While you're at the clinic, have the vet show you how to feed your little charge. (For more information on feeding, see the section "Feeding the poor little orphan" later in this chapter.)

In my area, several vets offer discounted services to help people who rescue animals. You can at least ask. Also ask the vet to answer any questions you may have about the kitten. The following list includes some of the questions you'll want answered:

- ✔ What sex is this kitten?
- ✔ How old is he?
- ✔ What does he weigh?
- ✔ What kind of shape is he in?
- ✔ Does he have worms, ear mites, or fleas?
- ✔ Does he have any injuries?
- ✔ Is he dehydrated?
- ✔ Does he need any special care?

The Responsibilities of Being Mom

The queen has two things on her side: She has mama-cat instincts and knows just what to do for her kittens, and she has plenty of time on her paws. Unfortunately you don't necessarily have those luxuries. But there are quick and easy things you can do to make that tiny kitten feel safe and loved.

Making him feel comfortable and safe

A lone kitten may be used to littermates, so place a small stuffed animal in his box.

I have discovered SnuggleKitties (see Figure 17-1). They are plush animals with a cavity that holds heated dry rice; they simulate the kitten's mother in size and even have a heartbeat. Even the youngest kittens clamor around it. At first it provides a mommy-like comfort. Later on, you can use it to teach appropriate rough play. (For more on how to have a happy and well-socialized kitten, see Chapter 18.)

When I get a really stressed kitten, I give him a couple of drops of Bach Flower Essence Rescue Remedy to help calm his fear and help him adapt to his new situation. Flower remedies are very gentle and can be given even to newborns without risk. Get it at your health food store.

Figure 17-1: SnuggleKitties come complete with a heat source and heartbeat.

Feeding the poor little orphan

Don't reach into the refrigerator and grab a bottle of whole milk. Kittens need a formula closer to their mother's milk. You can buy a special formula at your veterinarian's office, pet supply store, or, in a late-night emergency, some of the 24-hour discount stores. Lately I've even noticed kitten formula available on the pet aisle in the grocery stores. You can also use canned goat milk found in the canned milk section of the grocery store. When you purchase a milk replacement, buy only formula made for kittens. Puppy formula isn't the same thing.

Kitten formula hardens in the fur surrounding the mouth like concrete. After feeding your kitten her bottle, use a moist cloth and a soft toothbrush to clean around his mouth. The toothbrush does the same thing that mom's tongue does.

Making a healthy choice

Formulas come in two forms: ready-to-use-liquid and powdered. (If your kitten needs a boost, prepare a batch of glop — I provide the recipe in the "Kitten glop" sidebar in this chapter.) You need to consider a few things when choosing a kitten formula:

- **Liquid formula:** The liquid kitten formulas are easy to use; just warm and pour into the bottle. Although they're fast and easy, consistently mixed, and never lumpy, they do have a downside: They can cost you a fortune if you're raising a large litter. And if you only have one tiny kitten, the milk in the opened can may spoil in the refrigerator before you have a chance to use it all.

Kitten glop

When kittens come to you in rough shape, you can feed them this formula used by breeders and rescuers worldwide. Feed glop to orphaned kittens who need a nutritional boost. Glop turns out pretty lumpy so be forewarned.

To make glop, you need

   8 ounces water

   1 package Knox unflavored gelatin

   8 ounces whole evaporated milk

   2 egg yolks

   2 tablespoons high-calorie mayonnaise

   2 tablespoons high-calorie yogurt

   1 teaspoon Karo or corn syrup

   Liquid pet vitamins

   1 capsule of acidophilus

   1 drop grapefruit seed extract

Dissolve gelatin in boiling water. Mix gelatin and water with the rest of the ingredients. Refrigerate. Glop becomes jellied when cold. Scoop out only what you need and heat to body temperature. You can freeze servings in ice trays and store the glop in your freezer.

✔ **Powdered formula:** Powdered formulas cost less per serving than liquid and have a much longer shelf life. While more affordable (a real consideration if you're caring for a large litter), powdered milk formulas take time to mix, and sometimes lumps clog the nipple of the bottle. On the plus side, powdered formulas give you more control over the formula concentration. If the kitten begins to suffer from diarrhea or constipation, the formula can be diluted or strengthened as necessary. You don't waste nearly as much because you only mix up what you need to get you through the next 24 hours.

If your powdered formula clogs the nipple, you may be tempted to give the bottle a little squeeze to dislodge the clot. Don't do it: When the clog breaks free, you could accidentally force formula into the kitten's lungs.

I feed my orphans Just Born Kitten Powder because it contains *colostrum,* an ingredient present in the queen's milk right after she gives birth to her kittens. Colostrum contains antibodies to help the kitten fight disease. If the kitten comes to me really dehydrated,

I mix the powder with unflavored Pedialyte instead of water. And kittens need beneficial bacteria in order to digest the milk. I help them along with Pet Ag's Bene-Bac or acidophilus.

Knowing how much and when to feed

Your kitten has a tiny tummy. Feed him two tablespoons of formula for every 4 ounces of weight. Most kittens have an automatic cut-off valve. They just spit the nipple out of their mouths when they're full. Don't overfeed your kitten. Follow the feeding instructions on the formula label. Very small kittens should be fed every four hours.

In the beginning, if a kitten's weak, I get up every few hours and check on him. After he's a week old, I can usually sleep through the night. A healthy kitten tells you when he's hungry.

Getting it down the hatch

You can feed your foster kitten with a bottle, dropper, syringe, or feeding tube. When dealing with very young kittens, I prefer to use an eyedropper because a little guy often can't get the nipple in his mouth, and even a tiny kitten can control the flow of the formula (see Figure 17-2). If you use an eyedropper, only release a drop at a time. As the kitten grows, she will be able to suck the formula out of the dropper by herself. Let her control the flow. If the kitten starts to choke, hold her upside down until she quits coughing.

If you chose to feed your kitten with a bottle, make sure you keep the neck of the bottle full of milk so the kitten doesn't start to suck air (see Figure 17-2). Kitten bottles are available at most pet supply stores and even grocery stores. Be careful when you cut the hole in the nipple — if you make the hole too large, the formula can flow too fast and choke the kitten; if it's too small, she won't be able to get any formula.

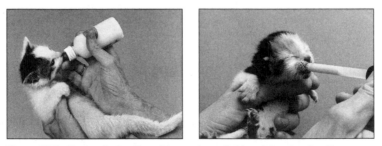

Figure 17-2: Try bottle feeding older orphans (left) and dropper feeding younger orphans (right).

If your kitten won't eat, ask your vet for some lessons in *tube feeding,* a procedure where the vet inserts a tiny feeding tube down your kitten's throat directly into his stomach. Tube feeding looks like a medieval torture technique, but it can save your kitten's life, because you put the food directly in the stomach and you know exactly how much the kitten takes in. But you shouldn't try this unless your vet or vet tech has shown you how and sold you the materials. Improperly done, the tube could slide down the trachea and send the formula straight into the lungs, killing the kitten.

Feeding in the proper position

When I feed a kitten, I prefer to sit with my bottom about a foot away from the back of the chair so I can lean back at a 45-degree angle. Then I place the kitten on my chest where he's properly situated for a comfortable dining experience. It looks like I'm actually nursing a baby. I think the kitten enjoys it because he feels my warmth and he can hear my heart. Some people hold the kittens in their hand at a very slight angle to nurse.

Never feed the kitten flat on his back. He may choke on his formula.

Burping your kitten — No kidding

A kitten is just a baby with fur, and like a human baby, when he's full, he needs to be burped. Place him against your shoulder and gently pat him until he burps. Only use one or two fingers and almost no pressure — just a gentle tapping. As long as he continues to lick his nose, he still has a good burp in him. It may take a while, so be patient.

After each feeding, be sure to wash all the utensils in hot soapy water and rinse well.

Pee all that you can pee

But wait, you haven't finished your motherly duties. Very young kittens (under 3 weeks) can't pee or poop on their own. You have to help them.

After your kitten eats, take a cotton ball moistened in warm water and massage the kitten's private parts. Moving the cotton in soft, gentle circles mimics the mother's tongue and stimulates the kitten to do both jobs at the same time. Gentle is the operative word. Don't use any more pressure than you would to wipe a human baby's eyelid. The cotton ball should take on a slightly yellowish color from his pee. If it's a dark yellow, he's dehydrated, and you need to give him a little drink of water every hour or so.

Keep an eye on the kitten's poop. It should be firm and brown or mustard-colored with the look of a little bitty log. If he doesn't go for a few of days, add a little more water to the formula. Like kids, each kitten is different, and some don't poop every day. (If, after 48 hours, he still fails to poop, call your veterinarian. Wait only a day, if he's lethargic or weak.) If he gets diarrhea, cut back on the strength of the formula a little. Kittens dehydrate very quickly with the squirts. If he looses a lot of fluid through the runs, your vet may need to give him fluids under his skin. If you wait too long, you could lose him. Run to Chapter 18 for all the poop on diarrhea.

When he's done, swab him off with warm moist cotton balls until his little privates are clean. You can even use a baby wipe, but buy the ones that don't have alcohol in them. Alcohol stings.

While you're cleaning your orphan up, check him for fleas. You may be surprised to find that the kitten is literally crawling with them. Fleas are bloodsucking little beasties that can also infect your kitten with nutrition-draining tapeworms. (You can read more about safe flea eradication in Chapter 9.)

As the kittens mature and become more active, they crawl about and pee or poop onto their bedding. Change the sheets frequently, because kittens can get diaper rash or pee scalds just like human babies. When the fur down the inside of their legs gets a spiky look, you need to give them a little butt bath. Warm the water until it's body temperature, then rinse off the fur. If a kitten has poop collected in the fur around his tail area, you may need tearless kitten shampoo and a flea comb to get it out. Coat his irritated bottom with petroleum jelly or a triple antibiotic ointment to soothe the scald.

Keeping him clean

Multiple kittens just can't stay clean. Unlike a single kitten, who tends to stick around in one place, kittens in litters tend to crawl all over each other just stimulating the pee and poop right out of each other. Although the same thing happens with a mother present, she quickly handles the situation by giving everyone a good tongue bath. If she's not there to clean them up, they stay covered in pee and poop. Again, you've got kittens with diaper rash.

Sometimes a cotton ball sponge bath just won't cut it. Times like these call for an old-fashioned solution to a stinky dilemma: a bath complete with warm water and tearless cat shampoo. But as soon as you're done with the final rinse, bring out the hair dryer and blow him dry on a mild warm setting. Don't delay drying him off. You don't want him to chill. Read about kitten baths in Chapter 11.

Weighing In on His Progress

The best way to tell how your kitten is progressing is to weigh him regularly.

Weigh your kitten on a digital or small postage scale. Get a weight when he arrives and at about the same time every day until he's weaned. He should gain about a half ounce a day for the first few weeks. If the kitten is losing or just maintaining, try feeding him more often, about 3 ccs every 3 to 4 hours. (See the section "Feeding the poor little orphan" for information on hand feeding a kitten.)

Chapter 18

Combating Health and Behavior Concerns Common to Orphans

*B*eing a little kitten is hard work and harder still when your mom's not around to feed and bathe you or teach you what you need to know about being a cat. Not only do orphans have the same health problems as all other kittens, but they also have a few more because no matter how big the heart of the human caretaker, he's just not as good a kitty mom as the real thing.

This chapter discusses many of the health and behavior problems associated with orphan kittens. I give you some early warning signs and tell you what you should do when a crisis arises. You may notice that in most instances, I tell you to go to the vet. That's because issues you wouldn't even notice in a mature cat can kill a tiny orphan. Symptoms can become deadly overnight, so it's important to know the facts and remain on guard.

Looking at the Main Health Risks for Orphans

A kitten receives immunity to disease from her mother's milk for the entire time she continues to nurse (usually up to the ages of 6 to 14 weeks). Unfortunately, because your orphan doesn't have the benefit of mom's antibodies, she's much more susceptible to diseases than kittens with a four-legged mom.

If she appears "not right," go ahead and take her to the vet. Chances are that any problem isn't just going to go away. A tiny kitten can go from seeming okay to sleeping on death's doorstep in no time at all. Watch her closely to for

- Diarrhea
- Congestion or goopy eyes
- Fleas
- Poop or unwashed pee clinging to her back legs
- Excessive crying especially before or after eating
- Refusing to eat

Some of these symptoms are more serious than others. I help you walk through it.

Your doctor may prescribe liquid meds to treat the following illnesses. To medicate, just open kitty's mouth up slightly and slide the syringe or dropper in from the side. Squeeze. Don't push the syringe straight in, because you could actually force the medication down into his lungs. You can medicate an uncooperative kitten by grabbing the skin behind the neck forcing him to hold his head back just a bit. Squirt.

Hypothermia

Before they need food, kittens need warmth. Even in a chilly environment, a normal kitten is able to burrow under a pile of his siblings or snuggle next to mom to keep warm. But a kitten alone needs *you* to maintain his temperature.

If your orphan kitten seems chilled, raise his body temperature slowly by putting him next to your body and covering him. This allows his organs to function properly. Don't feed him until he has warmed up to at least 95 or 96 degrees Fahrenheit. When he's warm, place him in a warm nest of blankets (see Chapter 17), which should stay around 85 degrees Fahrenheit. Try not to warm the kitten too quickly with a heating pad.

Dehydration

Kittens dehydrate quickly. Usually it's caused by the runs or not taking in enough formula. When a kitten's outflow surpasses his intake, you can give him 3 or 4 ccs of unflavored Pedialyte every hour or 1 cc every 15 minutes. If he's severely dehydrated, have your vet inject some fluid under his skin.

To monitor how hydrated or dehydrated your kitten is, you can

- ✔ **Look at the color of his pee:** Red, dark yellow, brown, or even intense yellow pee rates an immediate trip to the vet, because the pee's way too concentrated and your kitten's very dehydrated. Yellow pee should be watched to make sure it doesn't get any darker. Give him some unflavored Pedialyte and see if that lightens things a bit. Light yellow says, "All is well." Nearly clear pee means he may be over-hydrated. Give your vet a call and see what she thinks.

- ✔ **Check his mouth and eyes:** A dehydrated kitten has gums that feel sticky; his mouth doesn't feel moist. The gums have lost their elasticity, and the tongue is very pink. The eyes have crusty stuff in the corners. Some vets consider this the most accurate method to test for dehydration in kittens under 6 weeks old.

- ✔ **Tent his skin:** This method is more accurate for kittens over 6 weeks old. Pull the skin at the back of the neck out and see how long it takes to spring back into place. Skin that snaps back immediately or only takes a second indicates that the kitten is fine. If it takes one to three seconds, take the kitten to the vet. Skin that doesn't return to the body requires an *immediate* trip to the vet. This kitten is severely dehydrated. She needs fluids injected under the skin.

Hypoglycemia

Hypoglycemia is an abnormal decrease in a kitten's blood sugar levels, which happens when the kitten is fed infrequently or not enough. The kitten becomes severely depressed, with muscle twitching and finally, convulsions. I had a 4-week-old kitten who suffered from it as a result of a belly full of internal parasites. My vet gave him glucose and wormed him. He completely recovered.

You can treat hypoglycemia on the spot with a drop or two of Karo syrup (or a generic corn syrup) placed on the tongue, followed by an immediate trip to the vet. Make sure you increase the amount and the frequency that you feed your kitten. I discuss how often you should feed your kitten in Chapter 17.

Diarrhea

Diarrhea is one of the hardest things for a kitten foster mom to deal with. So many things can cause diarrhea, and a kitten dehydrates so quickly! Add to that what a mess it makes (especially if you have more than one bottle baby) and *you've* got a major headache. The sooner you get your kitten to the vet and find out what's going on, the less it costs and the more likely she is to survive.

Diarrhea can result from major diseases like feline leukemia, feline distemper, and feline infectious peritonitis (see Chapter 9). Food changes, overfeeding, or a formula that doesn't agree with the kitten can cause diarrhea as well. But more often than not, parasite infestations and a lack of beneficial intestinal bacteria cause the runs. The frustrating thing is that often they don't show up when the vet's looking at the poop under the microscope. When this happens, I ask the vet to go ahead and treat for coccidia. This ailment is very common among kittens and most of my bottle babies have it.

If you fear overfeeding is the culprit, add one-third more water or unflavored Pedialyte than the instructions recommend when you mix the formula. And you need to restore the healthy intestinal bugs by feeding a little yogurt with active cultures, putting a little lactobacillus from the health food store in the formula, or giving the kitten a daily dose of Pet Ag's Bene-Bac (beneficial bacteria); you can get it at any pet store.

After your vet has started the kitten on treatment for the runs, the medication may take a while to kick in, especially if he's treating for coccidia. If your kitten has an especially bad case and you're afraid she's becoming dehydrated, talk to your vet about prescribing something for her to slow the poop. If you don't, dehydration could become life threatening (see "Dehydration" earlier in this chapter).

After I've begun treatment of whatever's bothering a kitten's bowels, I give my weaned kittens a tablespoon of pumpkin to help slow the flow. Some kittens really like it. For unweaned kittens, you can put some pumpkin in a blender and add a tablespoon to a bottle of formula.

Reading kitten poop — Think of it as tea leaves only more disgusting

Bodily fluids say a lot about your kitten's condition. You can look at an orphan's poo and tell if she's dehydrated, overfed, or has protozoa living inside her intestines. Take a look at this poopy color chart:

✔ **White poop with a cottage cheese texture:** Either the kitten formula's too rich, you're overfeeding him, or he's not digesting the formula. Try diluting his formula with unflavored Pedialyte. Call your vet just to be safe.

✔ **Grayish and runny:** Your kitten may have a bacterial infection. See the vet immediately.

✔ **Greenish:** Bile isn't being absorbed or you're overfeeding. Dilute formula by one-third with unflavored Pedialyte.

✔ **Mustard or brown colored and slightly soft to firm:** Perfect. Hope that it keeps coming!

✔ **Yellow/whitish with clear slimy stuff:** Possible intestinal irritation or over-feeding. Dilute his formula by one-third with unflavored Pedialyte until his poop returns to normal, or call your vet.

✔ **Yellow and stinks bad:** Probably coccidia. Go to the vet.

✔ **Bloody:** Could be coccidia, parasites, or distemper. See your vet now.

✔ **Black:** Indicates bleeding. Go to the vet now.

If the poop appears to by dry and hard, your kitten could be dehydrated. Firm or formed but slightly soft poop should make you smile. Everything's just fine. Anything of a more liquid nature requires a trip to the vet. The more like water the poop, the quicker you should get him in the car.

Now I'm not a fan of using over-the-counter medications on these little guys, because many products made for humans don't sit well with kittens, but sometimes you have to. Always check the label, especially when considering giving your kitten over-the-counter drugs. Although many people have written that Kaopectate is okay for cats and kittens, recently the manufacturer reformulated the adult product. It now contains salicylate, a form of aspirin that's harmful to your kitten. Instead, opt for Children's Kaopectate, which contains no salicylates or alcohol. A less expensive option is to order Kaolin Pectin, formulated for animals, from KV Vet Supply. Give the company a call at 800-423-8211. Avoid Pepto-Bismol or any product that contains salicylates.

When your kitten has watery poop squirting out of her bottom, you've got to keep her clean or she's going to get scalds from the poop and the pee. Give her a shower in body temperature water (see Chapter 17). I use a tearless cat shampoo, but if you haven't had a chance to get cat shampoo, you can use human baby shampoo once or twice. But human shampoo will dry out the kitten's skin. So go invest in some mild kitten shampoo because you may be bathing two or three times a day. Towel her off and finish with a blow dryer set on low heat. Don't blow the air in her face.

If you have a litter with the runs, bathe everyone several times a day. Put them in a carrier and set the dryer (on a cool setting) above them. They dry off in just a few minutes.

If you can't manage a bath at that particular moment, use baby wipes (without alcohol) or a damp washcloth to clean up the poop or give a bottom rinse. You still need to blow the kitty dry, though.

After my soggy kitten has dried out, I put Neosporin or Vaseline on her bottom, belly, and down the inside of the legs to shield her from poopy irritation and to prevent kitten diaper rash.

Feline distemper or panleukopenia

Feline distemper is more dangerous to orphans than to any other segment of the kitty population because of their vulnerability and lack of mom's antibodies. The virus is airborne and can be contracted from another cat or even from infected clothing. Always wash your hands before and after handling your kitten. Among older kittens, this disease kills up to 90 percent of those infected. Unfortunately, with bottle babies it's close to a clean sweep. For more detailed information about feline distemper, see Chapter 9.

Fleas

When people first started bringing me kittens, I never thought to check for fleas. Now, I immediately grab my flea comb and look for flea dirt. That icky black stuff left behind by the orphan's no-rent boarders is actually flea poop. To get all the dirt on fleas, comb through Chapter 9.

If you have an orphan kitten, you have to have a flea comb. When you buy one, get the extra fine teeth. Don't waste your money on the plastic ones because the fleas just pass right through the teeth.

You simply can't use any topical flea products on orphans because they are so small (unless your vet recommends it). Don't use a flea shampoo on him either.

Your options are limited if your very young kitten has fleas. Talk to your vet. If you have a great deal of patience, you can flea comb until you get them all. A friend of mine gives the kitten a flea bath using only baby shampoo, water, and a flea comb. Lather the kitten and the fleas show up against the foamy background. The fleas get trapped in the soap bubbles and can't run off; you can comb them right out. Don't forget to dry the kitten well so he doesn't get chilled.

Fleas aren't just uncomfortable for the kitten; fleas can suck so much blood out that a tiny kitten could shortly suffer from flea anemia, not to mention another gift courtesy of the flea: tapeworms.

Parasites

Most stray or feral kittens come to you infected with worms or parasites. That means the kitten could have any number of bugs living in his guts. Diarrhea is one of the most common symptoms. But the kitten could also have a potbelly, little appetite, bloody poop, weight loss, or just look unhealthy. Parasites to watch out for include

- ✔ Tapeworms
- ✔ Roundworms
- ✔ Coccidia
- ✔ Giardia

Because most strays come to you with a crop of their own pets, you should take a poop sample to the vet on your first visit. He can check it out under a microscope for eggs or organisms. Orphans should be treated for worms at 3 weeks; only use medicine your vet gives because dosing is so critical. Don't try to treat the parasites yourself, especially in a kitten this young. Continue to give the medication as long as the vet recommends and repeat doses as directed. You may need to go back and kill a second crop that hatched after the first treatment.

The best way to keep your kitten from being reinfected is

- ✔ Keep his sleeping area clean; wash the linens regularly.
- ✔ When you start litter box training him, remove the poop every day.

✔ Disinfect the litter box with a bleach solution.

✔ Try not to have too many kittens in one area.

✔ Get rid of fleas, ticks, and mice that may carry parasites.

Constipation

Anytime you change your orphan's diet, his poop is affected. Whether you switch to a different brand of formula, from a ready-to-use formula to a powdered, or you start weaning, it either gets things in motion or clogs up the works. When I start weaning my kittens, they usually get the poops, although I do get the occasional kitten who gets plugged up.

Don't use a commercial human enema on your orphan. They're toxic and make her situation go from uncomfortable to critical. For a constipated kitten I add a few drops of olive oil or canola oil to the formula to grease the skids. Give her some unflavored Pedialyte to make sure she's got enough moisture in her body to pass her poop. If the condition continues for more than 48 hours, contact your vet.

Upper respiratory infections

All kittens are more susceptible to disease than adult cats, but because orphans don't benefit from their mom's immune system they're leading candidates for upper respiratory infections. As soon as you notice sniffles or sneezing, take your orphan to the vet. You can't begin treatment too soon with kittens so vulnerable.

Feline calicivirus and feline herpesvirus are the two most common kitten colds. Like a human cold, the viruses themselves can't be treated, but the symptoms can be managed, so get him to a vet before the snotty nose gets too severe. To find out more about what can be done to help kittens with these viruses, flip to Chapter 9.

If your vet has prescribed medication, be sure and give it for as long as he's recommended. If you stop medicating too soon, you leave some of the stronger bacteria alive in your kitten's body. When they reproduce, they come back with a vengeance.

Fading kitten syndrome

Fading kitten syndrome (FKS) is the most devastating situation any foster mom or dad must face. A kitten who appeared to be healthy rapidly fades away for no apparent reason a few days to several weeks after he's born. I've had it happen with 4-week-old kittens.

Vets have several theories of what causes FKS, including blood incompatibility or a virus the mother carried. Others use FKS as a catchall phrase for a kitten who dies for no recognizable reason. Sometimes the orphan has internal deformities that don't cause problems until the kitten grows past his heart or digestive tract's ability to function.

Kittens with FKS may not grow and gain weight like the other kittens in the litter. They may stop sucking on the bottle or grow progressively weaker. The weaker kittens with FKS usually fade a few days after birth, but stronger kittens can put up more of a fight. These kittens simply don't respond to any treatments and die regardless of what you do for them. FKS is more common among purebred cats than among the kitty population at large.

Addressing Orphan Behavior

Kittens find out how to be happy, well-adjusted cats from their mom. If she's not around to teach those lessons, the kitten has to fill in the blanks herself, like an unsupervised kid or a human baby raised by wolves. This section goes over a few problems that are unique to orphan kittens.

Helping a lone kitten adjust

Between the ages of 2 and 7 weeks, a kitten begins to pick up on socialization behavior. During this critical period, a kitten figures out how to play gently from his brothers and sisters. Mom teaches him to use the litter box and what's safe and what to fear. When the queen and siblings aren't there, all those lessons are missing, and the kitten may act out.

Without other kittens around to play with and learn social and predatory behaviors from, a kitten turns to the foster mom. He acts out instinctive behaviors on that person. If the foster permits rough play, that becomes the pattern for the kitten's relationships with people. Bite 'em hard and keep 'em coming back for more! I have to admit I raised a few of those, before I learned to be a good foster mom. Without exposure to other people and pets, a kitten becomes shy and fearful of animals. Such kittens have a condition called *over-attachment* to the person who is feeding and grooming. That person becomes the center of his universe. This kitten can grow into a dominating and controlling cat.

The worst thing you can do to a lone kitten (or even a litter) is keep him isolated. Instead, engineer pleasant interactions with people and animals you know will be gentle with him. This interaction expands his universe from the foster mother with the bottle to other gentle people and animals.

The best way to keep your orphan from becoming possessive and domineering is to introduce him to other cats. Hopefully you have a friendly adult cat that he can hang out with. The older kitty, while not mom, can show him what's acceptable in the social world of cats. She can put him in his place, too. Introducing him to a trustworthy and friendly dog can teach him that dogs, while a little smelly, aren't bad sorts after all.

I had a Doberman named Streamer, who lived for kitten season. He loved nothing more than bathing my foster kittens. Of course, the kittens didn't appreciate it much because a dog's tongue makes them wet, and they smelled like dog spit. But those kittens were able to go to homes with dogs because they weren't afraid of them. On the other hand, I couldn't leave my Dachshund with the kittens until they reached about 5 weeks and they didn't act like rats anymore.

If you decide you want to keep your foster kitten and you don't already have a kitty, a quick fix to the behavior dilemma is to get the kitten a cat. When the kitten can't be exposed to other cats, introduce him to interactive toys that can discharge some of that predatory energy. Read about interactive toys that mimic prey in Chapter 15. You can use stuffed animals to wrestle with the kitten.

Never let your orphan play with your bare hand. This teaches him that biting and scratching fingers is fun, which sets a bad precedent. The behavior could continue after the kitten goes to his new home. Instead use a Kitten Mitten. I go into more detail about it in Chapter 15.

Whenever a kitten gets too rough, I pull my hand away from him, get right in his face, and hiss. Then, as the human in his life, I refuse to play. Never hit a kitten to correct him.

Problems with orphan litters: Watching out for the little suckers

I've raised single kittens and combined litters of as many as 11 kittens together. The more kittens you have, the more complicated things get. When raising orphans, loners are usually healthier than litters.

All kittens have the instinctive need to suck on something. Anything will do if mom's not around. That is, any old body part — including siblings' ears and even, uh, well, the little naughty bits. The offending kitten tends to obsess on his siblings' genitals. Often he goes after the same victim time after time. While rather amusing at first glance, it's a real pain in the rear for the recipient, literally. I had a kitten so inflamed that I had to take him to the vet to get him to potty. Another foster mom I know had to put a kitten to sleep because his sister severed his penis.

Another problem is that the kitten is being stimulated to pee and poop, which means the kitten doing the sucking is taking in kitten waste. Gross! Now, I've spoken to vets who have told me that ingesting a little poop won't hurt. But I've found that kittens who aren't suckers stay healthier (less diarrhea) than suckers. When a kitten starts sucking on a sibling, spray a little Bitter Apple on the receiver's privates. If that doesn't work, separate them.

Losing Your Bottle Baby

Sometimes they just don't make it. Bottle babies have a tentative paw on life from the very beginning. Caring for an orphaned kitten can be difficult, and even the most conscientious foster parent may lose a little one. If a kitten dies, you shouldn't blame yourself. Many of the kittens rescued by good Samaritans have been abandoned by their mother because they had health problems she sensed. These poor kittens usually pass away at birth, during the first week, or while weaning.

As late as 3 months of age, a kitten's growth spurt can challenge his body past its capacity. Most times he has a problem with his heart or digestive tract. Sometimes the first symptom you see is when you find him taking his last breath. You may never know why you lost him.

You can second-guess everything you did, but some kittens were never intended to survive. Your care gave him weeks in a warm loving home that he wouldn't have had. Knowing that the kitten experienced love rather than dying alone can help to give you solace.

Chapter 19

All Grown Up: What Should I Do?

• •

In This Chapter

▶ Going over some kitten basics: eating, pooping, and playing

▶ Finding a good home

• •

*I*n this chapter, I tell you what you need to know to make your kitten self-sufficient. Discover how to get him to eat big kitty food, use a litter box, and play nice. If you decide you can't keep your cute little foster kitten, I tell you how to find the perfect home. If you can't locate a no-kill shelter, I prepare you to find and screen potential families.

Enrolling in Kitten Kindergarten

You've gotten through the tough part: those late-night feedings and the constant worry. You've taken care of your kitten's most basic physical needs. Once upon a time she was a creature so helpless she couldn't even pee on her own. Now, she pees and poops just fine and she's getting harder to feed because she gnaws on the nipple. At about 3 weeks of age, you need to enroll your precious angel in Kitten Kindergarten. Before you can teach your foster kitten all the things a mom cat, or *queen,* would have taught her, you must prepare your lesson plans. The following sections explain how to instruct your kitten to eat solid food, use the litter box, and play gently with people and other animals.

Experiencing the joys of weaning

Sometime between the ages of 4 to 6 weeks your kitten may decide she doesn't want to eat her favorite formula anymore. She may chew the nipple on the bottle, scratch your hand when you try to feed her, and act like she's forgotten how to nurse altogether. These signs tell you your kitten is switching her mental gears from sucking to chewing to prepare for life as a cat.

Many weaning techniques exist. Some people start by placing the formula in a saucer for the kitten to lap. Others give tiny pieces of meat. Still others add a weaning powder to thicken the formula. The world needs this many techniques because no two kittens, no two litters, are alike. Some kittens, like my foster kitten Wally, are determined. At 3 weeks old, Wally became so impatient with me while I heated up his bottle that he walked over to the adult cats' bowl and chowed down on canned food. Instantly, he had weaned himself. He never wanted the bottle again. However, I've encountered 6-week-old kittens that refused anything but the bottle.

I use a number of methods and I may have to try a couple to find the one that works on a particular kitten or litter. Consider each of the following methods to find one right for your orphan:

- ✔ Make a mush of high-quality canned kitten food and formula and encourage your kitten to lick it from your finger. (High-quality food gives her less trouble with diarrhea and gives you a fresher-smelling litter box — see Chapter 7.) If she shows interest, then try to get her to eat it from a saucer. Gradually, reduce the amount of formula you add until she eats straight kitten food.

- ✔ Offer licks of lamb, turkey, or chicken baby food. Make sure the baby food doesn't contain onion or onion powder (see Chapter 8). This tasty sample often whets her appetite for more adventures with solid food.

- ✔ If you prefer to feed dry food, add boiling water to your kitten kibble and let it soak until it completely softens and cools. Mash it with a spoon until it turns into gruel. Add formula to it and warm it up to body temperature. I just pop it in the microwave on 50 percent or raw for about 10 seconds. Heat it; don't cook it. She may not try the mush on her own, so you may have to let her lick it off your finger or place a little dab in her mouth. After she consistently eats the mush, you can begin to add a little dry food to the mixture. (Make sure the dry kibble you offer your baby can actually be eaten. Some crunchies are so large they can't even fit in a 3-week-old's mouth, much less be chewed.) Gradually make the mixture crunchier until you have converted her to your dry food of choice.

Don't forget to put out a shallow pan of water so your kitten can get a drink. And place her bowl on a newspaper. If you don't, you may find yourself chiseling dried gruel from your floor. And don't panic when you give her the saucer and she immediately walks through the middle of it. Sometimes you may find your kitten dripping whiskers to tail with goo. That's part of the learning process; she learns about eating solid food from licking her paws. Just give her a bath and a gentle blow dry (see Chapter 11). She's probably going to enjoy several extreme-grooming sessions before she's completely off the bottle.

Until your kitten's completely weaned — which usually takes between a few days to a few weeks — you need to supplement her with the bottle. Orphans should be weaned by the time they reach 6 weeks old. As your kitten eats more solid food, begin to reduce the number of bottle feedings she gets. Even after my kittens are weaned I give them a liquid as a nighttime snack: If mom were around, she would continue to nurse after they'd mostly switched to solid food. I had one mom cat who nursed until after her litter was 5 months old. Wally, my self-weaner, was the only kitten I ever instantly weaned. Weaning takes time.

Wear gloves (I wear old, fingerless bicycling gloves) when you're feeding to protect your hand and wrist from all that thrashing and grabbing.

If you're having a hard time weaning your kitten, try warming up her food to make it tastier. Heat it up for 10 seconds in the microwave on 50 percent power or the thaw setting. Because cats are predators, their wiring tells them they can only eat something that has just been killed. If the food temperature drops, the cat senses it isn't a fresh kill and therefore, not safe to eat. Kittens operate the same way. If your kitten simply wants no part of solid food, wait longer periods between each feeding. Don't starve her, but make sure she's hungry when mealtime rolls around.

Kittens often suffer from the runs during this important transitional stage of their lives. If she develops diarrhea for more than a day, take her to the vet. You don't want her to become dehydrated.

Navigating litter box alley

When your kitten reaches 3 weeks old, you may notice his linens are damp or you may find some poop in his bed. Congratulations. He can use the bathroom on his own. Kittens, unlike puppies, arrive pre-programmed with potty instructions. It just takes three weeks to activate the program. The time has come to litter box train him.

You need to put together a miniature litter box for him. Because your kitten only stands 5 inches tall, don't expect him to be able to use a standard-size 5- to 6-inch high cat box. He's still having problems walking in a straight line. When I introduce the litter box, I use the cardboard boxes that some brands of canned kitten food come in. They're only 1 or 2 inches high and they're disposable. You can also buy kitten-sized litter boxes from your favorite pet supply store.

You also need to buy a cat litter that can't harm your kittens. Even if you use clumping clay litter in your adult cats' box, do *not* use it while box training your orphan. Kittens, like babies, explore everything with their mouths. Expect, when you put your kitten in his box, for him to immediately eat a mouthful. I prefer a crumbled corn litter, World's Best Cat Litter, or a wheat litter that passes through his system should he decide to go grazing. Even traditional clay is a safer choice that clumping clay. For more on cat litter, read Chapter 5.

Position the liter box where it's easy to get to, in an area where he hangs out. He won't have a very good memory at that age, so make the box as easy for him to find as you can. Consider placing it in the bathroom or a corner of the family room. When you put him up for the night, make sure the box is in there with him. Be sure to place the litter as far away from his food and water bowls as possible. Even kittens don't like to eat in their bathroom.

The first thing I do is to stimulate him to poop and pee into the new fresh litter in the box, by taking a warm, moist cotton ball and gently brushing it in circles around his genitals. The box now smells of purpose. Sometimes I even take used litter from my family cat boxes and sprinkle it in the kitten's box so the kittens can smell the pee and poop in his litter box. They smell my cats' pee and poop and they know just what that box should be used for.

Immediately after you feed him, place your kitten in his litter box and move his paw through the litter in a scratching motion. He may begin circling the box and squat: just like magic. However, he may take a more indirect approach by digging and playing. If he tries to leave, simply continue to put him back until he goes. He should figure it out rather quickly. If he keeps climbing out before he's done his job, then place him in the box so that he faces the wall. I've found that if he's not distracted by what's happening in the room and only sees a wall or a corner, he stays more focused on the job behind him. If only toilet training was this easy with dogs and kids!

You have to be consistent. Put him in the box after meals, when he wakes up, and after a play session. When he pees, praise him and tell him what a brilliant kitten he has grown into. Make everything associated with the litter box pleasant and fun. My kittens seem to spend more time in the box when I keep the litter a little deeper. That way they can dig to China.

If you're not around, your kitten may forget and head for the corner of the room. Don't scold him. He doesn't have a clue why you're upset. Clean up the mess, making sure you remove all the odor from the floor (see Chapter 14). Hopefully, you have him in a bathroom where messes clean easily and thoroughly. Also keep his box clean. Don't make him navigate around piles of poop.

Kittens often give themselves away. While he tries to make his anal muscles work, he may let out little sounds like a moan or a cry of pain. It may more appropriately be called a pep talk: "I can do it. I can do it." When you hear the kitten talking to himself, dash in and make sure he's in his litter box. If you find him squatting in the corner of the room, don't yell at him. Gently pick him up and just as gently set him in his box. No matter how many times you catch him making a mistake, don't drop or throw him in the box. That just makes him fear it and you. As he finishes, praise him and tell him what a big boy he's become. Always praise when he does good. And don't get worked up when he stumbles and steps in a pile of poop. He's still discovering how to control those legs. You try balancing in that position!

You may be litter box training him at about the same time you're weaning him (see "Enjoying the joys of weaning" earlier in this chapter). Weaning kittens often get diarrhea. If he can't control his runs, he can't figure out to use the litter box. Before you can expect him to perfect his potty habits, he must know ahead of time he's gotta go. For more on controlling the runs, turn to Chapter 18.

Introducing kitty to people and other animals

Bottle babies take a lot of work. Sometimes, I get so wrapped up in keeping mine alive, that I almost forget I need to socialize them as well. Whether you plan to keep your kitten or not, you want her to enjoy the company of people. An easygoing personality is a huge key to her future happiness and ability to adjust to new and changing situations.

When I first started fostering orphans, I kept them hermetically sealed and protected in the bathroom. Those kittens grew up shy and responded only to their family, hiding from strangers. Later, when my new neighbors found out I often had kittens, the orphans held court at certain times of the day with a constant flow of admirers. At first I was annoyed, but I had an epiphany when I heard back from the adoptive homes that these kittens had grown into well-adjusted cats who loved everyone, even strangers. The more things you expose your kitten to, the more outgoing and well adjusted she grows up to be.

Just spend time holding your kitten. Let her fall asleep in your lap while you check your e-mail or watch television together. At 4 or 5 weeks old, your kitten is going to start playing. If you have older children (over 6) or well-behaved neighbor kids, let them hold her and quietly entice her with age-appropriate toys like feathers. Your kitten can develop those all-important hunting skills and discharge some of that predatory energy. To find out more about introducing your kitten to children and other pets, read Chapter 6.

The worst you can do to a kitten emotionally is keep her in isolation. If you engineer pleasant interactions and carefully choose the visitors (including other cats and dogs) who pick her up and pet her, she may turn out to be one of those cats who astounds people with her outgoingness. For more on raising a well-balanced, friendly orphan kitty, see Chapter 18.

Other stuff you need to know

You need to know so many things about taking care of an orphan. Nature armed him with so many instincts that allow him to instantly know what to do with a litter box and how to keep himself clean. But there are other areas in which he's going to need your help.

- ✔ Brush your orphan with a very soft cat brush; this reminds her of mom's tongue and is good training for later, especially if she has long hair. Run the brush over her head and then along her back and even across her tummy using short, gentle strokes.

- ✔ Brushing may give you a warm fuzzy feeling, but nail trimming can keep you from feeling great pain and suffering. Unless you like the sensation of ten little needles pressed into your flesh, supporting a pound of kitten, you'd better get those nail clippers out. When he's little (under 2 months) a tiny kitten has very soft and fine nails that are hard to see with cat clippers, so it's safe to clip with human fingernail clippers. After he's 2 or 3 months old, switch to cat claw clippers or nippers (see

Chapter 11), because his nails become more brittle as he gets older. Hold your kitten's paw securely and nip just the very tip off — no more than ⅟₁₆ inch. Praise her for being good.

✔ When your kitten is 3 weeks old, you need to contact your vet about getting his first worming. At 4 weeks, he's ready for his first round of shots. At 6 to 12 weeks (depending on your vet), he can be tested for feline leukemia and feline immunodeficiency virus. (To find out more about when and which shots your kitten needs and testing for diseases, read Chapter 10.)

✔ After my kittens have had a couple of rounds of inoculations, I put them in a carrier and take them with me to the department store, the pet supply store, and even the bank. One bank vice president decided to adopt my kittens, Lilo and Stitch, on the spot. She waited another three weeks, until they had been spayed and neutered to pick them up.

✔ If you plan to put the kitten up for adoption, you may want to consider early spay/neuter (see Chapter 14). Kittens as small as 2 pounds and as young as 8 to 9 weeks old can be altered, providing they don't suffer from any health problems.

Finding Him a Home of His Own

Kittens are so cute. How can you resist? After all, you saved his life. Now you find yourself attached to and in love with that adorable little wad of fur. The decision to open your home to him permanently shouldn't be made lightly; Kitten ownership is a long-term relationship. Do some serious soul searching. Flip back to Chapter 1 and take the self-evaluation quiz, which gets you thinking about your lifestyle and the depth of the commitment you can make to your kitten.

If you decide to keep the kitten, you win it all: the kitten, the litter box, and a lifetime of love. If you decide to put the kitten up for adoption, read the following sections, which help you locate a no-kill shelter or a loving family.

You can find a new home for your orphan when he's at least 8 weeks old, eating dry food well, and using the litter box consistently.

Prior to putting her up for adoption you may be able to arrange a vet or humane society to get a low-cost or even no-cost rate for early kitten fixing. Altering assures that she can't have unwanted litters when she grows up. Although money comes out of your pocket, you can ask the adopter to compensate you for the money you invested. While the fee may make finding a home a little more difficult, it actually works to your advantage. If someone pays even a small amount as opposed to getting a free kitten, he or she tends to have a stronger commitment to the kitten.

Looking at adoption options

After your foster kitten is weaned and ready for adoption, if you don't have time to find and screen a new family yourself, you can explore other avenues. Call your local PetsMart or Petco (or other pet store that hosts adoptions) and find out what rescue groups it works with. Call the rescue groups. You can ask if you can continue to foster the kitten and bring her to the adoptions or find out if they have a foster home available. If you don't have these pet warehouses in your area, call animal control and ask if it works with humane groups or check out www.petfinder.org.

If you can't find an adopt-a-pet program in your area, I recommend placing your kitten with a no-kill shelter. These organizations don't usually euthanize unless the kitten has received a serious injury or is sick. Unfortunately, they seldom have available room. You can always ask them to add your kitten to the waiting list, but don't be surprised to find out she may have grown into a cat before a space opens up. However, if a family comes into the shelter and doesn't find what they're looking for, the facility can tell them about your kittens.

People often use the terms "humane society" and "animal control" interchangeably. The only thing they have in common is that they shelter animals. Municipal shelters are owned and operated by the city or county. Most of these have limited space and usually euthanize animals after a certain number of days. Other shelters are operated by humane organizations. Some of these are no-kill; others must put the animals to sleep after a designated period. Some of the humane groups have shelters while others must rely on volunteer foster homes to care for the kittens until they're adopted by a permanent home.

If you can't find room at a no-kill shelter and you must give up your kitten right away, take him to the municipal animal shelter only as a last resort. I'm not going to kid you; the odds aren't great. But it's better than a life of starvation and abuse on the streets. Some shelters have better adoption statistics than others. Find out what their adoption rate is and how many days they give owner-release kittens before they put them to sleep. Ask if they allow humane groups to rescue kittens from the cats on hand. That will give your kitten the best chances under the circumstances.

Placing kitty yourself

If you can't find a humane group to work with or if you have the time, you can open up your own kitten adoption service. You've spent a great deal of effort and love raising your little charge. Now you need to find someone with a good heart to give him a home.

Your first step is to get the word out. Put up notices that include your contact information and whether you have any stipulations like requiring a home inspection or that the adopter promise to alter or not declaw the kitten. Many of my foster kittens go to friends or friends of friends. Put the signs up in places where animal people go: vet clinics, pet stores, and animal shelters. Call your area humane society and ask to be put on its referral list. Also don't rule out other avenues like the bulletin boards at the post office, grocery store, fitness centers, and churches. But be selective of the places you post the signs. The more places you advertise the kitten, the more calls you get and the more screening you need to do. If you really want to give your kitten away, word the ad, "Free to the right home."

Draw up a contract. Ask for a nominal adoption fee, not only to cover the cost of a spay or neuter, but also to discourage the person from selling a free kitten to a laboratory, feeding her to a boa constrictor, or using her for other improper purposes. Ask to see identification and get a phone number. Legitimate adopters shouldn't mind your caution. Assure them you want to hear from them.

When you have someone on the phone, ask a lot of questions. Be friendly and conversational. You get more information than if they think you're interrogating them. Here are some questions you should ask:

- ✔ **Have you ever had a cat or kitten?** If they say they had one who died recently, ask them what happened. Sound conversational and sympathetic. "Oh, I'm so sorry. What happened?" If they say a car hit it, it disappeared, or the neighbor dog killed it, those are warning flags. On the other hand, they may say that they recently lost their 18-year-old cat to kidney failure. This is probably a pretty good home. Also, if they've never had a kitten, you need to educate them about the mischief kittens get into.

- ✔ **What kind of pets do you have?** Do they have a pit bull or a Jack Russell terrier that may be aggressive? How old are their pets? Are their pets spayed/neutered? Do they have current shots? Are they inside or outside pets? These are all good indications of how your kitten may be treated.

✔ **Tell me about your kids.** Many humane groups refuse to adopt tiny kittens to homes with children under 5 years old.

✔ **Who's your vet?** Call the clinic. They may not tell you if the family has been a poor pet owner, but you may be able to glean some information by the tone or hesitation of the person with whom you speak. If they were responsible cat owners, the office would probably be glad to tell you.

✔ **What is your landlord's pet policy? Have you already paid your pet deposit?** If they haven't, tell them they need to bring you a receipt. Humane societies across the country get former kittens back (long after they become cats) because adopters get caught without paying the deposit. Warn them that you plan to call the landlord to check prior to letting them take your kitten.

✔ **Do you know that kittens can live 18 years?** Are you willing to keep her that long? What happens if you have to move? This is one of the most common reasons for surrendering a pet to a shelter.

After the person has answered your questions to your satisfaction, and you're comfortable with him, you can make an appointment to meet him. You can meet somewhere like a pet store, or have him come to your home. Some people I know will only hand over the kitten after a home visitation. It's not a social visit; but to see if there's a pit bull tied to a tree in the front yard. While you may consider this extreme, many humane groups require a home inspection before completing the adoption of a kitten. I've had good luck whenever their vet contacts check out okay.

Go with your gut instinct. You are not obligated to hand over your kitten just because someone shows interest.

You may find it difficult to let the kitten go. It's all right to shed a tear or two. But if you ask enough questions and get the right answers, you can be reasonably certain that your kitten is going to have a happy and healthy life with her new family. When you get that holiday card with her picture in it, you'll know your kitten's happiness was worth all the trouble it took.

When the time comes, kiss your baby and send him off to a wonderful new life he wouldn't have had without you. And don't worry . . . now that you know how to do it, you can always help another motherless kitten who needs your care.

Part VI
The Part of Tens

The 5th Wave   By Rich Tennant

©RICHTENNANT

"I never appreciated having cats until I went bald."

In this part . . .

This part deals with the most stressful and the most joyous aspects of having a kitten. I tell you how to cope with the most common emergencies a kitten owner faces. I give you tips to help you recognize symptoms of poisoning and injuries and tell you what to do until you get your kitten to the vet. And at the opposite end of the spectrum, I also suggest some fun ways to bond with your kitten.

Chapter 20

Ten Common Kitten Emergencies and How to Deal with Them

● ●

In This Chapter

▶ Handing an emergency

▶ Giving first aid

▶ Administering CPR

● ●

Kittens are a nosy lot. They have to inspect everything. And their inquisitive nature brings to life that cryptic old saying about cats and curiosity: While quenching that insatiable curiosity, kittens sometimes wind up in an animal emergency room.

No matter how thoroughly you kitty-proof your home, your kitten will still manage to find some creative new hazards of her own. If and when that happens, this chapter can help you deal with some of the most common kitten emergencies, so you'll have the best chance of a happy ending.

Regardless of what has occurred, stay calm and assess the situation. If your kitten appears distressed or in pain, put a muzzle on her. Getting bit will only make matters worse.

If you happen to have the Bach Flower Essence Rescue Remedy (which is a flower essence mixture that you can buy at most health food stores and even some grocery stores), put a few drops in your kitten's mouth. He doesn't have to swallow it. It's absorbed through the mouth tissue. This treatment can help calm him down.

Freeing Foreign Objects from the Airway

Because kittens are so low to the floor, they can find a whole world of objects to chew on that you may not even know are down there. The time may come when one of those small objects gets lodged in your kitten's throat and cuts off her air. You can tell a kitten is choking when she makes coughing and gasping sounds. You may also see her place a paw at her mouth, gag, struggle to breathe, or hold her neck in an abnormal posture.

Removing a foreign object is usually easy. Simply restrain the kitten, remove her collar, open her mouth, peek down her throat, and remove the object if you see it. If you don't see anything, take your finger and run it around the very back of the mouth. Sometimes this will dislodge a foreign object. If you can't locate the object, and the cat is conscious, take her to the vet as quickly as possible.

If the situation is more serious or the cat becomes unconscious (you can tell it's serious when her gums turn blue from lack of oxygen or she goes limp), perform the Heimlich maneuver. Here's how:

1. **Hold the kitten upside down with her back against your chest.**

   This makes gravity work for you rather than against you.

2. **Using both hands, give five sharp upward thrusts to the soft area just below the ribcage.**

   Be very careful not to be too forceful or apply too much pressure, because you could break a rib and puncture her lung.

3. **Check her mouth to see if the object has popped loose. If you see something lodged down there, remove it.**

After the object is out of there, if your kitten isn't breathing, start nose to mouth breathing. Don't blow too hard. If the air isn't filling the kitten's lungs, try the Heimlich again. If the kitten still is unresponsive, perform CPR on your kitten. I tell you how to help your kitten in the "CPR and artificial respiration" sidebar in this chapter.

Dealing with Bleeding Cuts

Few things are more frightening to a kitten owner than the sight of a bleeding cut. Most of the time, such a cut turns out to be superficial — just a minor cut or scrape. To treat a small cut, place clean gauze or a clean washcloth against the cut and apply direct pressure. Within 90 seconds, the cut should begin to clot (it will eventually form a scab). If the bleeding hasn't stopped in five minutes, then it fits into the category of more serious bleeding.

You should be concerned if blood is gushing from a cut or puncture, or you see blood coming from the kitten's nose, mouth, ears, or bottom. If your kitten appears to be in pain, you may want to put a muzzle on her, so she won't be tempted to bite you out of fear and confusion.

For spurting or flowing cuts, you must act quickly and follow these steps:

1. **Using a clean cloth or piece of gauze, apply pressure directly to the cut.**

   If the cloth or gauze bleeds through, place a second one on top of the first one. Don't pull the first one off because you'll pull off the forming scab.

2. **Elevate the body part and put an ice pack on it.**

3. **Continue to apply the pressure for at least five minutes.**

4. **If you don't see any slow in the bleeding, you can apply pressure to *pressure points* on the legs and tail (see Figure 20-1), which are arteries just under the skin.**

   When you crimp the artery with your finger, it should greatly reduce the blood flow. The three main pressure points are located:

   • **On the upper inside of the rear leg:** Apply pressure above the cut in the inside center of the hurt leg.

   • **In the kitten's armpit:** Press on the inside of the front leg that's injured, right up from the elbow joint.

   • **On the underside of the tail, close to where it meets the body:** Place your thumb on the inside of the tail and your forefinger on top of the tail and press.

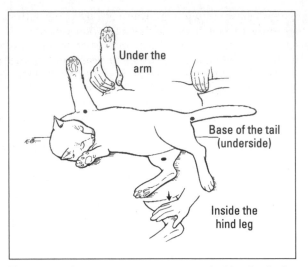

Under the arm

Base of the tail (underside)

Inside the hind leg

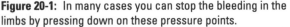

Figure 20-1: In many cases you can stop the bleeding in the limbs by pressing down on these pressure points.

When you just can't stop that blood flow, you can place a tourniquet on the limb above the cut. Use a tourniquet only as a last resort. Never use a tourniquet around the head or neck. Make certain you leave it on no longer than ten minutes at a time. With blood cut off to the limb, the tissue will start dying. Apply pressure again and loosen it for one minute every ten minutes until you get to the vet. You can read more about tourniquets and bleeding at www.veterinarypartner.com.

Treating Animal Bites

Outside kittens are always at risk of being attacked by other animals. Sometimes the attacker is a wild animal like a skunk and sometimes a roaming dog or a territorial cat. An attack by a large animal requires an immediate trip to the vet, especially for a kitten. Even if it doesn't look serious, your kitten could have suffered internal injuries, broken bones, and serious cuts and tears. Early treatment by a vet will prevent problems later like abscesses that may require treatment under anesthesia.

If your kitten is attacked by another cat and suffers minor punctures and abrasion, you don't have to rush the kitten to the vet. But be sure to treat the non-life-threatening injuries that penetrate the skin properly before they develop into an abscess.

An abscess can form when another cat bites your kitten, because cat teeth inject nasty bacteria like a hypodermic shot. If not treated immediately, the bacteria reproduce and create pus. Eventually, the original puncture heals over, sealing the infection beneath the skin. The area begins to swell, and the kitten develops a fever, goes off his food, and becomes lethargic.

If an abscess does form, you may have to have your vet anesthetize the kitten and open the wound to drain it. Or, if your kitten cooperates, you may be able to drain the abscess yourself. Simply wet a cotton ball with hydrogen peroxide and hold it against the scab until the scab softens. After the scab comes off, let the pus drain until nothing else comes out. If the scab opening is big enough, insert the tip of a syringe (without the needle) and inject some peroxide directly into the wound. Do this for three or four days, and the wound should clear up. (If you can't remove the scab, take the kitten to the vet.)

Bites from other cats put your kitten at risk of feline leukemia virus, feline immunodeficiency virus, and feline infectious peritonitis. And almost any mammal bite could put him at risk of rabies. Make sure your kitten has been vaccinated against these diseases. Check out Chapters 9 and 10 for more information about these diseases and the latest on the vaccines.

Soothing Burns

Your kitten doesn't have to be exposed to the stove or a heater to be burned. She can also receive caustic burns from chemicals. Brushing up against something like liquid potpourri (which can contain a caustic substance), she could burn her skin and then receive additional burns to the mouth or even internal injuries when she grooms herself.

How serious a burn is depends on how deep it goes in the kitten's skin and tissue and how big the affected area is. A superficial burn only affects the skin. Deeper burns damage deeper tissue and can be fatal if not treated.

If your kitten has been burned, flush the area with cold water, cover it with a moist cloth and take her to the vet immediately, because her fur may hide the full extent of the burn. Don't put any ointments, medication, or butter on the wound. If the kitten is suffering from a chemical or substance burn and you know what she's gotten into, take the container with you.

CPR and artificial respiration

Your kitten has been involved in an accident, or he's choking. He's unconscious, and you can't detect any sign of breathing, and his heart has stopped. It's time to perform artificial respiration and cardiopulmonary resuscitation (CPR), so remember your ABCs:

✔ Airway

✔ Breathing

✔ Circulation

For artificial respiration:

1. **Clear the kitten's airway and pull his tongue forward.**

2. **Remove any obstruction that may be blocking the throat.**

3. **Close his mouth.**

4. **Check for breathing.**

   If you can't determine whether he's breathing, place a tissue or toilet paper in front of his nose and see if it flutters.

5. **If he isn't breathing, put your mouth over his nose (get a good seal) and blow very gently into the nose until you see the chest expand.**

6. **Remove your mouth so he can exhale.**

7. **Breath into the kitten every 4 or 5 seconds for 10 minutes, then stop to see if your kitten has started breathing on his own.**

Next you come to the cardio (heart) or circulation part. If he has no pulse:

1. **Lay your kitten on his side and place your hand along the back of his spine.**

2. **Put your fingers around his chest just behind the elbows and squeeze gently.**

   You don't want to crush or break his ribs. Squeeze rapidly for 15 seconds.

3. **Check to see if he has a pulse.**

   You can feel it by touching the large vein on the inside of the back leg.

4. **Repeat the compressions as necessary while someone drives you to the veterinary clinic.**

   On a kitten try to do 100 compressions per minute and 20 breaths per minute. Continue until she breathes on her own, you reach the clinic, or until you haven't felt a heartbeat for 30 minutes.

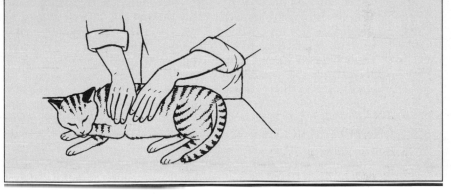

A kitten suffering from burns finds herself at risk of infection and fluid loss. She'll probably need to get intravenous fluids and antibiotics, special wound dressings, and pain killers. If she inhaled smoke, she'll need to be treated for that, too.

Handling Electrocution

Your kitten simply can't resist playing with exposed electrical wires. After all, wires wiggle and sway just like prey. Unfortunately, wires bite back with a vengeance. Electricity can burn your kitten, damage his heart or make it stop beating, cause *edema* (that's when fluids fill his lungs), trigger seizures, or kill him.

One last chance

If the kitten doesn't start breathing after you perform CPR, and you know he's going to die without a miracle, you can try one last ditch effort to save him. Try to stimulate the GV 26 Chinese acupuncture point. It's the split area between the lower nose and the upper lip. Take a pointed object like a pin, needle, or even a straightened paper clip and jab it into that area down to the bone and move it back and forth. When all else fails, there is a chance that this procedure could stimulate the heart and respiration. This may be hard to do, but he's unresponsive and limp. You don't have time to get him to the vet.

If you're there when your kitten bites into a power cord, unplug the cord or turn off the power before you touch him. Or push him away from the wire using something that doesn't conduct electricity, like a wood stick or broom handle. You don't want to turn into a victim yourself. Next, check to see if he's breathing. Perform CPR if your kitten isn't breathing and is unconscious. (You can read about CPR in the "CPR and artificial respiration" sidebar in this chapter.) Take your kitten to the vet immediately, regardless of whether the kitten looks or acts hurt. Fluids can start filling the lungs in just 30 minutes. Check out Chapter 8 to see how you can protect your kitten from electrical cords.

Your kitten may suffer from seizures while you're on your way to the vet. Turn to the "Surviving Seizures" section for information on seizures.

Counteracting Poison

You wouldn't believe all the ways a kitten can poison himself. He can drink poison straight, lick it off his coat, or even walk through a puddle of spilled cleaning solution and then clean off his paws. Most poisons smell bad to you, so you may assume that your kitten will be smart enough to avoid a cleaner or other toxic substance. Unfortunately, instinct has not provided him with as much poison savvy as you may like to think, and someday he may wander through a pool of pine cleaner, bite the wrong plant, or sidle up against your liquid potpourri. To learn about the most common household items that are toxic to your kitten, flip to Chapter 8.

Your kitten may have gotten into something nasty if he experiences one or more of the following symptoms:

- ✔ Repeated vomiting
- ✔ Drooling
- ✔ Repeated diarrhea
- ✔ Nervousness

- ✔ Difficulty breathing
- ✔ Change in pupil size
- ✔ Staggering or seizures
- ✔ Paralysis or coma

If you suspect that your kitten has come in contact with something poisonous, call the ASPCA Animal Poison Control Center (or APCC) at 800-548-2423 (each call costs $45). Tell the vet what he was exposed to, how much, and when. Also tell her about your kitten's medical history and any health problems he has.

Don't try to induce vomiting unless the APCC vet tells you to. Some poisons are caustic, and if you make the kitten vomit, it could burn his mouth and esophagus both going down and coming up. Also, don't try to induce vomiting if the kitten has slipped into unconsciousness. If the APCC vet recommends you induce vomiting, then give the kitten a few teaspoon of hydrogen peroxide, (the same kind that you put on wounds, not the kind for coloring hair).

Go to the vet immediately unless instructed otherwise by poison control. (If you know what the kitten has ingested, take the poison with you.) Call ahead to your vet and give him your APCC case number. That way he'll already have the necessary information when you arrive. Your kitten could go into shock or suffer a seizure so try to keep him warm. You can find more information on dealing with shock and seizures later in this chapter. If the kitten quits breathing or his heart stops, give him CPR (as described in the "CPR and artificial respiration" sidebar in this chapter).

To help mitigate the effects of poisoning, especially certain pesticides, you can buy activated charcoal from a fish supply store. It absorbs some of the poison before it enters the kitten's system. Grind it up to a fine powder, the finer the better, and give the kitten a tablespoon. But only give it to your kitten when your vet or Animal Poison Control contact tells you to.

To remove poison gunk that your kitten's rubbed up against, give him a good bath in Dawn dishwashing liquid. It cuts any oil that clings to his coat and, if you rinse it off thoroughly, won't hurt him. If he gets into paint or motor oil, use baby oil or Vaseline to loosen it and then give your kitty a bath. Also, be sure to flush his eyes out thoroughly with saline solution if substances have splattered in his eyes. I had one litter of 2-week-old kittens that came to me with splotches of tar or industrial grease splattered all over them including over their eyes. I used an antibiotic eye ointment, and the gunk loosened and came off without injuring their sensitive little eyes.

Treating Trauma

The two most common traumatic injuries are being hit by a car and falling from a window. They both result in similar injuries: broken bones, internal bleeding, crushed chest, concussion, and open wounds are all possibilities.

Even if the injuries look minor, take your kitten to the vet. She could have internal bleeding or fractures that you can't detect visually.

If your kitten comes home with scrapes, dragging a leg, and struggling to breathe, stay calm and keep her quiet. Be careful; she's hurting a lot right now, and if you try to handle her, not only could you injure her more, but she could also lash out and bite you. Put a muzzle on her so she can't bite. Stop any obvious bleeding and monitor her breathing. If she quits breathing, perform artificial respiration. Also watch for shock. You can read about how to stop bleeding in the "Dealing with Bleeding Cuts" section and how to perform artificial respiration in the "CPR and artificial respiration" sidebar in this chapter. The next section tells you about shock.

High-rise syndrome

So many kittens jump or fall from open apartment windows that the phenomenon even has a name: high-rise syndrome. Ironically, kittens who fall from 7 to 32 stories up are twice as likely to survive as those who only fall 2 to 6 stories, because a higher fall gives the kitten time to place herself in a proper landing position and relax on impact.

You can help keep your kitten safe from falling by

✔ Regularly checking to see if your screens are in good shape. Make sure they aren't warped and have no tears. Test the screens yourself. If you can't push it out, I doubt your kitten can.

✔ Keeping your windows closed when you aren't home.

✔ Never leaving your kitten unattended on a balcony.

Any wound where air escapes from a kitten's chest will make it impossible for her to breathe. Wrap plastic kitchen wrap around her chest to create an airtight seal until you get her to the vet. If the kitten has been impaled by a stick or other object, don't remove it yourself, unless it traps her. Removing the stick could cause uncontrollable bleeding or make breathing impossible.

If you must pick your kitten up, do it as gently as possible, trying to avoid any unnecessary movements of her body. Scoop her with a hand under her chest and the other under her hips. Place her on a towel. You can use it as a stretcher or slide a board under the towel. I have a kitchen cutting board just the right size for transporting an injured kitten. If boards or towels aren't immediately available, lay her in a cardboard box: It may hurt her even more to shove her into a carrier. Wrap the towel over her to keep her warm and to protect any open wound. You can attach strips of packing tape to the board (across the towel) to immobilize her and keep her from further injuring herself. Covering her eyes will also help keep her calm. Take her to the vet immediately.

Calming a Kitten in Shock

Shock is the body's reaction to a severe traumatic injury or allergic reaction — it slows the circulation, causing the organs to shut down. This can happen within 15 or 20 minutes of an accident. Any time your kitten suffers a major injury, watch for a weak pulse, shallow breathing, nervousness, and a dazed appearance. She could also have a pale tongue and gums. Treat for life-threatening injuries first. After breathing, bleeding, and heartbeat are under control, treat for shock. Restrain her, and keep her quiet and warm. Putting a towel over her head will help to keep her calm. Get her to the vet as quickly as possible. Shock's a killer.

If you suspect that your kitten is becoming shocky, rub some Karo syrup on her gums to help raise her blood sugar. You can do this even if she's unconscious.

Surviving Seizures

Seizures are terrifying. You can't do much about a seizure while it's going on, except to make sure your kitten doesn't hurt himself. Contrary to what you may have read, don't put a pencil or anything else in his mouth. He won't swallow his tongue, and you'll just get bitten. Only touch him to move him out of danger. Even though he's not aware of anything going on around him, throw a towel over him. The darkness may shorten the length of the seizure. Time the seizure. Note the beginning and ending time of each one. Your vet will want this information.

A kitten experiencing a major or *grand mal* seizure will stiffen and fall over, roll his eyes, and kick his legs violently. He'll often froth at the mouth and snap his jaws, so keep your hands away from his mouth. He'll probably pee and poop involuntarily. When he comes out of the seizure, he may act dazed and disoriented. Although seizures only last a minute or two, it could be the longest minute of your life. He can also have a less violent seizure called a *petit mal,* where he stares into space, bumps into things, has muscle twitches, and tries to catch imaginary bugs.

If your kitten has more than one episode or the seizures last longer than two minutes, put him in a blanket to keep him warm and take him to a vet. Longer seizures can cause fevers and brain damage. A kitten experiencing a seizure that isn't prolonged (under two minutes) can wait until the next day to see the vet, unless you suspect poisoning. Medical tests are in order. The seizures could be caused by any number of things, including head trauma, a brain tumor, flea anemia and hypoglycemia, various illnesses, poisons, and epilepsy.

Taking the Bite out of Frostbite

Kittens are more prone to frostbite than adult cats, so keep your kitten inside, especially when the thermometer dips. If your kitten has been exposed to extreme cold, check the tips of her ears, footpads, and tail. You may not see evidence of frostbite right away. It could take a couple of days for blisters or the pale, glossy, or white patches to appear on the skin. The skin will swell and turn red as the circulation returns to the tissue. Eventually the hair and the skin will slough away.

The first thing you need to do is get a frostbitten kitten out of the cold weather and thaw that injured tissue slowly. Don't put her feet or tail in hot water. Don't rub those areas, either. That will just hurt her. Instead, wrap the limbs in warm moist towels. When you see the tissue turning red, stop the moist towels and wrap her in a dry towel or blanket. Dab a little antibiotic ointment (without steroids) on the frostbitten areas. Take her to the vet.

Keep your kitten out of the weather. Her tender little toes, ears, and tail will be even more susceptible to frostbite now.

First-aid kit for kittens

A basic first aid kit for your kitten should contain the following:

- A muzzle to protect you from a frantic kitten

- Some 3 percent hydrogen peroxide for cleaning cuts and abscesses and inducing vomiting

- Dawn dishwashing detergent to wash goo and chemicals out of the fur

- Eye wash/saline solution to flush out eye contaminants

- Hemostats or tweezers for removing stingers and thorns

- A 12 cubic centimeter syringe for force-feeding

- A flashlight for looking in the mouth, ears, and other hard-to-see places

- Karo syrup to elevate the blood sugar during hypoglycemic episodes and shock

- A rectal thermometer to take the kittens temperature of course (a normal temperature runs between 100.5 and 102.5 degrees Fahrenheit)

- Non-stick gauze pads and bandaging to cover a wound or help stop bleeding

- Bach Flower Essence Rescue Remedy to calm the kitten (and you) down

- A very thick towel or blanket to help safely pick up your kitten, as bite protection, and to stop bleeding

- Phone numbers to your vet clinic, the emergency clinic, and the ASPCA Animal Poison Control Center

Chapter 21

Ten Ways to Bond with Your Kitten

*W*hen you bring your kitten home, he may be confused and scared — he misses his mommy. From now on, you *are* his mommy. Mimicking the things that mom did to make him feel comfortable and safe will bring you together quickly. Think about what a *queen* (that's the mother kitty) does for her kitten. She grooms, plays, teaches, and disciplines — the things your mom may have done for you.

Doing these things for and to your kitten help him to look at you as the mom cat he can depend on. That way, you're less like a scary giant stranger who stole him away from his real mom.

Dining Together

Your kitten's mom sat with her through every meal. Of course, she had to — she was nursing. Take a cue from the queen. Don't just dish out a bowl of food and walk away. Occasionally, sit down beside your kitten and visit with her while she eats. Talk to her. You can tell her about your day, and she won't complain that she's too busy to listen.

Treating Him like a Special Kitten

Bonito, in Spanish, means pretty; bonito is also a kind of fish. Your kitten will think you're *pretty great* if you occasionally treat him to some dried bonito flakes, which you can buy at any pet supply store. To your kitten, bonito flakes taste like fish-flavored air; you only need to share a couple of pieces to get across the point that he's pretty special.

If your kitten isn't crazy about the fish flakes, then try a lick or two of turkey baby food, but make sure it doesn't contain onion powder. (For more on foods to avoid, take a look at Chapter 7.) Neither the bonito flakes nor a dab of baby food will fill him up, so you don't have to worry about spoiling his dinner or adding too many calories. Two quick cautions: Don't overdo the baby food (you don't want to deal with diarrhea), and don't keep the bonito flakes in a spot where you don't want the kitten to hang out, like around the computer keyboard. He'll never leave you alone.

Offering Her a Little (Cat)Nip

Most kitties just love a little catnip. Even big cats, like lions and tigers and pumas (oh my!) respond like kittens to the stuff. But maybe I shouldn't say they respond like kittens, because enjoying catnip is an acquired taste, and young kittens usually don't respond. Although most kittens don't react to catnip until they're about 6 months old, I have had fosters that got turned on as early as 6 weeks. Some kitties get sleepy, and others become wired. Your kitten may experience euphoria for 10 or 15 minutes. Catnip isn't chemically addictive like a drug. But like candy, it sure is fun.

You don't have to go out and spend a fortune on catnip toys. One of the favorite toys around our house is an old sock filled with bulk catnip (which you can get at any pet supply store). The sock takes seconds to make — just stuff the catnip in and tie a knot in the end. After your kitty is done playing, seal the toy in a plastic bag: The catnip will stay fresh and appealing longer, and he won't grow bored with it.

Your kitten may also enjoy some homegrown catnip. Catnip growing kits can be purchased at any pet store. Catnip takes eight to ten weeks to grow, so I prefer the live catnip plants available from most pet retailers. Just break off a leaf and hand it over to your older kitten. You'll both be entertained.

You may have seen some cats writhe in unadulterated joy when you serve up the catnip, while others trot past without a clue. Somewhere around a quarter to a third of cats don't have that gene that lets them enjoy the pleasant chemical reaction to catnip. That doesn't mean these cats must go without plant-induced euphoria. Kittens and cats who don't respond to catnip usually respond to honeysuckle toys. Dampen the toy to release the aroma.

Massaging Your Kitten

Even before feeding her baby, the mother cat licked and massaged her kitten to stimulate his first breaths and his blood flow. You can make him feel like his mother is giving him a gentle massage again.

Wait until your kitten is relaxed. Then start the massage with slow caresses. Alternate moving with your full palm along broader areas like his back and sides. Using the pads of your fingers, stroke slowly under the chin and around the cheeks. Work your way under the neck, along the back, and even out to the tip of the tail.

Try to establish a daily massage routine at the same time and place — and follow the same massage pattern. For example, each morning while coffee is brewing, take four minutes for massage before your day gets too busy.

Grooming with a Soft Brush

Your kitten's mother used to groom her kittens until they were squeaky clean. But you probably don't want to give the kitten a spit bath to make her feel the way mamma did. Use a very soft cat brush instead. Make slow strokes beginning at the tip of the nose, brushing over the whiskers up to the ear. Keep the emphasis on working slowly. Next, run the brush from the tip of the chin right down to the chest. Caress along the shoulder and the length of the back. This gentle grooming not only bonds the two of you together, but it also gets her accustomed to brushes and handling. Try different textures against her fur like a glove with a missing mate or a bathing glove with rubber knobs.

Sleeping with Your Furry Friend

Your kitten felt very safe as he curled up against his mom's giant body. So sleeping with you is a reminder of sleeping with his mom.

Before he can go to your slumber party, though, he needs to be grown up enough to find his litter box on his own. I don't recommend sleeping with your kitten until he reaches about 4 months. By this time, he should be big enough to avoid you when you roll around and competent enough with the litter box that you can trust him for the night.

Disciplining with Love

Bonding with your kitten doesn't mean that she gets her way all the time. Sometimes, she's going to test the boundaries. But never hit your kitten. When she's veered off the path of appropriate behavior, do what her mom would do — hiss. However, hisses are effective only if your kitten is right beside you. If your kitten is across the room, make a loud noise: Clap your hands, stamp your foot, shake a soft drink can full of pennies or pebbles, and say "No" in a strong voice. Praise her by saying "Thank you!" or "Good girl!" when she does something right. When she's focused on something inappropriate, distract her with a toy. (To find out more about correcting kitten behavior, check out Chapter 14.) Gentle correction and distraction, instead of screaming and hitting, shows your kitten the rules without teaching her to fear you. Everyone's happy and that can only bring you closer together.

Going Fishing with Your Kitten

Nothing excites a kitten like the opportunity to chase after something and kill it. You can appeal to that aspect of your kitten's personality and also wear him out before bedtime with a "chase the prey" game. You can play with a toy called Da Bird (which makes a fluttering sound like the beating of a bird's wings when you flip it through the air — www.go-cat.com) as described in Chapter 15, or you can hang a toy mouse from the end of an old fishing rod or stick.

Cast the toy across the room like you would if you were going fishing. Then when kitty reaches the lure, start reeling him in. Hey — looks like you caught a big one! Don't reel too quickly. He needs to be able to catch that prey in his paws and know that he's the mighty hunter. A couple of tugs on the line and the lure makes a break for it.

At my house, our Turkish Van kittens, Herman and Vanna, used to run around underfoot and meow until they got to play cat fish. Playing the game is a great way to bond.

Making the Bed

What most people look at as a tedious chore could turn out to be the high point of your kitten's day. Drop the sheet or bedspread on top of her and then tease your kitten with your fingers. Those tantalizing moving things become prey she can overpower and kill. Or, reverse the game. If she's sleeping on top of the comforter, slip your hand underneath and run it back and forth. Making the bed is another one of those fun games that use up kitty's predatory energy, and because a blanket or bedspread covers your digits, your kitten won't associate your naked fingers with prey.

Playing with the Irresistible Pheasant Feather

If your kitten was a baby wildcat, he'd have to figure out early how to kill prey to survive. And domesticated kittens have this hunting instinct, too. Although you bring a kitten into your home and feed him, he still wants to hunt. I cringe at the thought of some little bird at the mercy of my guys, so I break out the pheasant feather (say that ten times really fast) and let them hunt to their hearts' content (see the color insert). Your kitten can pounce, chase, grab, and bite just like nature tells him to. Although it's the feather that excites him, he knows the fun stuff doesn't happen without you.

Playing with the feather also provides your kitten with some much needed rough play that he doesn't associate directly with a bare human hand. Attacking your hand may be cute when he's little, but you'll find a biting habit's a royal pain in the hand when he's older and stronger. With practice, you can make the feather flutter, glide, or flit. Although you don't want to make it too easy, let him catch and maul his prey from time to time so that he doesn't become frustrated. You can buy pheasant feathers at cat shows or hobby shops.

Index

• C •

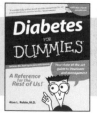

FOR DUMMIES®

A world of resources to help you grow

HOME & BUSINESS COMPUTER BASICS

PCs FOR DUMMIES
A Reference for the Rest of Us!
Dan Gookin
0-7645-0838-5

The Flat-Screen iMac FOR DUMMIES
A Reference for the Rest of Us!
David Pogue
0-7645-1663-9

Windows XP ALL-IN-ONE DESK REFERENCE FOR DUMMIES
9 BOOKS IN 1
Woody Leonhard
0-7645-1548-9

Also available:

Excel 2002 All-in-One Desk Reference For Dummies
(0-7645-1794-5)

Office XP 9-in-1 Desk Reference For Dummies
(0-7645-0819-9)

PCs All-in-One Desk Reference For Dummies
(0-7645-0791-5)

Troubleshooting Your PC For Dummies
(0-7645-1669-8)

Upgrading & Fixing PCs For Dummies
(0-7645-1665-5)

Windows XP For Dummies
(0-7645-0893-8)

Windows XP For Dummies Quick Reference
(0-7645-0897-0)

Word 2002 For Dummies
(0-7645-0839-3)

INTERNET & DIGITAL MEDIA

The Internet FOR DUMMIES
A Reference for the Rest of Us!
John R. Levine
Carol Baroudi
Margaret Levine Young
0-7645-0894-6

eBay FOR DUMMIES
A Reference for the Rest of Us!
Marsha Collier
Roland Woerner
Stephanie Becker
0-7645-1642-6

Digital Photography FOR DUMMIES
A Reference for the Rest of Us!
Julie Adair King
0-7645-1664-7

Also available:

CD and DVD Recording For Dummies
(0-7645-1627-2)

Digital Photography All-in-One Desk Reference For Dummies
(0-7645-1800-3)

eBay For Dummies
(0-7645-1642-6)

Genealogy Online For Dummies
(0-7645-0807-5)

Internet All-in-One Desk Reference For Dummies
(0-7645-1659-0)

Internet For Dummies Quick Reference
(0-7645-1645-0)

Internet Privacy For Dummies
(0-7645-0846-6)

Paint Shop Pro For Dummies
(0-7645-2440-3)

Photo Retouching & Restoration For Dummies
(0-7645-1662-0)

Photoshop Elements For Dummies
(0-7645-1675-2)

Scanners For Dummies
(0-7645-0783-4)

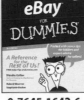

Get smart! Visit www.dummies.com

- **Find listings of even more Dummies titles**
- **Browse online articles, excerpts, and how-to's**
- **Sign up for daily or weekly e-mail tips**
- **Check out Dummies fitness videos and other products**
- **Order from our online bookstore**

TM

Available wherever books are sold. Go to www.dummies.com or call 1-877-762-2974 to order direct